Northbound
with Theo

A Man and His Dog Thru-Hike
the Appalachian Trail
at Ages 75 and 8

SOREN WEST

WALNUT
STREET
BOOKS

LANCASTER,
PENNSYLVANIA

walnutstreetbooks.com

Cover and page design by Cliff Snyder

Northbound with Theo
Copyright © 2022 by Soren West

Book photos by, or supplied by, Soren West, except: photos on
front cover and page 257 by Soren's grandson Thomas West;
page 276 by Mike Mayberry; and back cover by Jenny Schulder.

All maps, except page 4, © by the National Park Service, a department
of the United States government. The map on page 4 is from the
Appalachian National Scenic Trail Resource Management Plan.

Paperback: 9781947597464
PDF, EPUB, and Kindle: 9781947597471

Library of Congress Control Number: Data available.

Northbound with Theo is published by
Walnut Street Books, Lancaster, Pennsylvania

info@walnutstreetbooks.com

*To my wife, Bonnie, and our five children,
Soren, Christopher, Emily, Nathan, and Marian,
whose love and support was like a slow-burning
fire igniting my resolve to fulfill a life-long
goal of thru-hiking the Appalachian Trail.*

Contents

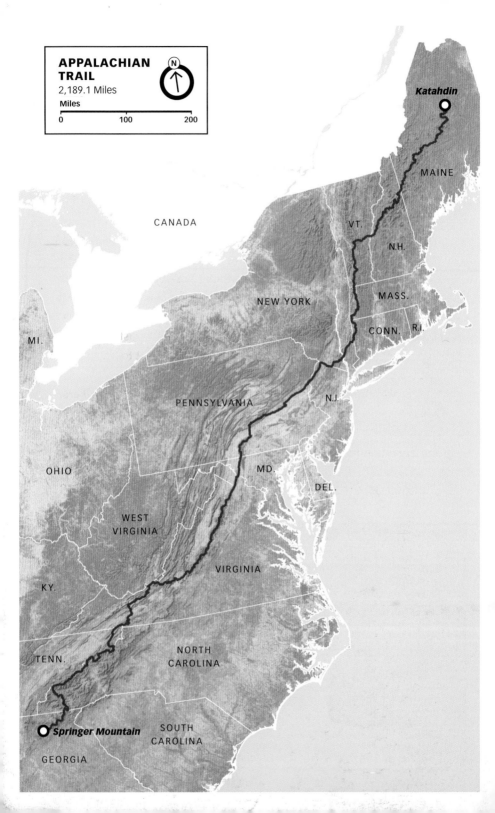

APPALACHIAN TRAIL

2,189.1 Miles

Miles

0   100   200

N

Katahdin

MAINE

CANADA

VT.

N.H.

NEW YORK

MASS.

CONN.   R.I.

MI.

PENNSYLVANIA

N.J.

OHIO

MD.

DEL.

WEST
VIRGINIA

VIRGINIA

KY.

TENN.

NORTH
CAROLINA

Springer Mountain

SOUTH
CAROLINA

GEORGIA

Introduction

The Appalachian Trail is a long ribbon of dirt, rocks, roots, fields, woods, hills, and valleys stretching from Springer Mountain in Georgia to mile-high Katahdin in Maine. For some of us, it lives inside like a song you can't stop singing. Its challenges and scenery capture our imaginations. But few of us can articulate clearly why we want to hike the Appalachian Trail—the AT. It's just out there, tugging at something within like gravity, ever present to those who just have to climb.

People who do the whole trail in one year are called thru-hikers. More than 3,000 people attempt such a hike every year, but only a quarter to a third finish. While there are more men than women on the trail, that margin is disappearing.

About 80% of thru-hikers are northbound. The remainder are southbound. Or they flip-flop, meaning they hike to or from

somewhere in the middle to the north or south end of the trail, and then do the other half. Many start a flip-flop at Harper's Ferry, West Virginia, the home of the Appalachian Trail Conservancy (ATC) whose mission is to preserve and manage the trail. The ATC keeps a picture and log of every thru-hiker who stops, helping make Harper's Ferry the psychological center of the AT.

The trail passes through 14 states: Georgia, North Carolina, Tennessee, Virginia, West Virginia, Maryland, Pennsylvania, New Jersey, New York, Connecticut, Massachusetts, Vermont, New Hampshire, and Maine. One-fourth of the trail is in Virginia.

Typical 3-sided shelter, inside and out

A direct flight from end to end of the AT is 1,100 miles. The long ribbon of dirt, however, is twice that, at close to 2,200 miles, up and over, but rarely around, some 510 mountains. While the distance changes because of necessary rerouting, the hike is longer than a crow's flight from Philadelphia, Pennsylvania, to Caracas, Venezuela, or to Calgary, Canada, or to Kangerlussuaq, Greenland. The elevation change is the equivalent of 16 ascents up Mount Everest—from sea level!

There are approximately 180,000 white blazes marking the trail, each two inches by six inches. They are found on trees, rocks, fence posts, and roads. Sometimes the distance between blazes is long enough to cause hikers to wonder if they've gone off the trail. And sometimes they have. There are 260 shelters on the trail, most three-sided structures of log or stone.

By far, most thru-hikers are in their 20s. The next largest group are in their 50s or 60s, with very few 70 or older. I was the fifth person to finish at 75 or older. As of the end of 2020, there are ten of us.

Of course, there is a good bit of wildlife on the trail. Certainly deer, bears, and snakes. Rarely seen are wild boars, bobcats, and coyotes. In Maine there are moose. In general, there is little danger from wildlife because they want to avoid you as much as you want to avoid them, except to see them at a safe distance. But care must be taken with food.

Maybe one percent of hikers bring a dog. I count myself very fortunate to have hiked with my eight-year-old golden retriever, Theo, who carried saddlebags with his own food and my water.

Theo posing in Tennessee

Those who take to the AT have Benton MacKaye and Myron Avery to thank. MacKaye studied forestry and planning at Harvard College. He was a dreamer who, in 1900 atop Stratton Mountain in Vermont, envisioned a trail along the peaks of the Appalachians. He wanted to provide wilderness recreation for congested East-Coast city-dwellers. Myron Avery, a Harvard-trained admiralty lawyer, was a get-it-done kind of person who frequently bucked heads with the dreamer as he pushed hard to get the trail built.

The dreams and hard work of these two men have helped countless people come down to earth to climb toward the heavens. Join Theo and me for all four seasons in the wilderness of the AT.

CHAPTER 1

Dog

The Trail's Call— The Dog's Gaze

I've always been in search of something—something beyond the confusion inside and the struggles of daily life. Mountains stand there. You don't argue with them. Humans tear them down and run riot over and around them in off-road vehicles, but a mountain is permanent, grand, and eternal. It may be shot through with an underground highway, yet still it stands.

Mountains call to many of us in a way we simply can't resist. They may ask that we reach into our depths to join them, especially those that stretch into the heavens. They require that we take the long view, past endless obstacles. They offer us a vision and stir a deep and consuming hunger that will not relent until we reach and struggle to attain their heights.

As I spent myself climbing all 510 mountains of the Appalachian Trail, I was not alone. Another being came with me, not two feet off the ground, always at my heels, muzzle in my lap, by my side or leading the way. One who almost always kept me in his sights, following me no matter how far I went or how high I climbed.

Never mind the snows or rain or heat or rivers to ford, Theo was always with me.

I've come to accept that Theo often knows me better than I know myself. He can look at me with a steady gaze, his kind face evoking the child within me. My long-ago inner self wakes up to the gentle presence of this creature who loves me with minimal judgment. He is steadfast, ever-present, totally dependent, and completely devoted. Our affinity was instantaneous. Our 250 days on the trail together simply cemented our bond with mutual adoration.

Connecticut Kennel

I grew up in suburban Connecticut. My dad commuted into New York City where he worked as a salesman for a large paper company. He had gone to Mount Hermon School in northern Massachusetts, and then to Yale, and from there followed his classmates to New York. He had high aspirations for my only sibling, an older brother who had ADD before anyone knew what that was. He had a high IQ, but school was not for him, even though seeing that he had a good education was a great source of pride for our father, whose heart was riveted to his firstborn.

I learned to take care of myself in the shadows and to be independent, and at times sadly self-reliant.

Our trip to a kennel in Connecticut only made me more so. I didn't know it as we drove there, but we were on our way to pick out my brother's dog. I would have no input that mattered. Mom, Dad, and my brother were taken with a proud dog standing on his doghouse inside a large private pen. He had curly, dark, rusty-red fur on his back and legs, with brilliant white fur on his chest and paws. He was part collie and part spitz, of moderate size, with a short snout. While my three family members were captivated by this dog, I wandered off to a row of smaller pens slightly uphill from the proud pooch.

There I saw a dachshund whose belly dragged on the floor of his wire pen. He came waddling toward me with a look that begged for the attention my wounded heart longed to give him. We appeared to be of the same breed. It seemed we might be comrades in the struggles of life. We wanted to be together. I wanted to comfort him, just as I wanted to be comforted.

"Can we get this one?" I asked.

"No. Your brother's going to pick out the dog." His choice was the proud one who would become known as Rusty.

The dachshund stayed and I got on with my life, but that little dog seeking love and affection never left my heart.

Theo

In late spring of 2008, I was sitting on a beat-up couch in an old barn in Manheim, Pennsylvania, 30 minutes north of our home in Lancaster. Both towns are in Lancaster County, where Amish farmers preserve their early American ways, using no electricity and tending their fields by mule power.

Across from the couch was a rugged old desk where the owner managed the paperwork associated with breeding and selling golden retriever pups. My wife, Bonnie—Bon, as I call her—found this breeder in our local paper and liked her instantly because the ad read,

Bonnie and Soren

"Conducting interviews now." Those words suggested that the breeder was not running one of the puppy mills which, unfortunately, do exist in the area. We were at the barn to pick out my Father's Day present. This would be our third golden retriever.

My wife is not a roll-on-the-floor-with-him kind of dog lover, but she appreciates a handsome dog with a nicely proportioned head, snout, and body. Good breeding and manners are a bonus. She loved our former golden, Rumpole, for his show-dog quality. He fed her sense of canine beauty.

At the same time, my wife knows well my down-and-dirty dog love and appreciates it in me—and the dog. Perhaps it was my nightly dogless walks after Rumpole's demise that prompted her to search the pet ads in our paper. It was she who set up the interview in Manheim, and it would be her $700 for the less than show-dog puppy.

Theo came home at 12 weeks

We were out behind the barn at the kennels, taking our time getting to know the dogs, as the breeder was getting to know us.

There was no particular magic at the kennels. The pups were nice, but there was no "Aha!" They all had brown-paper-bag coloring; they were clean and soft but not classic.

The breeder led us back into the barn and directed us to the couch with the comment, "I think I have just the dog for you."

"Interviews" in the ad meant she would not place just any dog with the buyer—it had to be a good fit. Dog and owner had to have something in common. A bullheaded, type-A person would not do well with a shy and retiring or fearful pup.

I'm sure the breeder could see we were a loving family. There are seven of us: parents, three boys and two girls. The animal-loving sisters, 24 and 34, had come along for the ride and the obvious thrill of seeing and handling newborn puppies. Bon sized up the brood with her discriminating eye as the rest of us ooooohed and aaaaaahed.

As Bon and I sat on the couch with the girls nearby, the breeder disappeared toward the kennels, until. . .what was it that came around that desk, no more than 6" off the ground? A brown-furred, loose-skinned part of my heart. A boy! He looked straight at me and I at him. I don't want to say the obvious—but it happened. We bonded in a heartbeat. He came right to me, and I was instantly transfixed by his soft, oversized coat, his warm brown eyes, cold, wet nose, and a tail that wagged my heart like captured prey.

No question—I was holding my Father's Day present.

The breeder showed us how docile our new pup was. She picked him up, cradling his spine in her arms. A dominant, aggressive dog would balk at that and try to turn over. Theo accepted the position, and today will roll over, legs in the air, exposing his entire underbelly for a rub. I can hardly resist his bidding.

Bon was happy to look on, but the girls wanted their turn with the heavy, slippery, brown fur-bag of floppy bones. A docile bundle of love who had no idea what was coming years hence. And neither did I.

Rescue Dog

In time, the exceptional and exhilarating puppy days were over, and numerous relatives and family friends all had their time on the floor with Theo. His growing muscle mass and expanding skeletal structure were filling in some of the ample folds of his loose skin, but it still seemed as if he were wrapped in a thick overcoat a few sizes too large. When fully grown, he filled out in perfect proportions, a thrill to behold each day when I returned from the office.

When I came home from the world of my serious concerns and walked through the back gate, there he was. Waiting for me with patience I wish I could emulate. He'd been out of sight and out of mind as work consumed me. But whenever I saw him, he filled my weary mind like an ocean breeze or a dip in a lake on a hot day. I was transported to another world, his world!

There were no mortgages in his world. No bills. No judgment. No hate. No grudges. Just the moment. "He's home! Together! Wag!"

Whether he was lying on his perch by the back door or sitting up ramrod straight awaiting my arrival on the walk to the back gate, Theo immediately drew me up and out of my daily concerns and duties like the rescue basket lowered from a helicopter to a capsized sailor. Daily, Theo saved me from drowning.

He saved me, too, from a storehouse of anger and a reservoir of tears. If I was beginning to grumble about some computer glitch or time-consuming telephone menu, Theo, most often at my feet, would stretch up and put his muzzle on my knee. He did the same with anyone whose emotional temperature seemed to be rising from sadness.

In the Moment

Theo lives in the moment. If he hears "Walk?" "Ride?"—instant action. Up! Move! Walk in circles! Wag tail! Go to door! Move back! Go to door! Move back!

Since we've been home from the trail, I've given many talks, sometimes in full gear, along with Theo wearing his saddlebags. I have no idea what goes through his head at these times. Is it, "Oh, noooo! Not again!"? Or, "Goodie, goodie. Let's go. Let's go!"?

People ask me, "Did he have a good time on the trail?"

I honestly don't know. His personality is so steady. Like Bonnie, he's solid as a rock. Unchanging, reliable, stable. He's the same at home as he was on the trail. All I know is that he wants to be with me no matter where I go.

He proved that over 2,200 miles, shivering with me in our tent, panting in the heat, and rolling countless times in leaves, grass, dirt, and dust to shed the feel of saddlebags day after day. Someone

asked my oldest son, "What if Theo dies on the trail?" His instant answer nailed it: "He'll be doing what he wants to do—following his master."

When asked if Theo had a good time on the trail, I should probably answer, "Oh, yes, he had a good time. He was with me."

In the Lead

As we hiked, Theo decided which of us would lead. From our first shakedown hike in Vermont until our AT finish six years later, Theo would scamper up or down ahead of me and find a place to lie, jowls between paws, looking back to monitor my progress.

On descents, it was critical that I enforce the "HOLD" command because, unchecked, he would bolt by me and could easily knock me over with possibly tragic results. He learned to stand right at my heel until I gave the "Okay, Puuup" or "Go ahead, Puuup" and off he'd go, brushing by me at a pace only a mountain goat could match. The command, "HOLD!" however gave me time to brace myself.

One time crossing a stream in the South, I was making my way over stones, balancing myself with my trekking poles, when Theo rushed by me, knocking me into the water. This incident gave birth to the command I often delivered: "Hoooold, HOOOOLD, **HOOOOLD!**" with increasing urgency until he got the message.

Early Training

Theo received some training as a young pup from a man who had worked with a dog whisperer. His methods were a little too alpha for me. Maybe such clear boundaries promote happiness for all concerned, but, the fact is, I'm a little looser and freer in my handling of dogs, including Theo. I don't want a show dog or one so regimented that he becomes my little robot. I want a little of the wild and playful dog left.

Theo's trainer thought him one of the smartest dogs he'd worked with and wanted to train him to detect breast cancer. But that was not to be. Together, Theo and I learned some basic training from him, and that was all we needed. The rest would evolve as we grew together.

Stay!

And grow together we did during our eight months and six days on the Appalachian Trail. We were the best of friends in the woods, on mountain tops, and in the valleys. But there were a few times when "we had words," and they were always my fault.

At several places on the trail, sets of stairs are positioned as an inverted V to take hikers over a wire fence, some barbed, some not. If they were regular stairs, Theo would be up and over them in a flash. But when the stairs were simply 2x4s, he would pass underneath, crawling through on the diagonal.

I arrived at the first set of 2x4 steps in the company of another hiker. I asked him if he'd stay on the near side of the steps, as I crossed over, and direct Theo to the entrance as I called him through to me. Worked like a charm.

The second time I came to such steps, we were on our own. I directed Theo to "STAY" while I crossed over. This was the wrong command.

I got on the ground on the far side and tapped the area under the steps with my trekking pole, trying to reach the entrance on Theo's side.

"Over here, Theo." Tapping. "Over here. Theo, over here!"

Nothing was working. He knew just one thing: "Ain't no way I'm stayin'!"

He charged the wire fence, ducking as low as he could. He had gotten under barbed wire fences many times without incident and without rushing it. But the bottom strand of this fence was a good bit lower and happily not barbed. He plowed ahead and was stopped in his tracks.

"STAY! **STAY!**" I urged forcefully, pushing him back.

Fence steps: if 2x4s, dogs underneath

He charged again without success. I repeated my command with rising anger in my voice.

He charged again.

On the third try he got through, tearing the bear bell, intended to alert bears of our arrival, off the top of his saddlebags. I retrieved it and put it in one of his pouches, miffed at his disobedience—until I realized he thought "STAY!" meant I was abandoning him. His answer: "NO WAY!"

As we walked along, the source of his fear and my error sank in. I apologized to him in soft, compassionate tones. I felt very sorry for instilling fear in him and marveled at the strength of his attachment to me.

I've come to realize that I am life to Theo. I am the air he breathes. The STAY incident was simple for him: Fear. Fix. Follow. End of story. We're together as we're meant to be and we carry on. . . and on. . . and on. . . together.

For 250 days, we were companions 24/7. On my mission. Not his. His mission is simply to be and remain with me. To know at all times where I am, or to have my assurance that I will return—and never, NEVER leave him behind.

We did "have words" a few other times as our adventure moved farther north, as you'll see.

Animal Nature

While the bond Theo and I feel for one another began at first sight, my knowledge of animals and how to act around them goes back to childhood.

I was fortunate as a boy to attend Major Self's New Canaan Mounted Troop in Connecticut. I'll never forget Major Self pointing out that, when you throw a ball high in the air, a horse thinks it's a person and will get spooked.

She also told us that you need to talk to the horse as you approach it, especially when you do so in a stall with his head away from you and his rump and hind legs nearest you. Let him know in a firm but gentle voice that you are approaching from behind. "Hello, big boy. Hey, big fella? Good boy. Ready to be groomed, big guy?" Gently put your hand on his rump and stroke toward the back, with the grain of the fur, as you step into the stall alongside him. Or her. . . .

I have learned that large animal veterinarians are grateful to owners who raise foals and, from birth, touch them all over, gently, kindly, and with zero threat. Vets manage such foals with more ease. They are used to touch and do not balk when examined.

I have followed this lesson with Theo. I touch him all over, including firmly massaging his strong hind leg muscles and rump. He loves my touch and waits for me at the foot of the stairs in the morning for his wake-up rub. I get down on the floor and hover over him loosely, rubbing his chest and whispering sweet gibberish in his ear. Grammar's out the window. Communication takes place in my tone of voice. He knows words because of their sound and how they're delivered.

I have tried to avoid the trigger word "walk" so as not to excite Theo prematurely. He has learned exactly what that means by both sound and tone, I'm sure. It's hard to fool a smart dog.

Theo has taught me to talk with my eyes. If I am upstairs, Theo will wait for me near the bottom step. I'll stop part-way down, and, if he is eager to go out, he'll turn his eyes toward the door. I'll answer with the same gesture and say, "I know. . . I know. . . ." If I anticipate his needs and look at the door first, he'll get up and start circling with excitement.

Sometimes we look at each other from a distance, with what has to be mutual love and respect. I'll talk to him in the softest, gentlest voice I can muster, trying to get him to blink his eyes at me. He will, and I'm certain he's saying, "I love you, too."

CHAPTER 2

Hiking

The Whites

I had hiked on the Appalachian Trail as a 12-year-old when I was at camp on Lake Winnipesaukee in New Hampshire. We'd done a 67½-mile, five-day trek in the White Mountains over several peaks, including Franconia Ridge. That experience would find a place in the recesses of my being and lodge there for years to come. Just two years later, at age 14, I said to my roommate at prep school in Massachusetts, "Let's hike the Appalachian Trail," meaning the whole thing! The term "thru-hike" came years later.

We gave it some serious thought, but it never happened. Like a great whale, the AT sounded into my depths. My kids tell me it surfaced for air frequently when they were little, but it was not until late fall of 2005 that it breached in an awesome display—as inspiring as mile-high Katahdin, the ultimate destination of a northbound AT thru-hiker. "Katahdin" is a Penobscot word for "Greatest."

I was walking from the living room into the foyer of our beautiful home at the western edge of Lancaster City when I realized I was going to turn 65 in June of the next year. That's when the surface of my subconscious mind broke open and the great leviathan burst into view high overhead:

▍ MY 65TH BIRTHDAY ON KATAHDIN!

The die was cast. I would realize the ancient goal of hiking the entire Appalachian Trail.

Devil's Gulch

Fifty years after I first thought to thru-hike the AT, I was thinking of it again. The whale had breached, and there was a good chance it would really happen. Every year from 2005 until 2015, I would say to my staff and my family, "If I can close my office by year end, I'm going to start the AT next spring."

My legal career was winding down, and there were no associates to carry the baton. My self-reliance made me a give-it-to-me-and-I'll-do-it kind of guy. Associates I'd hired were not that way. My heyday was ending. Younger lawyers were getting the cases and spending gobs of money on advertising, which I couldn't afford.

I take some pride in what I accomplished at the bar and in the service I provided my loyal clients. I trained two president judges, placed children for adoption, earned significant compensation for people who were seriously injured, and saved lives with a suit encouraging owners of tractor-trailers to light up their perimeters at night. But now it was time to move on, even in my advanced years, to fulfill my deep-seated desire—on foot.

In the summer of 2010, I traveled to Vermont to take my first steps in preparation for the AT. I had heard a good bit about The Long Trail running over the peaks of the Green Mountains of Vermont from the Canadian border to Massachusetts. Because of the metadata recorded with digital photos, I can tell you that Theo and I took our first steps on The Long Trail at 7:42 a.m., on Friday, July 30, 2010. We would not stop hiking until 11:00 that night. We missed a shelter in the dark and had to sleep on the side of a rocky hill where

I used a tree to prevent me from rolling down. Theo was uphill from me at the start and flat against me not long after. This was our first night in the woods together, very much together.

When we encountered our first tree fallen across the trail, Theo's response was simple: "This is as far as I go. You're on your own. I'm done. Stayin' right here." I thought if I climbed over the fallen sentinel, Theo would get the idea and follow. It didn't happen.

First obstacle on first shakedown hike

With further encouragement, he made it over, and soon there was very little that he couldn't handle on the trail.

On August 2, 2010, three days in, the trail passed right through Devil's Gulch, a jumble of large boulders surrounded by thick forest. In the middle, Theo slipped into a deep hole. I removed my pack and went in after him. I had to remove his pack to get him back up. At the surface, I replaced his saddlebags and tried to lift him to a ledge where he'd be able to climb out, but the slant was more than

Theo could manage. I was stumped as to what to do, and then I thought: "I'll just leave him. He'll figure it out."

I climbed out of the gulch and started hiking. It wasn't 30 seconds before he was walking right behind me.

The Nose Knows

We did The Long Trail in two two-week hikes from Canada down to the point where it meets the AT, which then tracks The Long Trail for 105 miles north of the Massachusetts border. About 12 miles south of Canada, we came to Jay Peak Ski Area, where the trail follows a ski slope on the north side. Theo preceded me in the climb.

Both the AT and The Long Trail use 2"x 6" white blazes painted on trees and rocks to mark the trail. As I expected, there were no blazes on the ski slope, but I didn't see any at the top either.

I climbed a nearby ridge. None. I headed down a slope. None. I walked back down the slope we'd climbed, looking for the last blaze to make sure it led to where we were.

We were in the right place, but I had no idea where the trail continued, until I saw Theo sniffing at a fence across from where I was standing. I walked westward toward him and, as I got close, I saw a break in the overlapping wooden fence and a blaze that had not been visible from where I'd been.

I don't know when I'd have found the way without Theo's sense of smell.

Mount Marcy

Theo and I hiked 480 mountainous miles in preparation for our AT adventure: 40 in New Jersey, 170 in Vermont, 30 in New York, and

240 in Pennsylvania. In November of 2013, we climbed New York's highest peak, Mount Marcy, in the Adirondacks. The trail was all ice, and the summit was enshrouded in clouds with cold winds blowing snow that obliterated the white blazes. My plan to descend by a different trail than we climbed was dashed. It was getting late, and we had to get down by the most certain path, the way we came.

When it got dark, we came to a fast-flowing stream we had crossed on the way up. I could hear the rushing water, but, with only the narrow beam of my headlamp, I could not find the place where it was safe to cross.

I looked around for a spot flat enough to pitch our tent in the snow and informed my hiking companion, "Theo, we're spending the night right here."

We both shivered a good bit in our tent, but doing so warmed us up and tired us out, aiding sleep, at least a little.

At sunrise I fed Theo, ate, and packed up in the tent. When I went to put on my boots, they were frozen. I unpacked my alcohol stove, which I had made from a Coke can, and cooked my boots to defrost them enough to get my feet inside—and we were off.

Final Preparations

Sometime in the fall of 2015, I referred the last of my cases, enabling me to close my downtown law office. I told people that my trek of the Appalachian Trail was not in stone, but it was in metal. I had changed my license plate to read: IK9AT16. You'll get it in time, I'm sure.

My wife and I renovated a loft space above our garage for an office where I now write. I cleared out my law office by donations, auction, and transfer to my new space.

I cleaned out my closets, the basement, and the garage and paid as many bills as I could. I rewrote my will and put down my burial wishes. My wife is not a worrier. She knows I am careful and capable. She also knew that if I were to die on the trail, I would be doing what I had long wanted to do.

Recoup, Regroup, and Return

Theo and I did everything right in preparing for the AT. We'd been in the woods for two weeks at a time more than once. We'd climbed difficult mountains and learned that we could handle our packs and survive on our food supply. We'd learned that our gear worked well for us.

I'd learned to carry only what I needed, or would wish I had in case of injury or gear breakdown. When I packed for that first trek in July of 2010, I brought all my camping gear upstairs from the basement, laid it out in the living room, and was hard on myself as I selected what to take. That small multi-tool item would be nice. Nah.

When I finished excluding the things I didn't really need, I packed the rest and weighed myself on the family scale. Then I weighed myself again with my pack on. Forty pounds more.

By the end of the second day on The Long Trail, I was exhausted. At the first road, I got a ride to the nearest motel. I took a hot bath, washed my clothes in the tub, wrung them out, and spread them on the lawn in the back to dry.

I ate well, slept well, and, after breakfast, decided I would take the day off and consider my situation. After studying the trail ahead, I came up with my motto going forward: Recoup, Regroup, and Return.

I laid out all my gear on the extra bed and went over it with a critical eye—the eye that belonged in the head that sat on the neck connected to the back that carried the pack up every mountain we encountered.

I had learned a very clear lesson from the trail: listen to your body. My body told me I didn't need my tent because The Long Trail rules were to sleep in the shelters, a rule easily accepted because there were rarely places to pitch a tent. I didn't need all of the clothes I'd brought. I didn't need so many plastic bags. I didn't need 10 pounds of what I had brought. I packed it up and sent it home. My shakedown hikes were teaching me what many on the AT would learn at Neel Gap, 30 miles in for northbounders (NOBOs) or at Shaw's Hostel, 120 miles in for southbounders (SOBOs). Each place offered help to break down over-stuffed packs, ship the excess home, and replace with lighter supplies if needed.

CHAPTER 3

Georgia

With preliminary hikes done and our gear selected and ready, we were soon to pack up and bid farewell to kith and kin. We would travel south 700 miles, a couple of Northerners heading deep into unfamiliar territory for an adventure in the kind of wilderness we had learned to call home. I did a one-way car rental for the trip and, to protect the car from Theo, covered the back seat with a sheet I would send home from the hostel where we'd stay for a couple of nights before our first steps under our loads.

Booties. We each had some. Four for him and two for me. Mine were down

First day out: booties for the grated steps

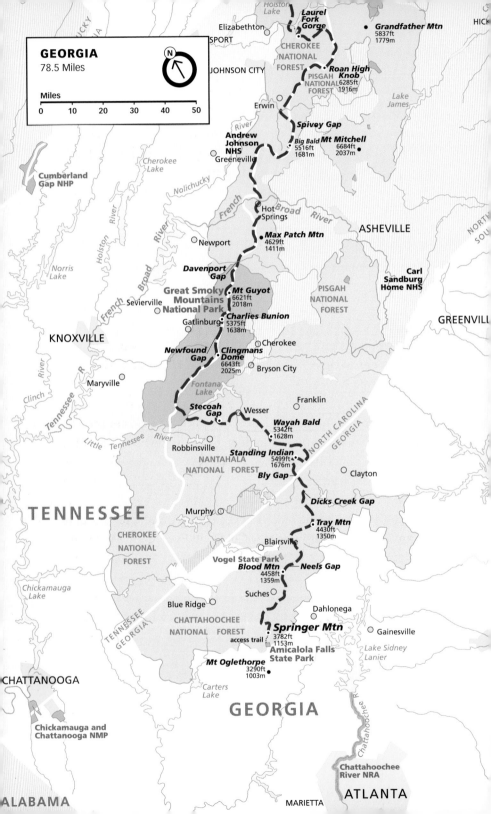

GEORGIA
78.5 Miles

N

Miles
0   10   20   30   40   50

Holston Lake

Laurel Fork Gorge

Elizabethton

SPORT

JOHNSON CITY

Grandfather Mtn
5837ft
1779m

HICK

CHEROKEE NATIONAL FOREST

Roan High Knob
6285ft
1916m

PISGAH NATIONAL FOREST

Erwin

Lake James

Spivey Gap

Andrew Johnson NHS
Greeneville

Big Bald
5516ft
1681m

Mt Mitchell
6684ft
2037m

Cherokee Lake

Nolichucky River

French Broad River

Hot Springs

ASHEVILLE

Cumberland Gap NHP

Newport

Max Patch Mtn
4629ft
1411m

NORTH
SOU

Norris Lake

Holston River

Davenport Gap

French Broad River

PISGAH NATIONAL FOREST

Carl Sandburg Home NHS

GREENVILL

Sevierville

Great Smoky Mountains National Park

Mt Guyot
6621ft
2018m

Gatlinburg

Charlies Bunion
5375ft
1638m

KNOXVILLE

Cherokee

Newfound Gap

Clingmans Dome
6643ft
2025m

Bryson City

Maryville

Fontana Lake

Little Tennessee River

Tennessee River

Clinch River

Stecoah Gap

Wesser

Franklin

Wayah Bald
5342ft
1628m

Robbinsville

NANTAHALA NATIONAL FOREST

Standing Indian
5499ft
1676m

Bly Gap

NORTH CAROLINA
GEORGIA

Clayton

TENNESSEE

Murphy

Dicks Creek Gap

CHEROKEE NATIONAL FOREST

Tray Mtn
4430ft
1350m

Blairsville

Vogel State Park
Blood Mtn
4458ft
1359m

Neels Gap

Chickamauga Lake

Suches

Dahlonega

Blue Ridge

CHATTAHOOCHEE NATIONAL FOREST

Springer Mtn
3782ft
1153m

Gainesville

Lake Sidney Lanier

TENNESSEE
GEORGIA

access trail

Amicalola Falls State Park

CHATTANOOGA

Mt Oglethorpe
3290ft
1003m

Carters Lake

GEORGIA

Chattahoochee R

Chickamauga and Chattanooga NMP

Chattahoochee River NRA

ATLANTA

ALABAMA

MARIETTA

booties to use at night in the subfreezing temperatures we would encounter in the mountains.

His were canvas sides with thin, hard rubber soles. I wondered if he would need them after years of road-walking with me up hills and down during my weekly exercise regimen. But I packed them in case. He carried them along with my Yaktrax micro spikes for ice. He also carried his dog food; a long, thin, vinyl-wrapped cable leash; his vitamins; an empty, spare, two-liter water bag; and my full water bottles.

In time I heard people recommending puppy chow for extra vitamins. I learned that grocery stores carried a 4.4-pound bag of Purina Puppy Chow, which I divided into two sturdy plastic bags, one for each pouch of his saddlebags.

Theo weighed around 67 pounds. The vet said he could carry one-third of his weight, but I'm sure he usually carried between 10 and 15 pounds.

Theo needed his booties on our first day and our first climb—up 604 grated steps at Amicalola Falls State Park. It was February 21, 2016, a rainy Sunday. The shuttle that got us to the hostel from the car rental in Gainesville, Georgia, also took us to the start of the approach trail beginning at the falls, 8½ miles south of Springer Mountain summit, the start of the AT in the South.

I didn't want to return home after hiking from here to Maine with any regrets. My attitude was Go! Do it! Every step! Miss nothing! When I was finished, I wanted to know that I had done what I set out to do, cutting no corners.

We passed through the stone arch leading to the falls and climbed the 604 steps to the top. These steps and many more landmarks on the trail loomed large in my imagination until I faced them head-on and took my first step.

There was no way I would have put Theo through that climb without booties. But getting his paw into a boot was like nailing Jell-O to the wall or pushing a wet noodle from behind. A little indignant, Theo accepted his fate and we began to climb, resting at a few landings en route.

At the top Theo led the way through mud to our first shelter, 7.3 miles in, according to a sign along the trail. Several guides and apps also provide distances, along with water sources, roads, towns, telephone numbers, rates, and amenities along the trail. Perhaps the most common guide is the book by David "AWOL" Miller, *The A.T. Guide: A Handbook for Hiking the Appalachian Trail*. I used the *2016 Northbound* edition. It is known to thru-hikers simply as AWOL. Miller left his job without leave in 2001 to do the trail, hence his trail name. He updates his northbound and southbound guides annually.

We stayed our first night at this first shelter with one other hiker. We would make our way to the official start of the trail in the morning.

Springer

At the Springer Mountain summit, we met several other hikers who wanted to get a jump on the bubbles which would follow. "Bubbles" are large groups who start together on the favorite days: February 29th (2016 was a leap year), March 1st, March 17th, April 1st, and May 1st. My calculations told me I would need all the time I could manage if I wanted to finish before the coldest winter weather set in. I had thought of starting in January, but I wasn't able to.

Here we are at the start of a trek to mile-high Katahdin in Maine, nearly 2,200 miles away. It was my idea. All Theo knew was that he was with his master in wet woods, wearing a contraption on his back. He accepted his saddlebags reluctantly at first, but, after a month or so, when I picked up his saddlebags, he'd walk over to me without being called. I heard of one hiker who, when he held the saddlebags for his dog, was met with a vicious growl. I heard, too, of a dog who refused to walk and another that got injured. The owners had to go off the trail, ending their hikes. Not Theo.

There had to be fewer than 10 hikers with dogs on the trail at that time in 2016, and most were day-hikers, I'm sure. Theo is the only dog I am aware of who walked the entire trail during our hiking year.

Theo was a little protective during our first month or so. If a southbound hiker appeared up ahead, he'd bark. Same if a northbound hiker came up from behind. But he loves humans, and there was no bite behind the bark. He has never felt the hand of a human except in kind, gentle petting, so he warmed up to every person he met on the trail or in town, and they warmed up to him, even at a distance. His fierce bark always turned to tail wagging. He'd even follow faster northbound hikers until he realized I wasn't keeping up, and . . . I had the food.

Springer Mountain summit — always close

The type of greeting Theo received varied with gender. Women got down on his level: "Hi puh-peeee. Aaaaah, he's so sweet." The guys stayed erect: "Hey. Nice dog."

We took our first step on the Appalachian Trail around 10:00 a.m. on February 22nd after the picture at the summit plaque. It was the first of 5,000,000 steps, but the mind can't grasp that, so we just started walking.

No Dogs

Neel Gap has the feel of a business interested mainly in business. They have places to bunk for the night with towels and showers. Of course AWOL had a write-up on the accommodations, but I had forgotten to note his "No Pets" comment. I arranged for a room which was promptly canceled when they saw Theo.

The guy was matter-of-fact. "No dogs."

Turned me off.

Theo didn't seem to care.

"Any recommendations?"

"Well, you've got Wolf Pen Gap Country Store in Suches, Georgia."

I called and they came for us, adding a shuttle fee to our tab. We'd stay two nights.

CHAPTER 4

North Carolina and Tennessee

Service Dog

An acquaintance who had done the trail with his dog several years before recommended that I register Theo as a service dog. He said dogs were not allowed in the Smokies or Baxter State Park at the northern end of the trail. Nor, for obvious reasons, in the zoo at Bear Mountain State Park in New York.

If your dog is not a service dog, you have to arrange to kennel him through the prohibited areas and have a driver deliver him to you at the other end. That is expensive and annoying.

I opted for registering Theo as a service dog to lighten my load because of my partial knee replacement. I carried only the card with a picture of the certificate. I needed the card only three times: at a motel our first night driving south; for a Ridge Runner who checks on hikers and trail status in the Smokies; and at Baxter State Park where the rangers are very serious about fulfilling the wishes of Percival Proctor Baxter, the 53rd governor of Maine. Governor Baxter donated the park land, which includes Katahdin, to be managed in trust under specific and strict terms, providing that the land:

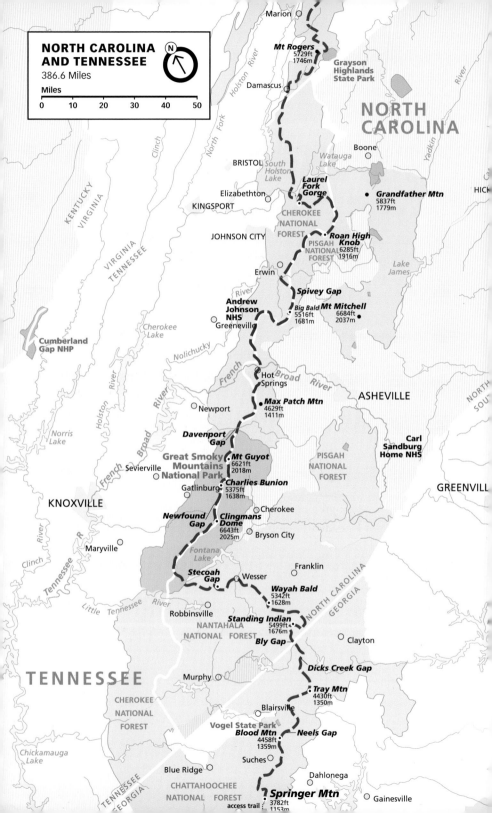

Marion

Mt Rogers
5729ft
1746m

Grayson
Highlands
State Park

Damascus

NORTH
CAROLINA

Boone

Watauga
Lake

BRISTOL   South
Holston
Lake

*Laurel
Fork
Gorge*

Elizabethton

● *Grandfather Mtn*
5837ft
1779m

HICK

KINGSPORT

CHEROKEE
NATIONAL
FOREST

JOHNSON CITY

*● Roan High
Knob*
6285ft
1916m

PISGAH
NATIONAL
FOREST

Lake
James

KENTUCKY
VIRGINIA

Erwin

Spivey Gap

VIRGINIA
TENNESSEE

*Andrew
Johnson
NHS*

Big Bald
5516ft
1681m

Mt Mitchell
6684ft
2037m

Greeneville

Cherokee
Lake

Nolichucky

*Cumberland
Gap NHP*

Hot
Springs

Broad

River

ASHEVILLE

French

Newport

● Max Patch Mtn
4629ft
1411m

NORTH

SOUT

Norris
Lake

Holston

River

Broad

*Davenport
Gap*

● Mt Guyot
6621ft
2018m

PISGAH
NATIONAL
FOREST

Carl
Sandburg
Home NHS

Great Smoky
Mountains
National Park

Sevierville

Charlies Bunion
5375ft
1638m

Gatlinburg

French

Cherokee

GREENVILL

KNOXVILLE

*Newfound
Gap*

*Clingmans
Dome*
6643ft
2025m

Bryson City

Maryville

Fontana
Lake

Clinch

Tennessee

R

*Stecoah
Gap*

Wesser

Franklin

Little

Tennessee

River

Wayah Bald
5342ft
1628m

Robbinsville

Standing Indian
5499ft
1676m

NORTH CAROLINA

GEORGIA

Clayton

NANTAHALA
NATIONAL   FOREST

Bly Gap

TENNESSEE

Murphy

Dicks Creek Gap

CHEROKEE

NATIONAL

FOREST

● Tray Mtn
4430ft
1350m

Blairsville

Vogel State Park
Blood Mtn
4458ft
1359m

Neels Gap

Chickamauga
Lake

Blue Ridge

Suches

Dahlonega

CHATTAHOOCHEE

TENNESSEE
GEORGIA

NATIONAL   FOREST

Springer Mtn
3782ft
1153m

access trail

Gainesville

> shall forever be used for public park and
> recreational purposes, shall be forever left in
> the natural wild state, shall forever be kept as a
> sanctuary for wild beasts and birds, that no road
> or ways for motor vehicles shall hereafter ever be
> constructed thereon or therein.

The Smokies are similarly managed, but perhaps a little looser. Nonetheless, it was difficult to come into these governed territories after being in the more lightly regulated wilderness. Rules were an imposition, but Theo took them in stride, even when I obliged and put him on leash in the Smokies. He just continued doing what he always did. He had learned to manage fallen trees with ease and would jump over most. But some, he went under.

Now that works really well with a leash, right?

I suppose it wasn't a problem if you handheld the leash and weren't using trekking poles. I had fixed the vinyl-covered cable leash to a hook on Theo's saddlebags and wrapped the excess around my waist. I was being fully compliant. I had paid the entrance fee online, filled out the paperwork in the box at the start of the park, and now I had my dog on leash. We were following the rules until Theo decided to go under a fallen tree. Then the entire assembly had to be undone and reworked on the other side.

One time I needed to step over his leash on a steep climb. He was uphill of me, leading, as usual. Up went my leg, back went my center of gravity, and down went the pack, followed by me, wearing it. The pack broke my fall, which broke nothing else. I had to roll off the trail and down a steep bank to right myself, and, as I did, my left leg folded up under me to the extent that my left heel contacted my left buttock.

I mention this because toward the end of our 480-miles of hiking to prepare for the AT, I had to back down mountains because of serious pain in the medial compartment of my left knee. Naproxen was no longer enough. I would need at least a partial knee replacement if I was ever to walk the full length of the Appalachian Trail. In May of 2014, I opted for a MAKOplasty procedure, in which the surgeon removed the painful joint surfaces and replaced them with prosthetic titanium plates. He positioned them using a robot and precise measurements of the joint made in a pre-op CAT scan. Three months post-op, I hiked 70 miles of the Horseshoe Trail with 30 pounds on my back.

I had done all the right things to restore my proper gait and to build the muscles around the joint, but I had never flexed it to the point where my foot struck my buttock.

Now I was sitting on my left foot on the side of the trail, muscles strained to the max, wondering just how bad this was. I carefully untwisted myself and found that I seemed to be okay, but for mild strain to the muscles around my knee. I climbed up the bank, and with an expletive for the leash requirement, returned the cable to Theo's pouch, never to be used again. I would risk the fine and, but for a couple of friendly and lenient Ridge Runners who monitor the trail, I encountered no authority figures.

Fellow Hikers

We carried on up the trail until another hiker caught up to us and, at my age, they all did. Probably in his 20s, he passed us with a "Hello," and kept on going. Then he stopped and turned around.

"Did you lose a pair of glasses?" he asked.

I reached to my face.

"Oh, my gosh! Yes. I guess I did."

He took glasses from a jacket pocket and handed them to me.

"Thank you!"

The jolt from the fall had dislodged my glasses, which happily landed not far off the trail. They were mostly for reading, less for distance, and I simply didn't notice with all the commotion and knee

Theo sitting in snow at a shelter in the Smokies, day 30

concerns. He saw them and carried them forward, hoping to find the owner. Hikers take care of each other this way. We all have a quiet respect for each other. There is a silent connection.

The Smokies

As we proceeded north in the Smokies, we came upon crowded shelters and snow. Thru-hikers were required to stay in the shelters unless they were full with local hikers; then we could pitch our tents nearby. The locals could kick us out of a full shelter.

I never saw this rule invoked, probably because everyone in the shelters was a thru-hiker. It was late March, and three bubbles of young, fast hikers were already on the trail. In a couple of shelters, the capacity was 12, with 20 inside. The double-decker platforms were packed. Extras slept on the ground, where some nearly froze all night without sleeping pads.

Each of the shelters in the Smokies has a stone fireplace in a side wall. Theo always cozied up to it, packed in with hikers huddling in front of the flames for warmth. But he'd sit comfortably in the snow come morning.

Happily, these shelters also had a large blue tarp hanging over the open side to keep the wind out. It got cold enough without the wind chill that water froze in my bottle right outside my sleeping bag. I was advised to bring a 0° bag but opted for my less bulky and lighter 32° bag in which I slept, wrapped in every stitch of clothing I had with me.

The cold in the Smokies should not be ignored. One year a hiker who had summited Everest thought he could handle these mountains and came unprepared. He died of hypothermia.

Since I would turn 75 on the trail, I was curious if I might be the oldest thru-hiker in 2016. But I thought not when I met "Tinker,"

Starting up Clingmans Dome

who showed up at one of the crowded shelters after dark, melting snow dripping from his long, white beard and beading on his bald head. He looked like Father Time himself, and I figured I was beat. But he was 69. So far so good.

Theo and I rose early on cold mornings and headed for the woods. We were the second ones out one morning. Deep snow was covering the trail, and some stuck to the trees covering the blazes.

We followed the footprints of the hiker who preceded us. "I hope he knows where he's going," I mused, remembering the story of the fellow following the taillights ahead of him in a thick fog in the English countryside. When the lights up ahead stopped, he yelled to the driver up ahead,

"Why did you stop?"

"I'm in my garage."

Theo and I made it to the next shelter at the foot of Clingmans Dome, the highest peak on the AT at 6,644 feet. We were the first up and out in the morning in snow over my boots.

I never wore gaiters, intended to keep leaves, bugs, debris, and snow out of your boots. They're extra gear and extra fuss to put on and maintain. My pants hung over my boot tops and all was well.

Clingmans Dome

I was thrilled to be out in the snow on a crisp, clear morning with my companion leading the way. Theo loves the snow as much as I do. One night on the top of Standing Indian Mountain, just north of the Georgia-North Carolina border, we practically froze in our tent. Even so, Theo jimmied his way out of my down jacket which I had zipped him in. I was so sorry that he was cold and felt like a poor provider, having nothing in which he was comfortable that met his winter needs. My conscience was eased, however, when he exited the tent in the morning and went outside to roll in the snow.

We started up Clingmans Dome under snow-laden evergreens and deciduous growth as the sun broke through. At the highest summit on the AT, it was bitter cold with howling winds. Frosty snow clung to dark bare branches as far as I could see.

Newfound Gap

After Clingmans, we came to another near-icon on the trail. New-found Gap is right on the North Carolina-Tennessee border, which the trail follows for over 215 miles. We were approaching Easter weekend, so there were lots of tourists around, especially by the

Rockefeller Memorial honoring the mother of John D. Rockefeller. It was here that Franklin Roosevelt dedicated the Great Smoky Mountains National Park on September 2, 1940, a few months before I was born.

Incidentally, "Smoky Mountains" has no "e" because the Tennessee spelling won over North Carolina's. They got their name from the frequent smokey haze covering the mountains.

Hikers always figure out in which towns they'll do laundry, shower, and resupply. I had decided that Gatlinburg, Tennessee, about 16 miles to the west, would be our stop. How to get there?

I was aware of no shuttles, so I inquired of some hikers who had called a van service. They welcomed me to ride into town with them. When the driver arrived, she said it was fine for me to ride along—until she saw Theo.

"You can't bring the dog. We don't allow dogs in our cabs."

"He's a service dog."

"That doesn't matter. He can't come."

"Do you know that's against the law?"

"He can't come. It's company policy."

I let it go. There'd be another ride.

Soon some young folks came over to me and Theo. The girl, as was usual, bent down to pet Theo and soon offered us a ride into town. We'd have to squeeze into the front seat of their truck, with Theo scrunched on the floor under my legs. We were just grateful!

There were two passengers in the small seat in the back, plus three with the driver, Theo, and me in the front. The driver, an ex-Marine, offered me a couple of his rations—MRE's (Meals Ready to Eat)—which I happily accepted as they dropped us off at the Motel 6 where I'd arranged to stay.

Gatlinburg

I took Theo into the woods behind the motel to do his business and returned to settle in for a couple of days. Before dark, I saw to it that Theo was comfortable, then walked into town to get the lay of the land and find a place for supper.

Gatlinburg is a bit of a honky-tonk town with roadside amusements and tourists, many with huge bellies and huge vehicles. The milieu is antithetical to the trail, and so is the pavement. It was here that I realized I would rather walk 10 miles in the woods than one mile on hard surfaces in town.

I found a place to eat and was seated at a table looking out onto a lighted sapling by a wide stream. I enjoyed a gin on the rocks with a shrimp cocktail as I looked out the window, unhappy with the superior judgmentalism I felt about the town and the tourists. As I sat there, this came to me:

There is no judgment
In the random ramifications
Of the branches of a sapling
Nor in the smooth waters of
A river turning white over rocks

I am grateful for what the warmly lit scene outside the restaurant window gave me that night. It's what Theo gives me with every glance. Perhaps the trail called to me long ago because I was the odd man out in my family of origin. Since I didn't fit in, I made my own path in a cultural wilderness, driven by a vow that grew out of adversity, rather than out of awareness, acceptance, love, care, or vision.

Theo and I camped out in Motel 6 until Good Friday, when it was time to get back on the trail. Before heading for the highway, I noticed a small thing with a big message. Half the body of a worm had been crushed under foot. The other half dragged the whitened, lifeless portion across the wet driveway at the motel. It was a good example for me of courage and persistence against great odds.

Ironically, nature in Gatlinburg taught me well.

Theo Gets a Ride

We stood by the side of the road with all our gear, Theo at my feet, my thumb extended in the direction I hoped to travel.

Many large SUVs passed us without a hint of stopping. I began reflecting that a tourist mecca was probably not the right place to expect down-home largesse. Maybe Theo was a drawback as he had been on the way in. He sat right in front of me with his saddlebags on, looking up at me for approval and direction. Knowing dog-speak as I do, I'm sure he was asking, "What are we doing now?

Are we heading back to the trail? Why are we standing here in the road? Doesn't matter. Just tell me what you want me to do and I'll do it. Count on it!"

I was a couple of SUVs from quitting and exploring other possibilities. Maybe we'd go to the garage at the corner and see if someone filling up could give us a ride. Just before I stepped off the road, a pickup truck pulled over east of us.

The driver told us we could ride in the back. He said he stopped because of the dog. He was in town from Alabama to pick up a beagle he had purchased. He really cared about dogs, and Theo again saved the day. A drawback? Not at all!

I threw our packs in the back, and Theo and I followed. There was a large crate in the bed of the truck, obviously for the dog the driver was in town to get.

The day was cool and cloudy, yet sunny. Theo and I enjoyed our ride as we wound and climbed back to the Gap. He hung his head over the side to get the ram air pressure up his nose, stimulating his profound frontal-lobe appreciation of life. I held on to his hindquarters and he mounted the side of the truck bed to maximize his pleasure.

Tourists and Thru-Hikers

Back at the familiar parking lot, we were more in sun than shadow. We hopped out, thanked our kind driver, and walked over to a retaining wall, where we had a broad, deep view into North Carolina.

Theo, my beard, and backpack were each people magnets. Some folks asked where we were headed, and I answered, as I did often in the deep South, "Dare I say, Maine?" That always prompted big smiles and not infrequent expressions of respect and awe. A small group asked if they might take our picture. Theo and I obliged happily.

The trail took off into the woods at the north end of the large parking area. Many tourists without gear were heading into the wilds to kick off their weekend. This section of the trail was the most well-worn I'd ever see on the AT. As we got deeper into the woods, the numbers thinned out in both directions. Those without backpacks were doing a round trip back to their cars. Thru-hikers would not be returning. Their destination was just shy of 2,000 miles farther north.

Theo and I hiked through the misty lowlands until we found ourselves on a narrow ridge where the sun sat low in the sky before sinking below the clouds. When it got dark, we hiked by headlamp until I looked up from the trail into the night sky. I turned the lamp off for a moment. The lights of Gatlinburg were far away. We were high in the sky, alone in a very dark night, the diamond-dusted heavens above. We took in the view and, notwithstanding the hour, lay back on the side of the trail, soaking in a firmament littered with stars.

Two Tent Nights

It was 9:00 or 10:00 when we arrived at the side trail to the shelter, which someone told us was full. There was a tent nearby with no sign of life. "Hiker's midnight" is 8:00 p.m., and surely sleep had gripped the weary soul within.

We found a tight spot on the other side of the trail and set up camp for a good night's sleep.

Morning dawned with golden sunlight that would last the whole day as we climbed up and down elevations between 4,500 and 6,300 feet.

By nightfall, we were at another shelter, arriving late as usual. We had to hike longer than others to keep a pace that would enable us to finish before Baxter State Park and Katahdin in Maine closed in mid-October.

This shelter was full, too, and so were the numerous campsites surrounding it. I enjoyed making do on a little island of land on perhaps an 8° slant to a pine tree at the foot and another 8° slant to the left where Theo would be. To avoid sliding in either direction, I put my empty backpack under my sleeping pad, making a shallow seat that would give me one of my best nights on the trail.

Sojo and Theo

Remember AWOL? That's a trail name. Every thru-hiker takes a trail name or is assigned one by their peers. One young woman was asked if she had a trail name and she said, "Not yet." That became her trail name.

Mine is "Sojo," for Sojourner. I gave it to myself, expressing the thought that I am just passing through.

Doing the AT is essentially walking from point A to point B. That's your single, daily objective. That's the big plan of your life on the trail. All the logistics and studies of trail profile, water sources, resupply spots, places to shower and do laundry, all of that serves the A-to-B journey. Katahdin was my goal as it is for every north-bound AT thru-hiker.

The community of Sojo and Theo on the AT was quite simple with very few rules. The goal of the adventure was so fixed and all-encompassing that complex rules were unnecessary. The Sojo / Theo Constitution was basic: 1) Just keep going; 2) Don't argue with Mother Nature; 3) Listen to your body; 4) Sometimes the fastest way forward is to stop; and 5) Hike your own hike.

A typical day reflected the simplicity of the undertaking: rise, eat, pack, hike, eat, hike, eat, hike, eat, camp, eat, sleep. That was our day every day—just keep going. And Theo followed, most often by leading.

Follow Me!

We did reach a place near Pearisburg, Virginia, where it was essential that Theo follow me as we walked along the side of what could be a dangerous road. We had descended a long, wide trail that came out of the woods at an intersection with a paved road which we would soon need to travel.

I had heard that this area was reputed to be an unsavory place inhabited by ex-cons. Nonetheless, at the intersection we found four guys serving up food, love, and Christianity under a canopy. I was a little uncomfortable with their proselytizing, but it turns out they were good company and generous with their food.

After this pitstop, we descended a hill on the paved road to get back to the trail. Theo wanted to walk beside me in the road. I kept saying, "FOLLOW ME! FOLLOW ME!"

I feel a little stupid confessing this, but I had never taught Theo the command, "Follow me." Those words didn't mean anything to him, but I kept repeating "FOLLOW ME!" gesturing to the ground behind me. I raised my trekking poles behind me forming a V, hoping to channel his steps where I wanted him to be.

On the trail he was often behind me, and he would stay there if I urged him not to pass in a precarious situation. The trail was a narrow path, naturally promoting walking single file, but the road was wide open and, thankfully, not too busy.

Again, my anger. Again, my fault. I apologized just as I had after the fence incident, in the most tender voice I could muster. Finally we made our way back into the woods, and our troubling ordeal was over. I doubt Theo carries the kind of sting people do after we have dissension or discomfort with another human. If I encountered tension or misunderstanding with anyone I met in town or on the trail, I tried to handle it the best I could, figuring it would fade into history as we headed north. I suspect Theo got over my little fit of anger in fewer steps than I would.

Are You Coming?

I think Theo worried more about me as we walked than I would about him. In the lead, he would wait for me to catch up. Sometimes in the late afternoon or evening, he'd pass me and climb onward, as if to say, "We can do it. I know we can. I can smell the shelter. Just follow me. We can do this."

Theo became the most loved dog—if not the most loved hiker—on the trail in 2016. Later in the White Mountains of New Hampshire someone would say to me, "I saw you in the Smokies. I remember your dog."

Leash

Theo never got upset or distracted around other animals. We walked right by goats along the Horseshoe Trail in Pennsylvania with no problem. I remember walking along the main drag in Helen, Georgia, past some geese who, even at 50 yards or more, got all excited about Theo. I did some shopping and returned to our room, past the same frantic squawking. Theo was unmoved.

The Top of Georgia Hostel required that all dogs be on a leash, but it became obvious that Theo was no ordinary dog. He was pure love in a furry gold coat, ready to please in return for hands-on attention. "You don't need the leash—don't bother," came the welcome comment from staff member Paula, who had a dog named Ella.

It was at Top of Georgia Hostel that I met Journey Man, a retired social worker who had served PTSD soldiers. Like me, he'd had the AT in his sights for years, and now he was doing it! He lives in North Carolina, and the state social worker organization had voted him the Social Worker of the Year and submitted his name to the national organization. At a summit several mountains farther north, he had a call from his wife who told him he had been selected Social Worker of the Year at the national level as well. It was an honor to hike with him, and I am happy we have maintained our friendship.

At the Nantahala Outdoor Center (the NOC, pronounced "knock"), an iconic stop in North Carolina, I took Theo into a restaurant along the Nantahala River. Hikers and their packs were gathered at the long bench outside. Inside, Theo drew the always-inquisitive looks from staff.

"He's a service dog," I'd say.

"Okay. He can come in. Just keep him with you."

Theo's always a little scattered about where to go or what to do in a new location. As we all know, a dog is a four-legged nose, and the nose is his guide. Scents come from all 360°, prompting behavior like the medieval knight who "ran out of the castle, jumped on his horse, and rode off in all directions." Notwithstanding his ubiquitous olfactory awareness and driving instincts, Theo will follow me and obey me, no questions asked, if only I keep the instructions coming.

A short "Come," a tiny whistle burst, a clap of the hands, or a call of his name bring him to me in a flash. Noting his strict obedience and his calm response to "Stay," people accepted him and his elevated status.

Food or Friends

Theo? I think "loyal." Me? He thinks "FOOD!" and "scratches."

But if I'm getting angry at something, even under my breath, he knows where it's going before I do, and he'll come over and soften my mood. So am I just "scratcher" and "provider"? There must be more to the indescribable bond between human and animal than that.

When we got to the North, I fell maybe 50 times—we'll get to that later. But I note here that I recall only one time when Theo came over to me as if to comfort me. All the other times, he'd just lie down and take the time to rest. Was he laughing to himself? "You silly fool! Think you're pretty cool standing so tall on two legs, huh? Wake me when you're ready." Or was he being sensitive to my dignity?

I kept notes on AWOL pages covering sections of the trail we had already hiked. My notes for this day include a reference to "The Colors of the Wind" from the Walt Disney movie *Pocahontas*. Together, Theo and I painted with all the colors of the wind—with gold and green, white and blue, with black, dull silver, and all the hues of a clear raindrop. We were painting with the bright yellow and orange of fire and the grey-white wisps of wind-blown fog and mist; with the grey-blue chill of ice and the breathless white of snow and frost. The colors of our journey folded in on one another day after day, season after season, storm-and-blue-sky cycle after cycle. It was a breathless time of wind-blown colors rising up without and within. A symphony of life on the loose.

American Dog

We met a hiker from overseas. He was a friendly man, but he had a thing about Theo. He liked Theo but also toyed with him.

Whenever he saw him he would say in an accented and theatrical voice, "American dog! American dog!" He did it so consistently and vociferously that I was getting annoyed. It did not seem loving of the dog. Instead, he seemed to regard Theo as his plaything, a vehicle that he used to take the stage and be noticed. I was ready to say something to him if it happened again.

We had been crisscrossing the North Carolina-Tennessee border many times and, at Doll Flats, where we left North Carolina for the last time, I set up my tent and ate supper against a log. Who came along but this hiker with his usual "**AMER**ICAN DOOOOG!" greeting.

I asked him if he would mind calling the dog by his name, "Theo." He hesitated with an unmoved expression and tried to mouth the word, "Teeee-o." That was close, but not on the mark. I repeated the name, thinking he was serious about using it.

I said, "Theo is a dog. He's not a toy." I spoke softly, kindly, seriously. I added, "It seems that you are always acting. I wish I could get to know **you**—not the actor." He went quietly to his tent, not too far north of mine, and never spoke to me again except to acknowledge my "Hi," on the few times we met after that.

I'd made a small stand for the quiet dignity of a dog and for a sincere connection with my fellow human. I believed I had done what needed to be done, and the rest was beyond my control.

Uncle Bob

The next day dawned bright and clear as Theo and I headed north toward the 400-mile mark. The trail, though easier, was typical of so many miles in the South. Dirt, leaves, few obstacles, mile-making terrain with the occasional curved descent. We were climbing an extended, modest grade when a German hiker came up behind me.

We stopped and chatted. His pack looked like it had supplies for three. It was stuffed to the gills and rose above his covered head. He had shoulder pads under his straps—little wonder.

He was "Uncle Bob" to his sibling's children, so he took the name with him on the trail. He was clearly in excellent shape and was hiking all over the world, including the Appalachian Trail.

Uncle Bob and I hiked together for a while, long enough for me to learn he made a habit of cooking and eating along the trail before he arrived at camp—a conservative method of keeping bears away.

I was not as careful as Uncle Bob. Perhaps I relied on Theo to scare away bears who, I'm told, don't like dogs they know to be used in hunting. Fortunately, we never had a dangerous bear encounter. In bear country, I ate away from my tent and hung all food, snacks, and wrappers with rope between trees at least 10 feet off the ground.

I would hang Theo's saddle bags, stuffed with his food and all food wrappers, which I collected in plastic bags to pitch in town. I was meticulous about leaving camp cleaner than when I got there.

I kept my food in a green stuff sack (a cloth bag with a tie) for breakfast, a blue one for lunch, and a red one for supper. I'd hang all of these as well in bear country.

Over time my meals evolved. In the winter, I didn't have to worry about food spoiling so I might carry butter, mayonnaise, and the like, but eventually I settled on a pretty regular menu. For breakfast, it was two packs of high-protein oatmeal, granola, nuts, raisins, lots of brown sugar, powdered milk, and hot water. I loved this meal! And it was topped off with fresh ground Starbuck's French Roast coffee, which was steeping in extra hot water in my cook pot while I ate. Then I'd pour it through a fine mesh, add a little sweetener, and enjoy it—maybe even with a doughnut which I'd eat with a spoon if it crumbled. Theo got several pieces.

Lunch was a large tortilla in which I'd roll peanut butter and jelly, each from a plastic jar—never glass. Peanut butter was the most popular source of protein on the trail. It and jelly are heavy but worth it!

For suppers I had tried out dehydrated foods, but after a while they all tasted the same. I eventually shifted to the more expensive and more palatable freeze-dried foods from Mountainhouse, Backpackers Pantry, and Good2Go. With these, as with breakfast, you just add hot water and eat. But while breakfast was instant, freeze-dried foods had to steep for about 12 minutes in the plastic package they came in. There was beef stroganoff, lasagna, and, my favorite, chicken and dumplings.

Water was another heavy item but obviously indispensable. I, or I should say Theo, carried three Gatorade bottles, two holding 20 fluid ounces, and one 32 fluid ounces. He also carried a spare two-liter, heavy plastic bag with a black canvas handle on either side of a very heavy Ziplock top that I needed real strength to open and a large stone to close. Once filled, there was a small plastic cap to a small spout for easy access.

Water had to be filtered to remove Giardia and harmful bacteria. An ultraviolet light is needed to remove viruses. I was told, and proved it to myself in my preparatory hikes, that the earth is the best filter there is. So if the water came right out of the ground, I didn't filter.

To heat water, I used an extremely lightweight, Coke-can alcohol stove. For fun, I made over 500 of them in my basement and gave them all away at hiking conferences. In the Smokies, I met "Minuteman" who had a jet-boil stove by MSR (Mountain Safety Research). It was a lot heavier than my stove, but it started easily and heated water in a flash. I bought one in Gatlinburg. It was worth the weight, but I do feel I sacrificed a little of the primitive hiker for a modern convenience.

And then there were snacks. Many hikers carry trail mix consisting of nuts, raisins, and M&Ms, or squeeze containers of a high-energy concoction, or beef jerky that did not appeal to me. Oreos and Snickers were my favorite. Theo never got people food at home. He got just a cup of dried dog food in the morning and a large dog biscuit at night. On the trail, however, snack time went like this: "A bite for me and a (small) bite for you" until we were ready to start hiking again. And at breakfast on the trail, he'd get twice as much dog food as he did at home for the whole day—and at supper, twice as much again. Since we're back home, I'm much more lenient.

Stove bought at Gatlinburg; boils fast and worth the weight

Watauga Lake

We stayed at Black Bear Resort near Hampton, Tennessee, for a couple of nights to rest from the trail, do laundry, resupply, and plan the days ahead. AWOL has information about all of this. I'd read about the terrain, elevation changes, available water, shelters, and campgrounds and figure how many miles we could manage until the next resupply spot. If we were going to be in the woods five days, we'd need five-day's worth of food, less one breakfast and one dinner because we'd have those meals before we left and when we arrived.

Stops like this were also the times to recharge the battery I'd use to recharge my phone on the trail. When fully charged, the battery would recharge my phone three times. To assure I would always have power, I put my phone in airplane mode, using much less power. For my headlamp, I carried one extra set of two AAA batteries and was never in the dark.

While at Black Bear Resort, I made my way to a McDonalds in Hampton for WiFi and spent most of the day paying bills and attempting to blog. I soon abandoned this effort because of many technical complications and a learning curve I wasn't willing to tackle in the woods. I had bought a small, lightweight tablet and a light, folded, Bluetooth keyboard to use on the trail. With vinyl-covered wire, I fashioned a stand for the tablet, and the set-up was super.

Back at the resort, I caught up with other hikers or continued with planning. I never watched TV or the news. They held no interest for me.

Leaving the resort, we found ourselves in what looked to my imagination very much like bear country. The name of the resort and a sign at the trailhead, explaining that the Watauga Lake Shelter was closed because of bear activity, only added to the suspense.

After passing by a beautiful waterfall and making a long, steep climb and descent, we came to Watauga Lake where I swam and had lunch. Theo stayed dry. In spite of his breed, he is not a water dog. He sunbathed as I swam in underwear black enough to look like a bathing suit. I loved the looser living and pared down demands of my life in the wilderness. Animals thrive and so did I in this more relaxed setting.

After dunking and eating, we rounded the lake and passed the closed shelter where I stopped for water. When we came to a good-looking campsite at the northern shoreline, I was tempted to stay. But I thought of food smells and bears' need for water, remembering Uncle Bob's advice—he cooked on the trail, and then hiked on to his camping spot, away from the smells bears can detect seven times better than a bloodhound.

Monster

Theo and I moved on past the lake and up onto the knoll of a service road where we saw five hikers in a circle. Juan quietly played a banjo. We joined them, pitched our tent by the side of the road, and ate.

I hung my bear bag of food from a big limb away from camp, using the "sophisticated" Pacific Crest Trail method. I carried eighth-inch-thick nylon cord with me and tied a loop at one end using a slip-knot. I fit the loop around the neck of one of my Gatorade bottles of water and swung the bottle from the rope, releasing it so it would go over a heavy limb about four feet from the tree trunk, and then drop to the ground. I removed the bottle and fastened all items to be hoisted out of reach to the loop. I then ran the other end of the rope through the loop and pulled all the items up to the limb. I reached as high as I could up the rope, higher than a bear's reach, and fastened a stick in the rope at that level. Then I lowered all items down to that stick, about 10 feet off the ground.

Bear bag hanging; Pacific Crest Trail method

I must confess, when I first encountered this "sophisticated" bear-bag-hanging method, I wondered about the rest of the rope that's left hanging down below the bag but thought, "Well, people tout this PCT method as very good—the best!"

I rolled up the loose end of rope as I high as I could and turned in a little after hiker's midnight.

At 12:37 a.m., I was awakened by a ruckus outside. "C'mon guys," I thought. "What are you doing up at this hour?"

Soon a large, powerful German hiker, who carried a 60-pound pack and was called Monster, said, "Sojo. You awake?"

"Yeah."

"We think a bear got your food."

I checked. It had—by just reversing the "sophisticated" Pacific Crest Trail hanging method I had used the night before to elevate the food out of his reach! The Watauga Lake bears were used to people visiting the lake and to hikers hanging their food. I had followed all the PCT bear-bag-hanging steps to the letter, but the bear was as sophisticated as the designers of this "safe" method of food storage.

Bears are very smart. Unfortunately, humans can be less so by leaving garbage around public areas near where bears live. This teaches bears that there is food where humans hang out, and they learn every trick in the book to get to it.

Fortunately I had not suspended Theo's saddlebags and his food in the tree with mine. If I had, the saddlebags and contents would be gone, along with all my food and the GPS Spot tracker which I kept with my supper food bag to remind myself to send the signal to my family each evening so they'd know where I was and that all was well.

It was also fortunate that the bear smelled my food before he smelled Theo's, which was in the vestibule of our tent!

I had just resupplied my meals, so now my cupboard was bare. In the morning, a fellow hiker emptied his food on the ground and said, "Take what you need." Along the way to the next town, Damascus, Virginia, other hikers would see us through.

Skunk

On our last night in Tennessee I had a frightening experience. The bear at Watauga had come and gone without my seeing him. But this time a giant skunk came upon me in the dark, right at my feet. Theo and I had done 19.9 miles that day, and we were camping alone just off the trail on the right side. I was not going to chance bears discovering food in my tent, so I devised a foolproof method of hanging my food and Theo's saddlebags.

It was dark as I fastened the bear bag and Theo's pack to the rope, which I would hoist to a spot a good distance between two trees. I began to pull on the loose end of the rope, aided only by the light of my headlamp, when, all of a sudden, this monstrous skunk came scurrying about my feet. I looked up at the branch above and nearby on the ground, trying to imagine where he might have come from or be going. I couldn't figure out why he had shown up so quickly, or what he was doing there, except to get our food and spray me in the process.

I was struck both by how big he was and how bright his stripes were, a wide one on each side of his expansive back.

I couldn't see him well in the dark, but when I looked right at him, his stripes seemed almost iridescent in my headlamp.

Then I noticed that he moved only when I pulled on the rope. If I let it go slack, he stopped.

The "skunk" was Theo's saddlebags with reflectorized strips on each side to help me locate Theo in the dark.

"He" had scurried to my feet when I first pulled on the rope, because the saddlebags swung toward me as I lifted them off the ground.

Fright. . . then relief. . . followed by feeling quite silly!

Shadows

I was spooked on the trail two other times by light. One was when a thin drawstring on a stuff sack pulled a large clip fastener across the tent floor in dim lighting, leading me to believe a monster bug was sharing our quarters.

The other was at night when I was walking through some low bushes with a small LED light in my hand. It cast eerie shadows of the leaves on the ground all around me. A second later I realized what I was seeing.

I didn't live in a constant state of catastrophic anticipation or fear, but at some level I was always ready to be surprised.

CHAPTER 5

Virginia

Mojo's

While Theo's gear scared me on our last night in Tennessee, he himself brought me great joy and kindness our first night in Virginia. On April 20, 2016, day 60 on the trail, Theo and I found a place to stay in Damascus. I chose a bed in the bunkhouse, stashed my gear, took a shower, and weighed myself. I had lost 25 pounds over 470 miles. (I would lose more weight in New Hampshire and Maine.)

I dressed and headed for MOJO'S, the spot in town to hang out with its WiFi, coffee, sodas, and good food. You could hang there all day if you wanted to. It seemed some did. Service-dog Theo came with me. Would I ever leave him if I didn't have to?

I always asked first if I could bring Theo into restaurants or other public places and would advise that he was a registered service dog. That opened doors for us. MOJO'S owner was short, wiry, and perhaps just a little testy. He wasn't sure about Theo or his official status (neither was I for that matter), and he kinda kept an eye on us.

I ordered eggs and French toast for me and pancakes for Theo. We ate them outside and, when finished, we both went in. Of course, people stopped and said Hi to Theo or otherwise ooooh'd and aaaaah'd about him. I always loved it!

I sat on a comfortable couch near the center of the room and soon noticed a young woman and her daughter at the counter. As the mother began a conversation with someone, her daughter was looking over at Theo. I caught Mom's eye.

"She can pet him if she'd like," I said.

They came over to meet us, and soon they both sat on the floor by Theo. The mother and I got into conversation for about an hour. I told her my trail name was Sojo, standing for sojourner or soul journey. I'd learn later that this description prompted her to stay and talk longer. I mentioned that I was going to turn 75 near the halfway mark on the trail. Both she and her daughter just kept petting and stroking Theo, who was in fur-lined heaven for sure.

As they left, I noticed the mother talking to Paul, the owner of the hostel where I was staying, gathering that, as a local, she knew everyone in town.

They left, and soon I returned to the hostel.

Sweet Surprise

As suppertime approached, I was in the common area outside, chatting with folks before departing for Hey Joe's Tacos & More two blocks away. I saw Paul before leaving, and he happened to ask me what I was doing around 6:30 that evening. I figured there was going to be a songfest or the like and told him I was off to Joe's Tacos but could be back by then. He said, "That would be good." I was slightly suspicious that something was being cooked up.

I got back to the hostel in plenty of time and just hung out with other hikers and "Skink," Paul's trail name from his thru-hike a few years before.

After a while, I saw two people coming down the drive alongside the house. It was the mother and daughter. I will admit, I had

Early Happy Birthday in Damascus, Virginia

wondered if she was behind Paul's concern about where I'd be at 6:30.

She was carrying a huge tray of incredible homemade cookies, each with a delicious crust, cream cheese, and fruit. One cookie had a candle in it. In short order, people gathered. Juan got out his practice banjo and played an early "Happy Birthday," while everyone sang along. These were the people who had rescued me at Watauga Lake when the bear cleaned out all my food!

Now in Damascus, I have a very pleasant meeting with a lovely woman and her daughter, and those who gave me food five days earlier show up to give again. God seemed to be smiling on my decision to hike the Appalachian Trail this year. I felt as if I was being told, "Soren, you have chosen well. I approve and am pleased!"

I was indeed blessed. I slept well that night alongside my silent companion, Theo, who had a lot to do with all of this happening.

The Women

I took a "zero" in Damascus—hiker talk for a day off the trail. I had calculated many scenarios for finishing on time, and they all included days off, even as many as one a week.

I found an outfitter where I could replace my food bags and a long-shanked titanium spoon for use with the deep freeze-dried food bags. I had also made arrangements for a new GPS device to be shipped to me at a reduced rate if I purchased insurance, which still saved money.

After these necessities, I hung out at MOJO'S. I found a table by the window where I set up and did tablet stuff all day, Theo at my side. We had many welcome interludes.

"How old is he?" asked one of three women at the nearby table.

"Eight," I replied.

"I have a golden back home," said another.

"We lost ours to cancer a year ago," said the third.

The women were in their late 50s to mid-60s. I had been aware of them near me, conversing like old friends. They were sophisticated and classy. We introduced ourselves.

When they asked my name, I answered "Sojo," as I would continue to be known here and farther north by this most unlikely group of hikers on the AT. I never guessed that I would revisit this encounter at MOJO'S again and again on the trail, a lovely surprise each time.

At some point during the day I ordered coffee from the short, slightly terse owner, and I reached for my credit card to satisfy their pay-as-you-go policy. By mistake, I handed him Theo's Service Dog card. Because of his original uncertainty about Theo, he thought I was pulling a fast one on him. We both laughed. Seeing how calm and obedient Theo was, he had come to accept him completely. Another happy moment in that day.

It Began to Rain

In the morning, we packed up and headed for breakfast at MOJO's, right on the trail. While we were enjoying the warmth and atmosphere one last time, it began to rain outside. No one knew it at the time, but we were headed into the wettest May in Virginia's history. Theo took it all in stride, and so did one of the five trail maintenance organizations in Virginia which posted alternate routes for washed-out bridges.

Virginia is the fourth state going north on the trail, and the longest by far. More than one-fourth of the trail passes through Virginia, over 540 miles. Hikers talk of the "Virginia blues," and some leave the trail because of them. You've proven to yourself that you can hike a long distance. Now you face more than you have done already—all in one state—and that doesn't even get you halfway to the finish.

For some reason, I didn't mind it at all. My wife has often commented that I don't seem to be bothered by the weather—hot, cold, dry, wet, freezing, or sweltering. Nonetheless, I've been fortunate not to have my home flooded or blown away. We've had wind and tree damage, but that's about it. Short of a volcano, tornado, flash flood, or the like, all weather is a kiss from Mom to me.

Our first night in the Virginia woods was at a misty pond in the company of a few other hikers, everyone tending quietly to their own affairs—setting up, cooking, and turning in. As I was pitching our tent, Theo went through his usual legs-up gymnastics, rolling back and forth and sliding head to tail as much as possible. A bank leading from the pond down to the stream was perfect for his exercises, until it got too steep and he nearly fell in.

Soon after I crawled into the tent with Theo, we heard the spring peepers in the pond trying to outdo each other. The strength of their chorus was indicative of the turn in weather that was about to happen. The more fresh water, the more they want to mate, and the more they call. Rain drives their mating instincts. I was very glad for my earplugs!

The predicted rain came in the middle of the night. Again I was grateful for earplugs but happy I could still hear the thunder. Theo and I were dry as a bone in our tidy two-walled home. I deeply appreciate the magnificent, efficient, and effective simplicity of our tent, which allowed us to be comfortable in otherwise inhospitable weather. In its own way it was every bit as cozy as a cold winter night at home by a blazing fire (for which I am famous!).

I think Theo loved being in our cozy quarters every bit as much as I did. We slept well that night.

Mount Rogers

This was Mount Rogers day—a significant climb in misty, overcast weather. At the foot we ran into some kind dog-lovers with dogs who welcomed Theo into their midst. I accepted a beer and a sample-sized bottle of bourbon which I would enjoy at the top.

Near the summit we emerged from thick woods into a clearing and soon found a small grove of pine trees. We had gone from the perfect pond to a perfect pine grove setting for the night.

I fed Theo, cooked my supper, and crawled in, comfortable that this was not bear country. I was quite happy with myself—enough to sip my Knob Creek Kentucky Straight Bourbon.

Ponies

Mount Rogers is the southern limit of Grayson Highlands, a wide expanse of land grazed by wild ponies. Once underway, we saw our first of these, including a mother and her foal. Theo and I were on

VIRGINIA   67

the right side of the trail; mare and foal on the left. Gradually the mare led her foal away from the trail and I figured all would be well.

Once the foal was at a safe distance, however, the mare made her way slowly back to the trail and, on arrival, jumped over and bit Theo in the rump. Another hiker, who professed to know something about dogs, checked out Theo and said he found no injury. The mare was just saying what a bear would say to us later—Move on! Then and now, we obliged.

500 Miles

As we came to the end of the grasslands at Grayson, I saw small stones arranged to read "500," with the AT symbol underneath. We had hiked 500 miles! It was an emotional time for me, especially as I sang the song, "500 Miles," with its verse, "I'm 500 hundred miles from my home." As I sang that line, I realized that I was, in fact, 500 miles from my home. We would hike that same distance again before I would be with my family in northern Virginia to celebrate my 75th birthday. I sang that song for at least a hundred miles as we hiked northbound to the family reunion.

Theo and I spent the night near the Old Orchard Shelter where we met Farel, Ziplock, and Falcon, whom we'd run into again farther north.

Sticks and stones would tell us how far we'd hiked

Canine Exhaustion

Virginia was hard on Theo. The weather was either warm or hot, and a good bit of the terrain was flat. My golden beauty had learned that I move faster on the flats. In the lead, when he realized that I was going to overtake him, he would move over to the side of the trail and let me pass. A few times I found myself way out in front, and I'd turn around to discover that Theo was still behind the last bend, out of sight.

At a campsite one evening, Theo was extremely tired. I videoed him as his head slowly sank into the leaves between his paws. After almost a full minute, he jerked awake and the sinking started over. Another time he made a branch his pillow.

Our campsite was a quiet, sunny spot and gave me enough time and daylight to watch my exhausted companion and to appreciate

Some dogs quit from exhaustion — not Theo

how his life was dedicated to following me, no matter the trials, the lack of sleep, the length or pitch of the climbs. What was in this faithful canine's mind, in his gut, in the marrow of his instincts, in the depths of his soul? "Better to be bone-tired than to be without him."

What a lovely, peaceful, slowly departing, late afternoon and evening in the leaves with Theo, under the sky, among the trees, caught in sunbeams fading from the day as I got ready for my tent and dreams.

Summer Gear

The next day we reached Marion, Virginia, where we stayed a couple of nights, awaiting summer gear being shipped from home, and where I would return the heavier items I used in the winter.

During the first day back on the trail, I discovered that my new, low-cut, Merrell boots were too tight in the toes, causing problems that would last until the Vermont border, more than 1,000 miles into my future. I would deal with removing toe spacers, moleskin, and duct tape night after night, and applying new ones morning after morning, grimacing day after day from interdigital blisters and very sore little toes. Plantar fasciitis of the left heel, caused by my stepping on a sharp stone, didn't help. I learned to knead my heel tendons each night. They, too, would heal by Vermont, in time for the difficult mountains in the North.

We Can Make Room

We moved from brilliant beauty to deep, dark, and mysterious woods at the end of a 20-mile day. En route, we crossed treeless mountain tops, called appropriately, "balds." I found myself fascinated by interesting patterns in the rocks lying in the trail. They stirred my imagination deeply about the early formation of our planet, just a heartbeat ago in geologic time, when rock was molten and could be shaped. What had caused the shapes I was seeing? The rock face of tangled latticework? How did this happen? And when?

There were many mysterious rock formations

We found ourselves deep in the woods on a ridge, which was frequently very rocky and difficult to traverse. The late day was misty and foggy. As it got more and more eerie, Theo and I were more and more alone, hiking deeper and deeper into the wilderness. It was then that I saw in the woods, some distance from the trail, this sign:

> **Recreating in Bear Country**
>
> More and more habitat is being shared by humans and black bears. Follow these steps to help ensure your safe experience in bear country.
>
> - Hike in groups and stay close together
>
> - Keep your dog on a leash. . . . Dogs can agitate bears or lead them back to you.

The sign included a picture of a big black bear.

"Okaaaay," I thought. "Stay calm. Stay alert, and just keep going."

We did keep going. . . and going. . . through the damp forest, up and over rocks, coming eventually to a three-mile descent to Jenkins Shelter. Within a mile of our destination, we passed a stream, and I filled up our bottles. And then it began to rain. Unless it's a deluge, I always have an internal debate: do I get out the rain gear, or hope the rain's not going to last? Do I even care if I get soaked? I always get a little soaked anyway, even if I do cover up.

I got out the gear in the dark and continued.

Finally we came to the shelter well past "midnight." The drenched camp was quiet and the shelter was full, with only about a foot of overhang left for us to squeeze under.

I put my pack on the shelter floor at the near end and stood under that foot-wide eave as much as possible. It was around 9:30. I wasn't going to bother cooking, so I dug in my pack for my lunch and breakfast food and took out some honey. I downed the food and sucked on the plastic honey jar. As I ate, the hiker nearest me whispered, "We can make room here for you."

Now, as I sit here at my desk all comfortable and cozy, with a roof over my head and a cup of coffee at hand, my fingers clattering away on the keyboard, I become emotional as I think back on that long, difficult, somewhat eerie day that could have ended differently, as many could have. I place myself again under that narrow lip of protection in the dark, as dear Theo, soaked pack removed, seeks shelter under the elevated floor, and I think of a fellow-hiker's kindness.

It is good to recall how even the lone hiker is part of a mobile community of like-minded people undertaking an extraordinary and, at times, dangerous adventure.

Thank you, fellow hiker. I don't even know your trail name.

Quietly, while standing under the minimal eave, I removed my rain gear and hung it on a couple of nails around the corner of the shelter where I had placed my poles. I extracted my sleeping pad, inflated it, got out my sleeping bag, and laid it out upon the pad. I hiked my rear end up on the elevated floor, removed my soaking boots and socks, found a spot for them in the front corner with my benefactor's boots, and then hung my pack on a nail under the eave. I crawled carefully, silently, over my sleeping bag, head away from the shelter opening and boot odors, removed my soaked clothes, and crawled in for the night, grateful.

Theo managed in his own way.

May 1st

We awoke to more rain and the communal event of getting ready for the day. Don't imagine vigorous chatter. It's a quiet time, each attending to his or her personal needs, dressing modestly, usually in one's bag, collecting and organizing gear, preparing and consuming breakfast, packing, and then heading off into the wet forest and over swollen rivers.

I called my oldest son, Soren, on this day just to chat. He said, "Dad, just FYI, today's Hollie's birthday." Hollie's my niece.

"Oh, is today May 1st?" I asked, sounding clueless.

"I can't wait till I don't know," he said, mindful of his very busy schedule.

Wild Card

I hiked on, and, in a couple of days, we were at another fairly crowded shelter. Someone said the weather report called for hail. At Marion, I had swapped my Fly Creek UL2 tent with its extra wall created by the rainfly for a Zpacks Duplex tent made of taut cuben fiber, which hail would pepper with holes. Fancying myself somewhat weather savvy, I decided to risk putting up the tent.

As I was setting up camp, a totally disheveled and obese hiker with loose-fitting clothes, a shirt that hadn't seen laundry detergent in months, and long, straggly, greasy hair, came down the side trail to the shelter. He certainly was not a thru-hiker and looked like he was up to no good. This thought only grew as we talked.

"What's your trail name?" I asked.

"I already told you my trail name," he replied. To which I responded, confident I had never seen this person before, "If you had told me your trail name, believe me, I would remember it."

I learned from another hiker that his trail name was Wild Card, which seemed fitting.

In the morning, mystery man left before us without a word. It was another overcast, wet morning. Better rain than hail, at least for the tent.

A little over a mile in, I crossed a paved road and headed back into the woods. Within less than 50 yards, there sat Wild Card in short growth along the right side of the trail. He was having a food break and did not look or act as if he intended Theo or me any harm.

"You spooked me when you asked me my trail name," he said.

I should note that, for a thru-hiker, nothing is more common than to ask a fellow hiker his trail name.

"I didn't mean to offend you," I said.

We shared some inconsequential niceties, intended by me to keep him calm and non-combative. I wanted him to think, "Hey! He's okay. No point in roughing up his day."

I bid him goodbye and we went on our way. He would surface later that day at a store not far off the trail where we had lunch.

Wapiti Shelter

Once northbound again, we came to a side trail to Dismal Falls. I decided to make the trek. Theo kept watch as I swam in the brisk waters below the falls.

Our destination was the Wapiti Shelter about 6.2 miles on. With the Wild Card incident, I was very glad not to know the tales about this shelter or the stories of Pearisburg, Virginia, not far away. Several hundred miles later I learned of a double murder here, followed by an attempted double murder in the area 15 years later by the same person. He was from Pearisburg, Virginia, a town with an unsavory reputation where we would soon be staying.

Woods Hole

By May 4th, Theo and I reached Woods Hole, a delightful and famous hiker hostel on the trail. I had called Merrell Boots about the bad fit, and they promised to have a new pair of Moabs at the hostel for me to exchange at no cost. Thru-hikers are suppliers' best salespeople, so suppliers do everything they can to see that we are satisfied. They also realize that thru-hikers are on an extraordinary undertaking, and they genuinely want to see them through in good stead.

Hold

Theo wanted to finish well, too, and took every opportunity to rest. If I stopped for anything, he would rest, taking cover from the sun under even the sparsest foliage. He would position his head as well as he could wherever he lay down. Cool, deep grass was a favorite spot, but a branch, a rock, a foot, or table leg all sufficed as a pillow.

After descending lush, rolling hills to a swampy area, we came to a footbridge over a small stream. Theo would not "HOLD" as I crossed ahead of him, yet it was imperative that he obey this command for his safety and mine.

Shade of any kind

"Panic" is the word that explains much of his behavior at such times. At home he would rush through the door as if he panicked at the thought of being left outside. Perhaps it was the same crossing the stream. Was I going to cross and leave him on the other side? For good? Shades of the fence incident drifted through my mind and maybe his. I tried to distinguish the HOLD command from the STAY command, both being temporary, but the first shorter in duration.

I crossed the footbridge first with a firm "HOLD" when we reached midway. I enforced a "STAY" when I saw that he had sneaked up behind me. I went back and crossed again and again, reworking the commands until I felt satisfied that he understood them well enough for me to release him. "Okay!" were two syllables he had no trouble following. Think starting gate at the Kentucky Derby.

Keffer Oak

After the swamp we crossed a road and climbed through more lush, green fields. The scene with cattle grazing reminded me of the romantic title of the book and movie, *How Green Was My Valley*. The barns, houses, and farms I could see on the distant hills made me wish I could hear the stories about life here—births, crops doing well or not, storms coming, along with good weather, life and death in and outside the houses in the valley. Loves and hates and we'll-get-by and maybe-we-won't. Life. In my veins, and in theirs. Theo and I paused, considered. . . and moved on.

Tonight we would camp under the Keffer Oak, "the largest oak tree on the AT in the South; over 18' around, over 300 yrs old. Dover Oak along AT in NY is slightly larger" (AWOL). The tree is older than our nation.

Audie Murphy

Soon Theo and I were having another rainy afternoon, but this time I opted not to put on my rain gear. We arrived at a shelter at the bottom of the mountain and, soaked through and through, decided to seek refuge there. When we made our way around to the open side, we were confronted with hikers packed in like sardines. I took a picture and decided that the best way to dry off would be to climb

Full house, so we kept walking in the rain

another mountain and create body heat. We set out, climbed, and pitched our tent at the summit four hours later.

The next day we visited the monument of Audie Murphy who died in a plane crash near where we had slept. Audie Murphy was the most decorated soldier of the Second World War, with 33 medals. He single-handedly took out an entire company of German infantry with a captured German machine gun. Atop a burning tank he withstood an advancing squad of German foot soldiers and tanks, leaving the burning tank just before it exploded. He suffered from PTSD after the war, before it was a recognized condition, and became addicted to sleeping pills.

His autobiography, *To Hell and Back,* was made into a movie by Universal Studios. He starred as himself, and for 20 years it was Universal's highest-grossing movie. He was 45 when he died in the plane crash on May 28, 1971.

Four Pines

We moved on, with plans to stay at the Four Pines Hostel that night. I had called Merrell again, seeking more help with my new boots. They said they'd send two more pairs to the hostel, and I could choose which I liked and send the others back. You can't ask for more.

The trail to the road leading to Four Pines took us over a ridge with steep angled slabs of rock on the descent. Farther north, people would ask me how Theo did on this descent. My answer: "Piece-a-cake!" For me, it was life-threatening, an assessment which others shared.

I had cell service to call for a ride from Four Pines when we got to the road. Our driver turned left before four large pine trees in front of a farmhouse. We passed a water shed and small barn on our left and climbed a slight grade, curving to the right to a parking area in front of a very large garage, which was the main hostel and general hangout. The walls were lined with tables, a refrigerator, and tool benches, with a shower in the front right corner. Beds, cots, couches, tables, and a potbelly stove completed the interior. The wall behind the stove was black chalkboard filled with trail names of hikers wanting to leave their mark.

All beds in the garage were taken, so I was invited to stay in the barn up on the hill or in the small barn we'd passed on the way in. I chose the latter because Theo and I would have it to ourselves. I brought my gear to our home for the night and took stock of the interior. Chickens roamed in and out unless Theo seemed too interested. They wandered the grounds at will, as did guinea hens in great number. I, of course, directed Theo not to chase any of these critters. Being the most amazing dog on the planet, he did not and probably would not have even without my command.

A Zero

A zero day at Four Pines enabled me to move to the garage. It was "Trail Days" in Damascus, and many hikers made the two-hour trip to the most trail-friendly town on the AT for the famous annual festivities. The Four Pines owners went every year with a trailer load of donated food and a van full of hikers. The town would be abuzz with swarms of hikers, parades, music, performances, outfitters, and lots and lots of food.

I opted to stay put to tend to business and keep my mind and efforts on heading north. I had arranged for two packages to be shipped to Four Pines, and I wanted to be there when they arrived, plus rest for the miles ahead. In addition to boots, I was getting new tips for my trekking poles, which had survived almost 1200 miles, including my shakedown hikes. I would return the boots without opening the box, reasoning that only time and daily care would cure my feet if I wasn't going to quit the northbound trek.

I took a bed in the back left corner of the garage for our last night at Four Pines. Neat, clean, and tidy were qualities absent from all parts of the garage, but the hang-out comfort could not be beaten.

Theeeeee-o

The most iconic spot on the Appalachian Trail in the South is McAfee Knob, southwest of Roanoke, Virginia. It was our destination on leaving Four Pines. Before we arrived, however, Theo put me through some paces. But first a "tail" from farther south.

One time Theo disappeared around a corner, and a most unusual thing occurred. He came trotting back toward me, all skin and no fur! Well, not exactly, but that's about the only way I can convey how absolutely startled I was by what I saw. He didn't have his saddlebags on! The lack of a pack made him look as naked as a totally unclad person walking down a city street. My brain was rattled at the sight.

Where were they? How did they come off?

While I'm in a mild panic of bewilderment, Theo is blithely sauntering along, kinda proud of himself for getting out from under his burden.

I went around the corner from whence he came so naked and entirely unafraid. No pack in sight.

Then I recalled that about a quarter-mile back, Theo had stopped to drink from a small stream crossing the trail. We went back. There it was.

I had allowed the two straps that go under his chest and belly to hang somewhat loosely. When he bent over to drink, the pack simply slipped off. He clearly felt no need to point out, "Oh, Master! Look what happened. My pack fell off." Nor did he bark nor hesitate nor linger behind to get my attention. No sir! Hiking free and easy was just fine with him.

In the woods after Four Pines, Theo went ahead of me around a bend, and as I came along, I didn't see him. I figured he was on up ahead. I never had any concern that he would get lost or abandon the trail or chase wildlife. There was reason to believe he could be thirsty, and I wondered if he had scurried on ahead looking for water. So I kept going.

Theo and I had met a fellow hiker, Highway, farther south, and he and I hiked together for a little while. But he was having knee troubles that caused him to lag behind as we moved on.

I never thought Theo would go off the trail or lose the trail. I asked some southbound hikers if they'd seen a golden retriever with saddlebags. They hadn't. If perchance he'd pulled off to the side of the trail for shade, which he did on every hot and sunny day when I paused for a picture, most likely Highway would see him.

Then Highway showed up. "No." He hadn't seen him.

I prepared myself to hunt as long as it took and dismissed any thought of continuing on without him. Since I am always talking to someone in my head, I imagined the conversation with my family: "I lost Theo in Virginia. He just disappeared and I never saw him again. I have no idea what happened to him. I'm so sorry."

I took off my pack, set it on the ground by a fallen tree with my trekking poles and red bandana, and hiked back toward where we'd come from that morning. I probably walked a mile calling, "Theeeeeeee-ooooh," as I went. Normally, if Theo's close, I can whistle and he responds instantly. For distances, I would clap. Calling and clapping availed nothing. . . until I got near the corner he had rounded before me.

There he was.

Somewhat sheepishly, he made his way down the leafy hillside at the corner. I was so glad to see my guy. Of course I didn't reprimand him. Dogs don't understand delayed reactions anyway. Reprimands

must be immediate and connected instantaneously with the incident or event you wish to alter.

I did not explore where he went or whether there was a trail up that hill that he might have thought to be the right way. Maybe he just wanted some shade, although it was not all that hot. I'll never know how Theo got lost that day, but we were back together, and it was time to return to my pack and poles.

McAfee Knob

We descended to VA 311, then crossed and headed up to McAfee Knob. There are perhaps three obligatory pictures for a thru-hiker: the start at Springer Mountain, McAfee Knob, and hugging, praying at, or somehow embracing the sign at the mile-high summit of

Katahdin. So, of course, Theo and I had the classic picture taken of us at McAfee Knob's jutting point, reminiscent of Pride Rock in *The Lion King*.

It was grand to look out on the 180° expanse from west on the left to east on the right, our destination in the north straight ahead. A long ridge to our right would lead us north from our perch out to Tinker Cliffs the next morning.

We slept back from the rock promontory in brush with no tent, cowboy-style, joining others in this prohibited activity, without shelter. Several visitors showed up at the knob for the 8:15 sunset, and more for the 6:15 sunrise. Theo made himself right at home with everyone and assumed his own Lion King pose as the sun rose over the knob.

Daleville

It was mid-May, and our next stop north was Daleville, Virginia. We hiked the four miles out to Tinker Cliffs, and, after our descent, there were another 9.2 miles to the edge of the forest, where I rested alongside a road into town. I was absolutely wiped, and fellow hikers on their way back from resupplying noticed. They pointed to a Howard Johnson that they knew accepted dogs, and off we went. Just shy of 730 miles in, I was wondering if my body was going to hold up.

On my small tablet with a Bluetooth keyboard, I wrote an article I had promised the Lancaster Bar Association back home, then accepted a little bourbon from Highway in a nearby room and turned in for a good night's sleep. After a leisurely breakfast with

a fellow hiker in the morning, I sent off the article and returned to my room to treat my clothes with Permethrin, an anti-tick spray that needed two hours to dry. I relaxed again and found my R/R/R, which I'd discovered on The Long Trail in Vermont. I recouped, regrouped, and would return.

We began hiking at 2:30 and did 11.2 miles before bedding down.

Took the Risk

The next day brought us to the Blue Ridge Parkway and beautiful views at vehicle pull-offs. We crossed the Parkway several more times heading north, always returning to the woods.

One return led us into Bearwallow Gap, where I saw a very tall man standing in bib overalls, a bright orange, short-sleeved shirt, and moccasins. He spoke slowly as he stood leaning casually against a tree and asked me if I'd seen a couple of fellas heading this way. I said I hadn't. He said he had dropped them off farther south some time ago, and they were going to hike to this spot where he'd meet them and take them home. He had his truck parked up the way, along the road, invisible from where we were.

"You hungry?" he asked.

"No, thanks. I'm fine." I answered.

"You sure?"

"Yes. I'm fine, thanks."

I wasn't sure who this country bumpkin was. For all I knew he had an ax up the road and was planning on pickling me for livestock back home.

We both made our way up the bank to the side of the road, he a little ahead of me. As we climbed, I figured if he really wanted to take me out, he could have done so already, down in the hollow away from the road. His gestures didn't suggest a violent man or an odd sort of fella. He seemed pretty decent and mild-mannered.

"You sure you're not hungry? It's steak."

His manner and offering were softening me.

"You make it hard to say 'No,' offering steak!" I said. "Sure."

He led the way and I followed, not knowing what to expect, but I had decided to take the risk. Not just for the steak, but to live out faith in humankind, faith in this fellow man. I was glad I did.

His vehicle was about 50 yards up a slight climb to the east and across the road. He crossed, and I followed into a clearing where a pickup truck sat. As I approached the open area, I saw a card table set up with a couple of chairs beside it. Beyond the table was a grill fastened to a propane tank.

My benefactor invited me to sit at the table as he got a partially cooked steak from the back seat of his truck and fired up the grill. In short order, he served me up one of the best steaks I've ever had. Of course, the trail turns almost any food into exotic fare.

I asked him his name, which, unfortunately, I did not write down, thinking I would remember it! But I do recall that his name had meaning related to his kindness. It was something like Will Good—and maybe that was it.

When I finished, there were a few gristly scraps left which I gave to Theo. After expressing my sincere thanks, we took our leave as he continued to wait for his friends.

I went back down the road on the truck side and turned right into the woods opposite the spot where we'd met. It was a pretty steep climb from Bearwallow Gap, a name which could have an eerie sound to it. As I climbed, I thought of how grateful I was that I trusted this kind man. I wanted to yell out from a point above him on the trail, "WILL GOOD IS VERY GOOD!" But I wasn't sure he'd hear me, or understand my meaning, and I didn't want to leave him confused. So I just thought what I would have yelled and carried on.

Bunky

We climbed up and over Cove Mountain to the Cove Mountain Shelter where I joined Feral, Pop-tart, and Bunky, an energetic, middle-aged woman who fell in love with Theo.

I set up in the shelter with these three hikers and prepared my supper at a table in front. I passed the tent of an older couple on my way to the privy. They would be spooked a little that night as they saw Theo's eyes glowing in their headlamp beams. All was well when they realized, "It's Theo!"

As we crawled in, Bunky wrapped her coat around Theo and hugged him as he lay on a section of pad I had bought for him from a hiker at Four Pines. It rained hard that night.

Hungry Hiker

The next day my shelter-mates and I all met by chance at the Middle Creek Campground, where we'd get out of the rain and have something to eat. As Theo and I began our climb up Middle Creek Road, the manager of the operation stopped to offer us a ride. We gladly accepted. The smelly, wet dog was no problem. "He can ride in the back," she said.

This was the first time I recall experiencing just how great is the thru-hiker's appetite for food. I sat at the counter at the campground store and ordered two eggs over light with bacon and toast. When I finished that, I ordered a biscuit and gravy (and the same for Theo). After that I ordered French toast, and then I ordered a burger.

Thru-hikers burn about 6,000 calories a day, so they can pack it in when good table food is available. I met only one hiker who said he did not lose weight in his thru-hike. Most people don't get all the calories they need and lose an average of 30 pounds by the time they finish. I was one of them.

Colors of the Wind

Back on the trail, it was another rainy day. Why didn't it bother me? Am I uniquely suited to what Mother Nature serves up, with rain just sauce for the meal? I don't know. But it is true that for me, the weather on the trail was just another color in the artist's palette of colors, all shimmering in the rain to the music of nature blowing life into the swish and clatter of leaves and branches overhead.

I must have some wild man inside. He may have made inroads into my soul when I was a boy who took to the woods in suburban Connecticut. My brother and I were raised there by our very social and alcoholic parents. Maybe I found solace then in the uncritical gifts of the earth. I am moved by the depth of spirit in Native Americans and their appreciation of the natural world which births and sustains us.

I remember a TV commercial featuring Will Sampson, a Native American actor of the Muscogee Nation, a large and impressive man. He was standing by the side of the road in Native dress as a car drove by. An occupant threw trash out the window landing at his feet. His expression never changed as a single tear ran slowly down his cheek.

That silent, emotional scene resonated with something unspeakable way down in the core of my being. I felt that the source and goodness of life itself had been violated in that moment of profound sadness.

I pray the Native American spirit is not lost for good. We consume so much of the earth. We walk and scar it with paths so we can get closer to each other and Nature. We fly in airplanes through a limited atmosphere to deliver messages about global warming. We live with insoluble paradoxes every day. May love for the gifts we have been given ever guide us through our maze of contradictions toward the highest good.

Granted a Reprieve

On that rainy day we just kept going through the wet and mist. We passed tangles of woody limbs and took in greens, purples, and yellows, accented against wet, brown leaves, damp-dark earth, and the rust-grey wood of decaying trees.

In time, Bunky came up behind us as we approached The Guillotine, two large rock outcroppings side by side, with a lethal boulder trapped between them as if designed to take your life. What forces brought this about? And when?

Was it caused by an eruption, or did the Ice Age push this rock into place? Did ice even reach down this far? This evidence of earth's history reminded me of looking into the Grand Canyon. The numerous layers of earth descending a mile down into the Canyon was like looking at the mind of God. The same here. A huge force had done its work just moments ago in earth's history.

Granted a last-minute reprieve from the guillotine, Theo and I carried on.

I feel for those hikers who are on a tight schedule because of school, work, visas, or some self-made compulsion. How much they rush by without really seeing. I felt blessed to be realizing my goal at this time in my life. Time, health, work, funds, and family all came together for me so I could have this experience. My gratitude will never wane.

At 1:00, Theo and I stopped for lunch. He rested his front paws over my right paw and relaxed, waiting for the last bite of my sandwich which I had become accustomed to giving him.

Our Private Knoll

Next was James River Day. I knew of this river from childhood when my young mind placed it in the Deep South associated with America's early history.

I took many pictures and Theo waited patiently. "If you're gonna aim that thing around the way you do, wake me when you're done."

Across the river was a steep climb, leading to a trail cut into the side of the hill. It was getting late, and neither AWOL nor the

topography promised much opportunity near the trail to set up camp. So we climbed a steep, densely forested hill off the trail to the right, up to its crest, hoping to find a spot where we could pitch the tent.

I'm sure that was Theo's plan, too. He was part of me. We might as well have been a six-legged hiker. "We" climbed and pitched and slept together in the tent that night, but not until Theo took advantage of the slope to get his double-duty, sliding-back-roll relief while I set up camp. It was a lovely sunny evening, and no one on the planet knew where we were. We had this off-the-trail knoll to ourselves. It felt like the sunset and the moonlight were all ours, too.

For some reason that I don't recall, I awoke near 2:00 a.m. and took a picture of Theo and me, Theo so close to my Crocs-under-pad pillow that it looks like he's my pillow.

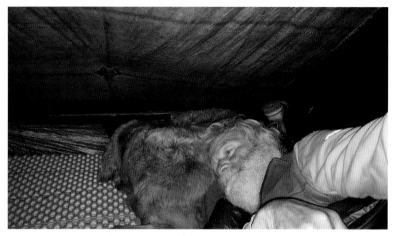

Theo at, not under, my head

An Eerie Camp

A few nights later we were at Piney River North Fork where, as seemed to be the case most of the time now, we were alone. The setting was eerie: sparse woods around a stream with no sign of any human presence, and large boulders strewn about, with an odd configuration of branches on top of the largest. I felt removed from everything familiar, as if we were in the wilderness of another planet. That night a mouse tried to get at Theo's food in his saddlebags, so I had to bring them into the tent, which is not wise when bears are around. I relied on Theo and his senses of hearing and smell to protect us. It rained very hard that night, perhaps keeping the bears away.

On rising, Theo was transfixed by the branches on top of the largest boulder, not far from our tent. He, too, sensed the eeriness of our campsite and growled as he backed away from whatever he saw.

Theo spooked

He moved slowly, keeping his eyes focused on the branches, until he was satisfied that perhaps they were not a living thing prepared to pounce.

Three Ridges

The Priest and Three Ridges were up ahead. We would take a long descent off Priest before climbing the trinity for a matchless view. Out on a rock ledge, we could see all that we had just traversed, great land masses rising up in a mildly hazy sky from another Eden.

I called Bonnie and sent her a picture of what I was seeing at that moment. Imagine Earl Shaffer from York, Pennsylvania, who, in 1948, was the first to hike the entire Appalachian Trail—imagine him sending a picture home to his wife to see what was going on as it happened!

We had a nice chat until other hikers came along. I took a picture of a girl standing too close to the edge for my comfort, and then one

of her companions took pictures of Theo and me enjoying the break from our labors in a most delightful spot.

Soon it was time to get underway, and nature felt it was time to return moisture to the earth. I put on my rain gear, but the weather quickly turned, so I doffed the duds, and, on a whim, bedecked Theo in my bandana. He looked indignant at my antics.

We spent one night by the Tye River and another in the woods, then found ourselves off the trail by happy mistake at Humpback Mountain the next day. We met a delightful group of graduate students on the way and, once there, Theo insisted on a selfie.

Animal Dangers

It was after Humpback that Theo and I saw our first bear. He was off the trail to my right, just sauntering slowly through the woods, paying us no mind. I'm sure he knew I was there—and that Theo was there.

The common wisdom around bears is:

> Don't surprise them—make noise (ring a bell, sing, talk).
>
> Don't look them in the eye.
>
> If they approach–
>
> • Make lots of noise.
>
> • Make yourself look big.
>
> • Don't run. Stand your ground.
>
> • If you're attacked, "Fight like hell!"

There is a motto to distinguish responses to brown grizzlies found in the West from responses to black bears in the East:

> If it's brown, lie down.
>
> If it's black, fight back.

The point here is that grizzlies apparently won't bother with you if they think you're dead. Apparently black bears will.

I have recently heard that water moccasins and copperhead snakes are territorial and aggressive. Fortunately, I have not encountered either of these, although the latter is supposed to be around on the AT. Otherwise, in my experience, animals in the wild really don't want to bother with you, at least not the ones I have encountered, including 13 black bears. One was in northern Pennsylvania where I also saw six rattlesnakes, which scurried away in the brush or lay coiled, tongues and rattles going, until we gave them a wide berth.

While I wouldn't want to test it, I have heard that rattlesnakes have been known to give a dry warning strike—in effect, head-butting you to help you wise up. Apparently the older snakes will inject only as much venom as is necessary for their purpose, while younger snakes will dump their whole load and can be more toxic.

We had many miles to cover after our first bear sighting. Destination: Waynesboro, Virginia, another trail-friendly town. On the way there I saw a list in a shelter of volunteer drivers who would shuttle you around as needed. I took advantage of this generous service and rested up with a zero day before heading back to the trail, where I saw my first snake and first rabbit.

Shenandoah

There was a one-mile climb into Shenandoah National Park from Rockfish Gap where we had exited the woods two nights before. At the start of the Park, deep in the woods, stood an "Entrance station and self-registration" for overnight permits. I filled out the form, left a copy and, with the wire supplied, attached my copy to my backpack as instructed.

As late afternoon arrived, I came upon a stream just off the trail to the right. It looked like a good spot to spend the night. I took off my pack and was about to fill my two-liter Platypus bag with water to filter when I saw a bear in the woods. He was at a fair distance and was taking his time passing by. Although he never looked in our direction, given his sense of smell, he surely knew Theo and I were there.

Not a good place to camp. We moved on and set up for the night in woods just across the Skyline Drive.

A Slow Pace

The next day we hiked over 16 miles to the Loft Mountain Campground and encountered our most aggressive bear. But first we came upon one of many toads I saw on the trail. I admired their courage and bumbling persistence in getting out of the way, notwithstanding the fact that their short hops served only to draw your attention to their location, otherwise incredibly well hidden by superb camouflage. Being able to hop was surely a lifesaver when they happened to get on the trail.

Hiking along, I reflected on my life in Lancaster County, Pennsylvania, compared to my life on the trail. Lancaster is home to a thriving community of Amish who reject the fast pace of the rest of us, whom they call "English." Although the Amish intersect with society, they choose to live somewhat separated from the modern world.

My musings were prompted by the contrails of a jet overhead. Its passengers were moving at one pace, the Amish at another, and then there was Theo and I. For months our pace had been, and would continue to be, much slower than that of an Amish horse and buggy. I was happy to be moving at human walk-speed.

Somewhere en route, speechless Theo endured a trek with both saddlebags on one side. This would happen a few times from one or two causes: his straps were too loose, or his load was unbalanced. I never cinched him up tightly. The balance thing could be a little tricky. Since he carried my water, I found the best way to even his load was to monitor which side I would drink from next. If need be, I would stop and move water around by shifting bottles or their contents.

Twice on the trail, Theo got one of his front legs through the chest strap. Just figuring out which strap was which in those situations required a rather intense effort as my poor friend tried to be pliable and docile. Once I figured out what was wrong, undoing it was another matter altogether and demanded a near torturous twisting of neck and limbs. Forget figuring out how my dear, I-hope-he-soon-sees-my-predicament companion got into this mess. Was it a case of his front cinch being so loose that he just stepped into it? Did he take an extra high step? Or did it happen as he jumped over a log?

Ooops! and Ooops!

Dead Ahead

A slightly hazy, late afternoon favored us with distant views westward as we continued our trek toward Maine. Back in the woods, our attention was straight ahead, following the footpath so wisely envisioned long ago atop Stratton Mountain in Vermont. And then—smack in the center of the trail—about 40 yards away, was the only black bear I ever saw dead ahead. I probably shouldn't use that term.

Clearly we were not going to continue forward until. . . .

"Theo, stay."

I really never needed to say that. He never—never!—bothered any creature on the trail. He never barked and never chased anything.

We stopped, of course. The bear looked up and saw us and then looked back down. Ever so slowly he moved up the hill to the left of the trail, westward. His gait suggested something like:

> Ok. I'll move. I don't have to, you know. These are
> my woods. You are the trespassers. Don't think I'm
> going to rush on your account. I'll go at whatever
> pace I please and you can pass when you're ready.
> Just don't bother me and I won't bother you.

There were several boulders between us and him. As he moved up the hill, a very large one hid him from view.

I wasn't going to stand there all afternoon never knowing where he was. So I took out my phone, set it on video, and started walking at a slow pace, wondering just what we would see past that big boulder. When we moved on, we could see that he was not very far off the trail. As he moved, I moved. When he stopped to forage, I stopped, camera rolling.

And then, slowly, he raised his head and looked over his left shoulder down the hill at us, not all that far away. Suddenly, in a single motion, he turned to his left, raised his front paws, and lunged toward us, stopping with a jerk.

Camera action tells me I reacted with a jerk of my own, yet I remember being rather calm. When the bear vacated the trail and returned to the woods, I reasoned that he did not want to bother with us. In keeping with this belief, I suspected he was giving us a warning and wouldn't come back. He was saying quite simply, "Take your dog and get out of here."

We obliged. The bear and I both kept an eye on each other as I continued to film our encounter. Theo and I moved on and saw frequent scatological proof that we were in bear country.

The next animal we saw straight ahead of us was far less threatening. Nonetheless, for many weeks, the odd dark stump along the trail heightened my awareness until its true nature became evident.

The Fawn

I had been hoping to find a campsite at Loft Mountain Campground but was informed by the ranger that it was Memorial Day Weekend, and the place had been booked since January. I could check to see if anyone would let us share their site. The first couple I saw welcomed me and Theo happily. They shared their wine with me that night and their pancakes and syrup in the morning as Theo basked in their kindness before we returned to our mission.

We weren't on the trail long when I came to an abrupt stop. About three feet in front of me lay a newborn fawn. Another step and I would have landed on it, the animal was so perfectly camouflaged. "Theo, stay." Without a sound, he remained right behind me.

I reached slowly for my camera in my front-left pants pocket, but as I pulled it out, the fawn bolted into thick brush on the side of the trail. I took pictures without aiming, not knowing what I was getting. On review, it appears that I got only brush, until closer examination revealed the fleeing fawn.

In a half-hour or so I came upon a female ranger. She told me that doe often drop their fawns in the trail, apparently believing that bears, wanting to avoid hikers, would not find them there. She also said they leave them right after birth to go hunt for food. I must have

arrived soon after delivery. A most distinct privilege for sure. God smiling upon me yet again.

But how did that fawn know to fear me? How did it know where and how to hide and be still? What an extraordinary amount of information is passed on through genes and DNA!

A Village

After a night at Lewis Mountain Campground we had a short day over moderate terrain on our way to Big Meadows Campground. The sun was out most of the day, waning with evening and incoming clouds. I had lunch en route just off the trail and, before long, a middle-aged hiker came southbound and greeted me with, "Is this the 75-year-old lawyer I'm supposed to talk to?"

Was there some kind of telepathic current running up and down the trail? I expressed my surprise: "How the heck did you know that?" I don't remember his answer, nor why he was supposed to talk to me.

I got the sense that every year, a village of about 3,000-4,000 people, dwindling by attrition to about 800-1000 as fall deepens, live and move along a thin stretch of land about 2,200 miles long, extending from Georgia to Maine. You learn to know a lot of the inhabitants in a village that size. As I moved farther north, I became convinced that I was part of this village. Yet a Yearbook of the 2016 hikers tells me I met very few of the thru-hikers during my year.

Echo

As we continued on to Big Meadows Campground, I came across a hiker I had met at Lewis Mountain Campground three days before.

Her trail name is Echo, and she is an amazing athlete, able to do 30 miles a day.

I put on my rain gear so I could do all my laundry and, so attired, had dinner at the lodge. When done, I got my laundry and returned to the tent just as it began to rain hard. Theo and I crawled in for a cozy night.

On the Moon

It was May 31st, four days from my 75th birthday, when I would be joined by 14 members of my family at the north end of the Shenandoah Mountains. I would stop somewhere along the trail to draw a stick figure which I would text to my family, preparing them for what I looked like. My limited artistic skills were up to the task.

It was a beautiful day as we left the campground, with quicksilver sunlight resting gently on ferns just off the trail. Views west, over hill and dale, made me think of my days of flying in the '70s and '80s. I wondered if I should get back at the controls when I got back home.

Our destination for the night was Byrd's Nest #3 Shelter, known by some as Byrd's Nest #3 Hut. Such places for camping on the trail are fairly similar, but their names change. They're "shelters" in the southern and middle states, and "huts" in the White Mountains of New Hampshire. In Maine, they're "lean-tos."

We arrived at the shelter at 6:20. It was a sturdy stone structure and sat near the crest of a hill in pleasant woods. There were people at a picnic table in front. I'd find a tent site, set up, cook, and turn in. But first, it was time to meet and greet. The conversation went like this:

"Did you ever hike on The Long Trail in Vermont?" asked the older fellow at the table.

"Yeah," I said, with a hint of "Why do you ask?" and "Where is this going?"

"Did you ever stay at Ma and Pa Bower's B&B in Richmond, Vermont?"

"Yeaaaaaah."

And then the woman asked, "Is your name Soren West?"

I was standing on the moon. Floating in outer space. In the depths of the ocean, able to breathe. I was Pavarotti applauded on a world stage.

I was experiencing an otherworldly sense because her question contained my name in the middle of a wilderness in the South, when I'd left all that was familiar behind.

The couple that ignited the rocket fuel within me had hiked The Long Trail in Vermont in 2010, when I was getting my legs under me for this adventure. I had met them at a shelter where I'd stopped for lunch, and we got briefly acquainted. Our conversation led to places to stay in town and, since they'd been on The Long Trail before, they recommended Ma and Pa Bower's B&B in Richmond as a good place to recoup and regroup. I took a picture of them at the shelter, and again when I saw them at the B&B. I also took a picture of their address by their comment in the guestbook so I could send them the pictures I'd taken.

Now the woman who had just said my name told me she had received my pictures and had felt bad ever since that she'd never written back.

Guilt. It's a horrible thing. Look at the burden this fine person carried all these years because she hadn't written to acknowledge my meager gift. My name must have been rattling around just outside her conscious mind until the sight of Theo and me yanked it out of the dark recesses into the light.

The younger hiker at the table told me I all but fainted when the woman said my name. Once we were over the shock of surprise, the same fellow took a picture of us and then told me where to get water down a nearby service road. He warned me that he saw a bear

They remembered me from The Long Trail in Vermont six years before

down there. I put my pack next to my tent and set out. As I turned the corner onto the overgrown service road, I heard a tremendous clatter in the bushes not 10 feet away, off to my left. It was a bear which, happily, was running away from me!

June

We left Virginia's wettest May behind and were greeted by a sunny June 1st, the month of my birth. I feel the march of time. Time past and time coming. The trail that blessed me with a challenge matched by its beauty is now a thread of natural reality entwined in my every thought.

I was reading recently in *Surprised by Joy* by C.S. Lewis. He looks back at his childhood and early formation and notes how his active imagination conjured up a world he called Animal-Land. I think of my own formation in the mountains of New Hampshire as a boy, preceded by endless romps in the woods around my home in Connecticut. I never conjured up an imaginary world of woodland sprites or elves, but I think the woods themselves became home to me, as if something deep within me knew earth as mother. Humans have no choice but to accept her laws, but, in that acceptance, is freedom. For me, it was freedom from my parents' drinking and my dad's judgment of me.

"Are you of this world?" he would ask, and then lean on me to escape his own tortured world. He'd tell me, "Money is the root of all evil" and "To thine own self be true," using me as a sounding board while preaching to himself. I learned to listen and even counsel from the natural love a child has for his parent.

My brother and I were given many advantages: horseback riding lessons, dancing lessons with white gloves, piano lessons, summer camp, and the best boarding schools. But something was missing. We were raised with fine, suburban, New York social graces—polite boys. But where was the bedrock of support for who we were as individuals—God-ordained persons to be discovered, loved, and nurtured in confidence, strong and true?

Silent and Waiting

Like a whale living in the depths of the ocean, the trail had lived in my imagination since I was 12, surfacing only occasionally, but always there. It rose to the surface in 1955 when I was 14, then sounded for years, rising to the surface now and then, but only long enough to exchange the stale air of inactivity for restored purpose and resolve—silent, waiting.

Now it was happening. It was June. My birthday. I would soon be with my family as I neared the end of my second 500 miles. I had stopped singing "I am 500 hundred miles from my home." My family could hear the whistle blow. The great whale's echolocation could be heard from hundreds of miles away in Pennsylvania. There was going to be a reunion.

Three-quarters of a century—my age when I would complete the Appalachian Trail. That year, 2016, is now history, but my accomplishment during it will never end. That common thread of earth heading northward will never leave me. Nor will Theo leave me. His ashes will be put in the ground with my shrouded body to return to Mother Earth. We will remain a part of nature together without end.

My hike from Virginia north would take me back to the future. New England was my past, my history, my formation. My family and home in Pennsylvania lay between the lonely exile and firm resolve of the South, and my history and future hiking in New England. My family is the common thread connecting every step. You'll hear how profoundly I needed my family's support in the months ahead, literally for every single step. We are sustained by an ocean of love that connects us.

Whatever the metaphor—ocean, universe, thread, river, train, whale—love flows in and out of us every bit as much as the life-sustaining air for which the whale surfaces. Every bit as much as the invisible bond that kept Theo following me mile after mile over our six years, from our preparing, to this extraordinary adventure together.

Waking on June 1st

Viewpoint

I began the month of June with a picture of Theo and me in our tent at 6:02 a.m. As I sat outside eating breakfast, I observed a tree stretching skyward in front of me. It was awkward with its limbs all askew, yet something about it prompted me to reflect about life— perfect in its imperfections. I had to share the moment with my Bonnie back home, soon to meet me at the northern end of Shenandoah National Park.

Theo and I were on our way at 7:30 on another sunny but hazy day, with more spectacular views westward over vast stretches of farmland and rolling hills.

Something interesting happened about an hour into our hike. As was frequently the case, there was a turn-off from the trail to a viewpoint off to one side. When we returned to the trail, Theo was in the lead and he turned right. Perhaps I had left my brain somewhere in the hazy sky above the distant farms, and I just followed suit until. . . I began to wonder if we were headed in the right direction.

Theo had a habit of starting back the way we came for a short stint almost every time we returned to the trail, whether after a snack, lunch, a view, or overnight. It was my job to set him straight. Perhaps this was his way of saying, "Let's go home," or maybe it was just instinct because he knew where we had come from, but not where we were going.

Today, however, I just blindly followed him, and when I questioned whether we were headed in the right direction, I could not remember if we had turned left or right to go to the viewpoint. If we had turned right, we were going in the right direction. If we had turned left, we were going in the wrong direction. How to tell?

I remembered that I had taken a picture of a rocky section of the trail shortly before the viewpoint. I would go as far as that rocky section, get out my camera, turn around, and check the view rock for rock.

Back we went to the viewpoint. We had gone the wrong way. We corrected ourselves and carried on to Gravel Springs Hut for the night.

I would see my wife tomorrow! We had planned for a day to ourselves before the others arrived. Daughter-in-law, Karen, married to our oldest child, is very adept at arranging things with impeccable taste. She chose the Wayside Inn in Middletown, Virginia, owned by George and Becky Reeves. Good times were ahead. My second 500 miles were nearly over, and I was about to see my family after more than three months.

Celebrating My 75th With Family

At the Inn, Theo made himself at home while Bon and I had a quiet catch-up and reunion dinner together at the Inn tavern.

Theo trying to relax

That night as we crawled into bed, Bonnie noticed a few spots on my skin and removed three ticks. I'm happy to say that I never got Lyme Disease, but Theo's tick medicine was so effective that, in our tent at night, the nasty critters would leave him and make their way over to me. I sprayed my clothes again with Permethrin before I left for the trail a couple days later.

June 3rd was travel day for most of my family, with a joyful reunion after their time on the road. My beard was a big hit. Everyone was kind and didn't criticize my loss of weight, although they were all amazed at how much I could eat.

After Saturday night mass, my first since Valentine's Day, Soren and Karen arrived. I had aged a year overnight. Hugs all around. Dog-lover Karen and Theo embraced.

Christopher amazed at my beard after four months

Karen and Theo—a warm greeting

My dinner that night was on the house, and dessert was a cake brought by Christopher's wife, Wendy. It was served with 75 lighted candles that took multiple breaths to extinguish. A female guitarist performing at the Inn came to our room to sing Irish songs and "Happy Birthday." I felt very loved that night and at breakfast the following morning.

Wendy delivers a warm cake — 75 candles!

Afterward, we took a family picture. It was 2:30 by the time we said our goodbyes and Bonnie drove me back to the parking area where she had picked me up three days before.

Family gathered for my birthday

(parents: sb=Soren and Bonnie; cw=Christopher and Wendy;
Soren and Karen's two – Hanna and Bergen couldn't make it)

Back: John Paul/cw; Thomas/cw; Karen and Soren

Middle: Nathan/sb; Marian/sb; Wendy; Beth/cw;
Hollie (my niece); Christopher; Emily/sb

Front: Isaac/cw; Bonnie; Soren; Theo/sb; Grace/cw

Back to the Dock

Everyone knew that the trail had me and that I would return to it, that my birthday was just a short interlude in the main mission of my life at the time. Like a huge ocean-going vessel moored at the harbor, my adventure was moored where I had left it—at the start of the next mile. It was a given. It was accepted. I would return to walking northward. Our goodbyes were not mournful. An underlying purpose was afoot, and we were all part of it in our own ways. It was time to return to busy lives and time to return to the trail.

Back to the trail, June 5th

We donned our packs, crossed the street, and I waved to Bonnie as Theo and I entered the woods and started hiking. A short way up the hill, I stopped and turned around to catch the back of her heavenly blue Forester after a U-turn for the drive back to Middletown. It was a poignant sight.

Tall luminescent grass

The Thin Brown Ribbon

June 6th: a day of gently rising mounds with the occasional climb of several hundred feet. A bright sunny day, birthday behind, home state ahead. I told my family as they left, "Don't forget, in a few weeks I'll be in the neighborhood." I was happy to know that family was now closer. Early morning light caught the extended tufts of tall grasses, illuminating them in a bath of life-giving energy as they sang soft and sweet silver-white notes in response.

I was back on the trail, back to my commitment to walk to Maine. My sights had been on my family for hundreds of miles. Now I would have to shift. I had climbed the mountain to my birthday, and it was no longer in view but behind me. What would take its place? I needed a goal. A target. Something out there to focus my vision, collect my purpose, unearth my resolve. I needed a battle to win. Something within myself to conquer. A place of dedication. A place of self-forgetting.

I AM directed Moses in the Old Testament, and he knew what he had to do. I needed an I AM—out there, in the trail that lay ahead, in the unknown. I needed an I-AM certainty in my bones. As I walked, giving myself step by step to my long-held purpose, I became aware that there was no room within for indecision or uncertainty. I had no question about the undertaking. It was a given. Katahdin was out there in our distant future, and that's where we were headed without doubt. Oh, divine purpose! We were underway again on the path to our destination.

But now—on to the intermediate steps—on to the goals within the goal. It was time to just keep walking—for days and weeks and months—one day and one step at a time.

The thin brown ribbon of trail turned into a jumble of large rocks and logs as the sun shone through the canopy of tall new growth from a bright blue sky beyond.

Night found us alone in a shelter as others camped in tents outside.

Trail Angels

June 7th. As I climbed out of the woods onto a dirt road, I was greeted by Trail Angels, people who just show up on the trail with Trail Magic—food and drink for hikers. These Angels were a middle-aged couple who had hiked across this very road one year ago to the day. Their trail names were Count and Lavender. The tailgate was down on their pickup, and it was spread with food. They had a table set up with more food, a cooler with drinks, and cloth folding chairs to "take a load off!"

I did just that and happily munched a couple of sandwiches and swilled a couple of cold drinks.

Of course, we got to visiting and introduced ourselves. When Lavender asked where I was from and I replied, "Lancaster, Pennsylvania," she hesitated a moment and then asked,

"Do you have a son named Christopher?"

"Yes," I replied.

This couple had thru-hiked the trail the year before. When they got to Vermont, my son Christopher was dropping off two of his sons to hike some of the Long Trail while he went on to give a talk in town. Count and Lavender asked if they could ride along and, en route, Christopher told them that his dad was going to thru-hike the trail in 2016 at age 75 with his dog.

And here I was with a white beard and a dog.

Trail Angels — a miraculous meeting

Lavender had written in her journal the night my son dropped them off, "Christopher has been so kind to us, I hope I get to give Trail Magic to his father next year." The circumstances that led to this encounter are astounding–

- That Christopher would be in Vermont where and when they were a year ago.
- That he would tell them about my plans to hike with Theo.
- That Lavender would make her journal entry.
- That they would return to the dirt road with Trail Magic on June 7th, a year later.
- That I would cross this same dirt road on exactly the same date as they had done a year before.

We were all flabbergasted!

I called Christopher on the spot and gave the phone to Lavender. He joined us in the serendipity, "God is smiling on your adventure, Pop!"

Tailspin

As Count, Lavender, and I tried to absorb the goodness of what was happening, along came a fellow thru-hiker, Tailspin. He was in his 20s and had a very pleasant way about him.

We all talked briefly while he removed his pack for a short respite. He didn't sit or eat but he did have a soda. He was soon ready to move on, and I decided to follow.

When I put on my pack, Tailspin noticed my lifter straps were extended. He shortened them for me, lifting my pack closer to the shoulder straps and my body. He was generous to care enough to observe and offer assistance. The whole time at this road crossing was blessed by the helpful instinct in humans—being there for each other. This is the way of thru-hikers who carry on day after day, impelled by a quiet inner drive which they recognize and honor in others with the same goal.

Bear's Den

By late afternoon, Theo and I arrived at the Bear's Den, a hostel just off the trail. It was a small stone castle built by a doctor for his wife who loved music and entertaining at this country estate.

A hundred miles or so south of Bear's Den, I had called Merrell from the trail. I explained my decision at Four Pines to keep the Moabs they had sent me, but my troubles continued. Merrell had an agent call me. She connected me with an outfitter in Purcellville, Virginia, and also said she was willing to meet me there to do whatever she could. In the end we agreed that I would go to the outfitters myself, and they would set me up with whatever worked best for me, all on Merrell.

When I called the outfitter, a kind man said he would pick me up in the morning before his shop opened and do what he could to get me in the right boot. Merrell had already approved this. I would see him at 8:00 a.m.

Rausch Gap **Swatara Gap**
LEBANON

WILM

LANCASTER

HARRISBURG

Duncannon
New Bloomfield

Susquehanna

YORK

Mechanicsburg

Churchtown

Carlisle
Boiling Springs

White Rocks

Gardners

Pine Grove Furnace State Park

Michaux State Forest

Gettysburg

Gettysburg NMP
Eisenhower NHS

Caledonia State Park

Fayetteville

Waynesboro

MARYLAND

River

PENNSYLVANIA
MARYLAND

Prettyboy Reservoir

BALTIMORE

Liberty Reservoir

ANNAPOLIS

CHESAPEAKE

Catoctin Mountain Park

HAGERSTOWN

South Mountain State Park

FREDERICK

Greenbrier State Park

Washington Monument State Park

Gathland State Park

Portage HS

Flood NM

Antietam NB

Martinsburg   Harpers Ferry

Appalachian Trail Conservancy

WEST VIRGINIA
VIRGINIA

Berryville

WINCHESTER

Harpers Ferry NHP

Shenandoah

WASHINGTON D.C.

Potomac   *River*

Snickers Gap

Manassas NBP

CUMBERLAND

Chesapeake and Ohio Canal NHP

Ashby Gap
Sky Meadows State Park
G.R. Thompson State Wildlife Management Area
Linden

WEST VIRGINIA

River

Prince William Forest Park

Geor

Front Royal

Frederic

Fred S

Rappahannock

South

Branch

Potomac

River

Luray

GEORGE WASHINGTON NF

Skyland

Big Meadows

Harrisonburg

Shenandoah National Park

GEORGE

Waynesboro

Calf Mtn
2974ft
906m

CHARLOTTESVILLE

River

James

Rockfish Gap

STAUNTON

NATIONAL

Reeds Gap

VIRGINIA

WEST VIRGINIA
17.7 Miles

N

Miles
0   10   20   30   40   50

CHAPTER 6

West Virginia

Harpers Ferry

Outfitted with new, lightweight boots which were like sneakers with a firm, hiking-boot tread, I was northbound with Theo under a tall, green canopy being whipped by strong winds. They were exhilarating—the kind that clean the cobwebs out of your soul.

In short order we crossed into West Virginia and traversed the infamous "Roller Coaster" on our way to Harpers Ferry. This was the location of the Appalachian Trail Conservancy (ATC), the organization primarily responsible for maintaining the trail. It was here that hikers had their picture taken and their information posted in ATC logs to keep track of all "2,000-milers," whether done in sections over time, or in one season as I was doing.

As I finished my business and was about to depart, I said to one of the attendants, "I've lost 25 pounds already." Her instant response was, "You'll lose more in the Whites."

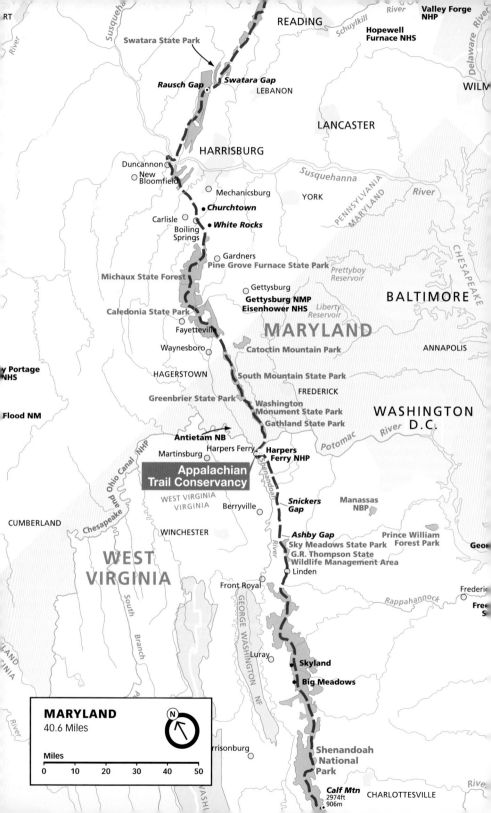

RT

Susquehanna River

READING

Schuylkill River

Valley Forge NHP

Hopewell Furnace NHS

Swatara State Park

Rausch Gap ● *Swatara Gap*

LEBANON

Delaware River

WILM

LANCASTER

HARRISBURG

Duncannon

New Bloomfield ○

○ Mechanicsburg

YORK

Susquehanna River

● *Churchtown*

Carlisle ○
Boiling Springs ○

● *White Rocks*

○ Gardners
Pine Grove Furnace State Park

Michaux State Forest

Gettysburg ○
**Gettysburg NMP
Eisenhower NHS**

Prettyboy Reservoir

PENNSYLVANIA
MARYLAND

River

CHESAPEAKE

BALTIMORE

Caledonia State Park

Fayetteville ●

Waynesboro ○

MARYLAND

Liberty Reservoir

ANNAPOLIS

y Portage NHS

HAGERSTOWN

Catoctin Mountain Park

South Mountain State Park

FREDERICK

WASHINGTON D.C.

Flood NM

Greenbrier State Park

Washington Monument State Park

Gathland State Park

Potomac River

Antietam NB

Martinsburg ○

Harpers Ferry

Harpers Ferry NHP

Chesapeake and Ohio Canal NHP

Appalachian Trail Conservancy

WEST VIRGINIA
VIRGINIA

Berryville ○

Snickers Gap

Manassas NBP

CUMBERLAND

Chesapeake and Ohio Canal

WINCHESTER

WEST VIRGINIA

South Branch

Front Royal ○

Ashby Gap
**Sky Meadows State Park
G.R. Thompson State
Wildlife Management Area**
○ Linden

Shenandoah River

Prince William Forest Park

Geo

GEORGE WASHINGTON NF

Rappahannock River

Frederic

Fre S

Luray ○

● *Skyland*

● *Big Meadows*

MARYLAND
40.6 Miles

N

Miles
0   10   20   30   40   50

Shenandoah National Park

rrisonburg ○

WASH

Calf Mtn
2974ft
906m
●

CHARLOTTESVILLE

River

CHAPTER 7

Maryland

Towpath

While there is much history and much to see in Harpers Ferry, northbound was my goal and we had to keep moving. We crossed the Potomac on the Byron Memorial Walkway (footbridge), adjacent to a railway bridge, and emerged in Maryland for a three-mile stretch on the C&O Canal Towpath. The slimy canal ran between the towpath and the railroad right-of-way. Given the length of this walk over gravel, I put Theo's boots back on.

Theo followed me most of the time, and I looked back occasionally to check on his boots. They seemed to be holding. However, about halfway along, a biker passed me and stopped to say he thinks the dog might have lost a boot. I thanked him and turned to go back. He said, "I'll get it," and my thanks was all the more vigorous on his return.

At the end of the towpath, we crossed a road and headed back into the woods for a steep climb to the Ed Garvey Shelter, where Theo and I spent the night with a few other hikers.

The Original Washington Monument

The next day brought us onto Civil War battlegrounds. Later that afternoon, as Theo and I were climbing toward the original Washington Monument near Boonsboro, Maryland, we encountered a young couple who encouraged us to take the side trail off the AT to the 40-foot tower. We did. At the top, the fellow asked my trail name. "Sojo," I said.

"You just had a birthday!" he responded.

Go ahead. Throw me off the tower! What the bleep is going on? I was still learning the just-a-village nature of the AT. "HOW did you know that?" I asked.

He had just finished a couple of weeks hiking the AT farther south and said, "A fella hiking with his son, Pops and the Kid, told me."

I wondered what prompted Pops and the Kid, whom I had met weeks before, to tell this section hiker about me. Was I a phenomenon at 75, hiking with my dog? I guess denial runs deep. Or maybe tuning into who we really are is hard to do.

We were back on the main trail and headed northbound by 6:30, then crossed US 70 en route to another shelter. A troop of Boy Scouts camped nearby.

Leaving Maryland

On our last day in Maryland, I saw a couple in the distance walking southbound. It looked like the woman had the heavier pack, and I was getting ready to rib the guy with something like, "Boy, you've gotten off easy! Looks like your pack mule's got the heavy load."

And then, "Oh, my God! Will! Melanie!" followed by hugs and kisses.

These were acquaintances from when Bonnie and I lived in Maryland. My wife had visited some of their relatives on her way to my birthday, and word of my hike got around. Will and Melanie wanted to do some of the AT in Maryland and imagined I'd be farther north. My age and pace brought us together.

CHAPTER 8

Pennsylvania

Waynesboro

Often on the trail, maintainers build steps into the path. They are never welcomed by thru-hikers. Instead of simply hiking along with Mother Nature, you suddenly are told 1) when to step; 2) how high to step; 3) and at what intervals to step. A thru-hiker avoids such steps by going to the bank at the side of the trail. Surely the intent is to be helpful, or perhaps to thwart erosion, but trenches or low diagonal walls are the best way to divert water off the trail.

Theo rather liked steps, especially when the intervals between them retained moisture and remained cool. If he got far enough ahead of me, he'd rest at such a spot until I came along.

Through Maryland, the trail went from long, wide, flat sections on abandoned Civil War access roads to rocky hints of things to come.

We would be in Pennsylvania by nightfall, so I called ahead for a room at the Burgundy Lane B&B in Waynesboro. One of the owners, Margaret Schmelzer, answered. She was very kind. "Just call when you get to the road, and we'll come pick you up." Soon we were at the Mason-Dixon Line and, for a brief moment, Theo and I were in different states.

While still in Maryland, I capture Theo stepping into Pennsylvania

David and Margaret Schmelzer could not have been more accommodating. They met Theo's and my every need during our first two nights in Pennsylvania. And Theo was free to roam at large in the clean, well-maintained home.

Rocksylvania

The next day was Sunday, so I couldn't get much done around town. I wanted to have Theo checked out before heading into the heart of what thru-hikers call "Rocksylvania, the graveyard of boots and paws." David said he'd be happy to take me to the vet in the morning. Theo had had a severe tear in a pad on the Horseshoe Trail in 2014, and he just kept walking over hot roads without a whimper. I did not want to have that happen again.

A couple joined me at the B&B breakfast the next morning, and we got acquainted. They took my email address, and I heard from them en route. Many who live in the AT village, or who visit it during a given season, tend to move on to busy lives and lose touch. So it has been with many we know only by their trail names, and with hostel owners who move on to the next year's class of thru-hikers. And yet, some we meet become friends for life.

After breakfast, it was time to tend to business. Because my hearing had gotten poor, David took me to the doctor. I had no wax build-up. All was clear, so what was going on? Next stop was the vet. Theo had a crack on his right front paw but, again, we got an all-clear. The crack was only in the black of the pad, and the vet said he'd be fine. He advised that if the crack opened down to the pink, I should use superglue to close it, and also superglue moleskin over the spot.

Shema

Errands done. Bills paid. David drove us back to the trail. He waved as we crossed the road from where he had picked us up two nights before. Soon we were on a long, wide, and straight stretch of trail through thick underbrush behind houses. Eventually we entered the woods that had become our normal habitat.

We were heading into home territory and would begin seeing people I know for miles to come: family and friends in Pennsylvania, New Jersey, New York, Connecticut, Massachusetts, Vermont, and New Hampshire. But after that, Theo and I would be on our own, heading deeper and deeper into shorter and colder days in the far north.

For now, we were going to a reunion with my paralegal and her husband at Caledonia State Park, a day away. We stopped for a late lunch at Antietam Shelter where two other hikers were set up for the night. We ate and soon left, but not before we all got to know each other a little.

The younger man had an elaborate display of food items around him, and he seemed to be taking considerable steps in preparing his meal. I asked if he was Jewish, and he said he was. I had reflected on the trail, ever since Georgia, that the Shema is perhaps the most brilliant thought in all of human history. "Hear, O Israel: The LORD our God, the LORD is one" (Deuteronomy 6:4). One!

> It is the hope of every marriage
> The hope of every nation
> The goal of every enterprise
> The hope for the planet
> The quest of every physicist
> The pride of Judah
> The hope of Christianity
> It was Jesus' hope—"That they might be one, as you and I are one, Father"
> (John 17: 21).

One. May there be but one God, no matter how many paths to the deity. May we stress what we share and let our differences be like the colors of so many different leaves in the fall.

There is a unity among thru-hikers. According to my notes in AWOL, I met several that day who shared the glory and struggles of the trail: Tiel-Rabbit, Shadow, Soggy, Dog-Nero, and Animal. They deserve mention—they are my friends—fellow sojourners on the AT. We connected, exchanged names, and went our separate ways.

How beautiful the 100-mile wilderness will be when I am there in October, taking in mile after mile of gloriously colorful, rolling foothills viewed from high up. All our differences add to the singular beauty of the human race.

Taj Mahal

We carried on to a place where several had set up camp for the night. It was tempting to join them at 6:30, but I decided to move on a mile or so to the next shelter, which proved to be the Taj Mahal with two separate structures—one for snoring and the other for non-snoring. I chose non-snoring, which didn't matter much because I was the only one there.

It was here that my small LED light picked up frightening creatures on the ground all around me. It took a little while for me to realize that what I was seeing on the ground were the shadows of waist-high leaves that entered my light beam. The leaves' nearness to the light exaggerated the movement of the shadows on the ground, giving them uncommon speed and distance, as if they were very much alive and quite agitated.

Halfway

At Caledonia State Park we met my loyal, faithful friend and paralegal, and her husband. They brought me a wonderful lunch, and Kim had some papers for me to review. Kim has been my right arm at the office for years, a longtime friend, and a fan of my writing. I hope I don't disappoint her with these verbal peaks and valleys.

Theo and I spent that night at a shelter with hanging flower pots—a little too domestic for my woodsman ways.

The next day, I took a break from the rain on the porch of a locked cabin, where I encountered Danny Kennedy and his girlfriend. Danny is a wounded warrior, partially paralyzed, blind in one eye, and legally deaf. He requires a medical device to keep his heart and lungs working. He has a gut-level, don't-mess-with-me attitude toward anyone who tells him "you can't." He had planned to do a thru-hike of the AT, but was settling for section hiking over several years. His girlfriend was supporting him. I admired and had a prayer in my heart for their relationship and their hike.

After they left, we left. They went south. We went north. The rain had abated, but diamonds still clung to the leaves. Theo followed right behind me. It was June 15th and, in short order, we were at a milestone—halfway to Katahdin:

> 1094.55 miles to Springer, Georgia
> 1094.55 miles to Katahdin, Maine

We had been hiking for 116 days. Twice this was 232. Would we make it, with all the difficult climbs in the north? "Just keep going. . . ."

Our first stop on the northern half of the trail was Toms Run Shelter. A few tents were set up, but I opted for the shelter, which Theo and I had to ourselves. In the summer, many took to their tents to avoid insects and, of course, the mice for whom the shelter is a hunting ground at night. They scurry around and over you, up the walls, across beams and down ropes from which food bags and backpacks are hung. They find the food.

With Theo sleeping beside me, I was less bothered—on the floor—by mice. They did get to my food a couple of times, but I survived.

Pine Grove Furnace

I had breakfast at a nearby pavilion in the morning as a light rain fell, and then we carried on through damp woods where I saw the first Queen Anne's Lace. There would be fields full of the flowers in Connecticut.

In time we emerged onto a road descending a gradual grade, leading to country houses on the way to Pine Grove Furnace State Park. It was the day I met Ken and Tina from Smiley's Deli in Lancaster. I had been a regular there, always ordering the same sandwich and ending my description with "and all the shakers." I was so consistent that I finally learned to identify myself as "Shakers" when I placed a phone order. In time, they put a "Shakers" button on each cash register. My lunch order went like this: I pressed memory 29 on my phone.

"Smileys."

"Shakers."

"Got it."

Oh, efficiency! You can imagine how I react to lengthy phone menus, including, "Please listen to this entire message as our menu options have changed. . . ."

Thank God for the Smileys of the world—and thank God for the wilderness!

Ken Smiley and Tina Martin—loyal friends from Lancaster

I included Ken Smiley as one of 10 recipients of my GPS Spot posts, letting him and Tina know where I was at the end of each day. They followed me as I hiked and promised to show up at Pine Grove Furnace and the Appalachian Trail Museum with two "Shakers," chips, and sodas when I arrived. Ken tracked me down when I posted a Spot at Burgundy Lane B&B to inquire when I'd be at Pine Grove Furnace. They got there soon after I did with the promised fare. We took our time over lunch and headed to the museum where we enjoyed soaking in trail history.

Woody the Woodpecker

Once back on the trail, I realized that I had left my backup battery charging on a ledge along the outside wall of the store. A few calls were all it took to find someone who would be heading to Boiling Springs, two days out.

Another problem fixed!

En route to James Fry Shelter, I saw my first-ever pileated woodpecker, the Woody the Woodpecker kind. It was huge and flew right across the trail in front of me, maybe 20 yards out—too fast for camera work. It was a rare and thrilling sight.

By late afternoon, we arrived at the shelter for a misty night's sleep.

Farmlands

Morning mists made the sight of tenters in the woods all the more cozy. Home is where your pack is and wherever you can pitch your tent. Under a bush, under a tree, near a stream, on a hillside, on a mountain top, in a field—in a parking lot if need be.

I grew up in the suburbs around New York City, where I was born and where my dad worked for 20 years. In 1972, after a couple of years of law practice in northeast Pennsylvania, my wife and I and our two boys moved to Lancaster, "The Garden Spot of America." I've been near this farmland for so long now that it has become my home. "Become" is the key word. It's not naturally "home" because I'm from up north.

There will forever be a substrate deep down in the archeology of my soul where rocks, mountains, and lakes are the natural features. However, a good quantity of rich topsoil has covered them over with rolling fields husbanded by the Amish, who have long preserved the ways of life known to early American settlers. The woodlands of the southern AT had now spit me out onto the mid-state's rich farmlands.

The path through these prolific fields took me to Boiling Springs, where I retrieved the battery backup for my phone at the ATC outpost there. At a nearby hostel I met Odie, who tries to encounter every thru-hiker each year for the production of a Yearbook. On a zero day there, Bonnie and a friend joined me for a picnic. It was June 18th. Bonnie and I each failed to note that the next day would be our 51st wedding anniversary. Somehow I remembered on what was, at 15 miles, probably the longest flat section of the entire trail. The rich greens and golds of nature's provision were a soulful elixir poured out in bright sunlight.

Here there were no cars named Spirit or Infinity, mocking in metal the deepest hungers of our heart. No four-wheelers tearing up the turf in a show of sadistic domination. Here were crops, food, goodness, precursors of the harvest. Bountiful blessing. A single colorful leaf in the trail, a treasure.

A single leaf a miracle

Middlesex Diner

Theo and I crossed a few highways as civilization moved in on the AT. Eventually we came to a walkway over US 11 into Carlisle, Pennsylvania. My youngest child, Marian (Mare), and her fiancé, Zach, were going to meet us here to hike a couple of hours with us and then turn around to head home.

We arrived well before they did and walked a half-mile, looking for a place to eat. We came upon the Middlesex Diner which seemed like a hap'nin' place in town.

I said Theo was a service dog and was seated at a booth. I took off my backpack, pushed it and my trekking poles to the wall, and then directed Theo under the table at the far end.

Since I was a good bit earlier than Mare and Zach, I decided to order, and when they showed up, after enthusiastic hugs and hellos, I asked the waitress to put their meals on my tab. She said, "Oh, your tab was paid by the gentleman who was sitting behind you."

I felt blessed and a little sorry. I was a white-haired, bearded fellow, who was maybe a little smelly, with a backpack which my benefactor surely thought contained all my worldly goods. And I had a service dog. He probably thought I was not only homeless but legally blind as well.

I had a twinge of guilt. Should I be wearing a sign: "Semi-Retired Attorney Thru-Hiking the Appalachian Trail"?

After Mare and Zach ate, we drove back to the trail, parking just east of it on the south side. Mare and Zach each tried on my backpack, and then we started hiking, passing through more golden fields, over fence stiles and a boardwalk through a swamp. At the north end it was time to bid farewell, which is always a little sad. My goal, however, was well fixed, like a steel rod pounded into the ground by a well-drilling hammer. It wasn't going to change. I hugged my first family co-hikers and headed north.

Before nightfall and a steep climb to the shelter, we came upon a sign by a spring that said the water at the shelter was uncertain, so get water here. I loaded Theo with all he could carry and did the same for myself, probably 6-8 liters in all.

The Doyle

The next day took us to another icon on the trail—The Doyle Hotel in Duncannon, Pennsylvania. En route, I came upon a perfect spider web that merited a photograph.

A spider's masterpiece

"Pennsylvania's rocks" are one of those elements of the trail that loom large enough to have a life of their own. Like Fontana Dam, The Smokies, Clingmans Dome, The Roller Coaster, the Whites, Mahoosuc Notch, the 100-mile wilderness, and Katahdin, you just had to get to each one and experience its mystique and lore for yourself.

The Appalachians through Pennsylvania form a ridge curving from the south-center of the state to the eastern border, from Warfordsburg, 40 miles west of Waynesboro, to Delaware Water Gap, north of center at the east end of the state. There would be a lot of long ridge-hiking through Pennsylvania, to be sure, much of it over rocks that challenged every step. The worst was north of Duncannon.

The Doyle loomed large on the AT because it, too, was difficult in its own way. It was a dingy, run-down, three-story, brick structure with no AC on the second and third floors where hikers slept, or tried to. The bar downstairs had your favorite beer along with passable food, served up by the owners, Pat and Vickey Kelly. The place runs on a shoestring, including a "Save the Doyle" campaign on the website to pay back taxes:

"Thousands of weary travelers coming off the Appalachian Trail have relied on the Doyle Hotel in Duncannon for a good night's rest and a shower. But now, it's the hotel that needs some relief."

I had made arrangements from the trail for my grandson Bergen to bring my original AT boots to me because my feet simply were not getting any better. I figured those original boots had worked for me at the start, and perhaps in time my feet would readjust to them. I knew, at least, that the boots were not too small because they had served me very well for over 500 miles. No other boots Merrell valiantly attempted to help me with had a proven track record behind them.

I treated Bergen to two dinners, and then to ice cream which he shared with Theo before heading back home.

The Doyle, Duncannon, Pennsylvania

Our room at The Doyle—with a fan—was on the third floor in the front corner overlooking the main street. It was hot, and I would sleep on top of the sheets in the altogether with the fan at max, Theo on the floor.

As we walked through the streets of Duncannon to The Doyle that day, a woman driving by called out the window, "His pack is lopsided!"

To which I answered, "I know—we're not going far."

"Oh." She was satisfied.

And so were Theo and I—at The Doyle.

Susquehanna and Raccoons

We left Duncannon the next morning and crossed the Susquehanna River and railroad tracks before climbing high above those landmarks en route to some of the famous Pennsylvania rocks. The next day was June 21st, the start of summer, a day some thru-hiker thought should be "hike-naked day." I was spared and spared others; however, I did see a bra in a tree along the trail.

Walking and walking, straight and straighter, long and longer, made it hard to know just where we were. There was no variation in terrain and few marked side paths. Finally we came to a stream where we stopped for water and lunch. I took off my boots to soak my feet in the cool water. Relief.

By late afternoon we came to a long descent leading to a campsite by a river. Magellan and Strider, a father-son team, were there. They had been camping together many weeks before when a bear came to one of their tents and completely destroyed it. They shooed him away, at which point he went to the other one's tent and did the same. They each bought new ones and kept going.

I set up my tent fairly near the river and cooked supper. I saw my first fireflies at this campsite and heard a raccoon fight in the middle of the night.

The Podiatrist

Our next night was at Pine Grove, Pennsylvania, where I visited a podiatrist, hoping he could help my feet. He examined my boots and replaced the insoles. He scaled off dried blisters and dead skin and then put lotion on my feet, rubbing it in with fingers that knew what they were doing. Aaaaaaaaah and aaaaaaaaah. . . . That was worth the hike from Georgia! If he'd have kept it up, I think I'd still be there.

He educated me on foot and toe management, putting a small silicon tube over my little toes and a spacer in between toes four and five. Then he packed up a good supply of extras for the road.

My son Soren joined us for breakfast. We talked of the trail and my feet. Many miles back he had said to me on the phone that I should get off the trail and tend to my toes now, or they could put me off the trail for good.

Now Ren, as we call him, is very quick. He can assess a situation in an instant and get right to the essence of where things are and where they need to go. With that background, here's the short phone conversation we had:

"Dad, you better get off the trail and tend to those toes now, or they could squelch the whole deal."

"Ren, I will amputate before I quit the trail."

"Okay. I'll send a sharp knife."

My Peeps

Always a lightning bolt response from Ren, and I love it!

Being a little anal, I was once scraping the bottom of my cereal bowl with Ren next to me. It must have looked to him as if I was about to scrape off some of the bowl's color. Then came the gentle bolt: "Dad. It's all gone."

While I'm loving on one of my children, let me mention what I have called my proof of God's existence. It's a logical impossibility, but also absolutely true, because I've experienced it time and time again: each of my children is my favorite.

It's simply fact. You've heard a little of Ren. Mare, the youngest, who had already hiked with me, I have long called my TBM,

Treasure Beyond Measure. A lithe, light, orderly, busy, compassionate, attentive, and productive friend, dancer, and massage therapist with an angelic voice. This stunning young woman knows how to ask her adoring dad for (almost) whatever she wants. Fully in control of her faculties, and knowing I'll laugh, she bats her eyelashes and says "Daaaaaadyyyy. . . ."

Christopher, our second child, a super husband and dad, whom I would never have pegged as a scholar in his early years, has become the world's most recognized authority on the teachings of Saint Pope John Paul II. He lectures all over the world. He's written countless teaching aids and published more than a dozen books on JPII, popes since his time, and the church. He's an avid skier, cliff-jumper, musician, and vocalist, most often accompanied on piano or drums by his youngest son, Isaac.

I tell people it's not a pretty sight to get me talking about my kids, but, it's too late now.

My wonderful children, by age, from right: Soren, Christopher, Emily, Nathan, Marian

Emily has an utterly profound grasp of the human condition, which is evident in her ceramics, painting, writing, songs, and love for troubled students she has counseled in the Lancaster school system. It is hard not to grow in essential ways in the glow of her keen insights and unfathomable love. And like her sister, she is gorgeous!

Now, Nathan, my favorite. Nathan has the driest, most culturally astute sense of humor. It extends to gestures and performances of all kinds. He is an actor, whose skills won him an award, and a linguist par excellence. While he was studying at the Sorbonne in Paris and living with a family near the city, his "French mother," whose whole family have become our friends, told us, "Naton could teach French to da French." The same is true of Spanish and Krio (spoken in Sierra Leone). Add to that German and a little Fon (a language spoken in Benin, Africa). Not to mention the music in his bones—his piano and voice, for which he has also received high praise, and his in-depth appreciation of classical vocalists and composers.

How am I so fortunate as to have such loving and talented children?

Dare I get started on the woman who gave birth to and raised them with sacrificial love? She, too, plays the piano and sings and is a meticulous actor. And as much as I love words, no one can put more heart into a sentence or paragraph than Bonnie. She can also cook up a tantalizing meal in minutes. She has many fans on many counts.

Bottomed Out

Okay, you've met my family, which includes eight extraordinary grandchildren. It's time to get back to the AT to resume my life on the rocks. That night in my tent, I hit a deep, deep low. The podiatrist's efforts brought only momentary relief, and my feet were really hurting. Pennsylvania's rocks were taking their toll. I wondered if the state where I lived was going to take me down. My resolve was strong, even against the pain, but I wondered if my body was simply going to quit on me.

For the first time on the trail, I decided to tune into whatever I could get on my cell phone. I watched *America's Got Talent* on YouTube. I am deeply moved by the courageous souls who stand up in front of thousands and belt out a song or present other extraordinary talent to the world.

"Golden Buzzer Moments" were on. Any one of the judges can hit the golden button in the middle of their desk and gold foil chips fall from the ceiling, signifying that the performer is deemed good enough to go directly to the finals. It was thrilling, and the talent was awesome.

I drank in each performance as rain pelted my tent and tears filled my eyes with joy for each beautiful moment of unrestrained affirmation. Every one of us craves that kind of approval—even that little dachshund that walked toward me in his wire cage so many years before.

In my view, no one on earth can give a more affirming thumbs-up than Simon Cowell. It is his tell-it-like-it-is honesty that sends you through the roof with his most sincere and compassionate approval. He truly cares for the brave souls who exhibit their wares to the world in his presence, and he feels genuinely privileged to witness the magnificent moments he celebrates with them.

Tears of joy and tears of deep hunger streaked my bearded cheeks.

I have longed for what I call my "Susan Boyle" moment. If I could have such a moment singing, I'd be thrilled. Somewhere within is a Pavarotti. My stage so far has been the shower, my car, and the trail (a little). There is an ocean of life and abundance in my soul that longs to come out, to be expressed and given away, to salve a savage beast. To inspire. To instill peace. To trigger love. To create a sunrise over a mountaintop. To pierce a cold, dark space with light and warmth. I would need nothing more in life. I could step off that moment into the home that lasts forever.

In my tent in the rain with sore feet, celebrating Golden Buzzer Moments, I was feeling that defeat was possible, even though quitting was unthinkable. But could my feet carry on? Somewhere within, I knew they would. I would make it all the way. In the conflict of my emotions, I cried out softly in ardent consternation, "I just want to hike to Katahdin."

I didn't expect the world to applaud me. That was okay. It was not a matter of my great talent but a matter of my simple determination. "I just want to walk—can I not even do that?"

Theo looked up at me from the tent floor. He knew what was going on. He sniffed out my need for love and approval. My need for success on the trail. He knew.

With melancholia, I fell off to sleep.

Empathetic Theo

Brother-in-Law Andrew

Tomorrow was another day. I was near Berks County, home to my brother-in-law Andrew, an oral-maxillofacial surgeon in Reading. He, and one of his partners who was interested in my trek, met me at Route 183 and took me to Cabela's for a fantastic lunch. Then Andy drove to a nearby drugstore and bought me all kinds of devices for my feet, plus the prescription drug Cipro for persistent hiker's diarrhea, an addition to my Pennsylvania woes. I returned to the trail well supplied.

Many more miles of long, straight hiking brought us to the Eagles Nest Shelter, which we had to ourselves. I cooked at one of the picnic tables out front and turned in.

Port Clinton

In the morning, Theo made himself comfortable (?) against the shelter floor as I packed. Then we headed for a ren-dezvous with Bonnie at Port Clinton while I was still in our home neighborhood. A long, steep descent brought us to this former hub of coal trans-port. Bonnie and I had lunch at the Port Clinton Hotel where the waitress brought water to Theo.

As we sat chatting and catching up, I debated whether to continue on up the steep

Can this be comfortable?

climb out of town or stay a night at the hotel. After several minutes of discussion, Bonnie looked across the table at me with loving concern in her eyes and said, "Soren, you need to come home."

I listened, debated with myself, and finally accepted the fact that she was right. I needed rest for my body, mind, and spirit. My feet and diarrhea were wearing me out. I accepted my wife's wisdom and the wisdom of my body.

On the way home, we stopped at brother-in-law Andy's home and soaked in the hot tub attached to his pool, beer in hand. From deprivation to indulgence. I needed every ounce of the love and kindness I received from Andy and Colleen, and at home where I remained for three full days.

Home

Theo and I had not been home in over four months. He was happy to be there and to sleep in his cushy bed. I was sufficiently content to be in our cushy bed, but don't recall any "Oh, thank God, I'm home with all the comforts" moments. Nothing would deter me from my decades-old purpose. I was indeed "divinely inspired, possessed by a god" to quote a definition of enthusiasm.

There are times when you know because you know. You have a moral certainty about your course of action. No obstacle will survive your inner drive. Your purpose feels God-given and divine—not airbrushed, putti-in-the-dome divine, but aching-toes, painful-heel, dehydrated-but-able-body divine.

Bonnie and I had lived at our current home for 21 years before I took to the trail. We each had established routines. Four months away was long enough for me to forget them all. Everything I did in the kitchen to get breakfast was no longer done on autopilot but by discovery.

At lunch one day, Bonnie prepared a full blender of milkshake with about a quarter-gallon of ice cream. To her great surprise I devoured it in about 30 seconds.

Bonnie was very solicitous about my well-being and nutrition on the trail. She went to a discount drug mart and purchased products that they highly recommended for my condition. She returned with many high-protein bars, some green powder, whey powder, probiotics, and a multivitamin. She divided them into Ziplock packets and wrote instructions on masking tape which she affixed to each. She wanted her husband well, and she wanted him to finish in good health, and she did all she could to assure that goal was met.

She was all I could ask for. Fully supportive. If my funds ran dry for lack of a case fee coming in, she would see that I had what I needed from the modest amount left from her inheritance. What I was doing was not her thing, but she adopted my goal as her own—for me—and she was as determined as I was to see me through to Katahdin. She devoted herself to my getting the job done in good health, so I would have the satisfaction of completing a goal that just never went away. She was the captain of the family team seeing me through this long, and sometimes painful, ordeal.

John Paul

Christopher and Wendy's oldest child, John Paul (JP), accompanied me on my return to Port Clinton. Loaded with the vitamins and supplements Bonnie lovingly purchased for me, and armed with her thorough instructions intended to thwart my stubbornness, I, with Theo and JP, set off for the trail. Our goal, after a late start and a drive, was the Windsor Furnace Shelter about 5.7 miles north of Port Clinton. Our start was a long and steep climb, the reciprocal of my descent several days before.

We hiked and climbed and rested, and climbed some more. Then we just kept on keeping on until it really was time to stop. Neither of us ever saw a sign for the shelter. I don't know if our noses were too fixed on the ground ahead, or if the sign was missing. However, we had been on rocks for some time, and the trail ahead and terrain on both sides were not promising as a place to spend the night. As a last resort, and for the first time, I pitched the tent on a clear spot smack in the center of the trail, confident that whoever needed to could make their way around us.

JP spent a night in the tent and one in a shelter, after miles of rocks, and returned home the next day. He had driven us to Port Clinton and got a shuttle back there to drive home. I will forever be extremely grateful that he joined me on my return to the Rocksylvania AT. He gave me a major morale boost for the ordeal and the will to carry on.

What is it about the trail? We spend most of our lives in some sort of twilight between womb and tomb, between the natural and the eternal world. In the twilight, we create vast amounts of stuff, including this writing, while in the core of our being, we long for connection with the real. Not ink on a page, or the electronic interpretation of 0s and 1s on a screen, but REAL! Dirt-under-foot, mountain-in-the-sky real. Our aspirations are infinite and our competence so finite. There is such grandeur and such devastation in the human soul, with but a knife edge between the two.

Knife Edge I

I was born in Manhattan and raised just outside the city that was Mecca to me. As a 12-year-old, I commuted into New York for a speed-reading program to address my irregular eye movements as I read.

I'm ambidextrous. I throw a baseball right-handed and a football left-handed. When I pole-vaulted for four years in prep school, my coach never recognized that I jumped off my left foot and went up the left side of the pole, instead of the right, which my jump demanded. I still got to 10' 6" with the old stiff poles, but my right thigh banged into the metal with each jump and eventually got very sore. When I pole-vaulted for my school on a year's exchange program in England, I took one jump and the coach flipped out. My wires had gotten crossed, and he saw it immediately.

My eyes have never known which way to go when I read, and I work at that every single day of my life. Moby Dick, who looked in opposite directions at the same time, fascinated Melville—and me.

Gard (short for "Gardner," my father's name) was my brother. He had ADD and would eventually become an alcoholic like our parents. I was the White Knight in the family (the color has yellowed over the years)—and the dreamer. Mom was not an intellectual but very creative. She made clothes for herself, friends, and actors on Broadway. She could look at her subject and begin cutting. A very strong, no-nonsense, get-it-done woman! She was not physical with her children—a little aloof. She made it clear, her husband came first. I love her dearly. I love my whole family—all three of them. All gone.

Knife Edge II

Dad drank in New York. Mom drank at home. When he found her drunk, he beat her black and blue around the eyes. My brother and I always knew when it had happened because Mom would be wearing sunglasses in the morning when we got up.

My dad didn't really know what he wanted, and neither did I. So I simply followed in his footsteps and went to Mount Hermon and then to Yale, just as he had.

At Mount Hermon, my very demanding English teacher encouraged me to submit a piece I had done for class to the *Atlantic Monthly*. I so appreciated what I had received from him, that I tried to pass it on when I became an English teacher at a boarding school in Connecticut. I lasted a year and a half and decided to leave for law school. When I told my father, he shot back,

"You're no lawyer!"

"Well, I'm going," was my immediate response.

Knife Edge III

One night my brother and I left our bedroom to stop Dad from beating Mom. He chased us back to our room, where my brother found a hatchet and threatened him with it if he came any closer. After near-death experiences with alcohol, my brother got sober at a rehab campfire in Arizona, where he was able to recall this incident. I was in the room but do not remember it, except as it was told to me by my brother.

Somewhere in those early years, I resolved that I would never hurt a woman the way my father hurt my mother. I learned to vent anger not with blows, but with words. If I wasn't cut out to be a teacher, then perhaps I could do battle with words on paper and in the courtroom.

So off I went, damaged goods, to study law. I caused my own amount of suffering in the years to come, but my loving wife and children have stuck with me and shown me the way, when I should have done my part in showing them. But I have never given up, not on the trail and not in life. Sir Winston Churchill is reputed to have said, "If you're going through hell, keep going." And "Never! Never! Never give up!" I pray my legacy contains this lesson.

I ended up fighting for the underdog in briefs and courtroom battles. I served some well and some not so well. I did my best in all circumstances, and sometimes that was not good enough. There was an underdog in me that never got out ahead of the pack.

A therapist once told my wife that my lack of trust was off the charts. For me, it wasn't safe out there. There was no teamwork in my childhood home. I hardly remember meals with my dad except on Sundays. I don't remember having friends over. My brother and I were on our own. When our neighbor's dog bit me, I had to get the neighbor to take me to the doctor to remove the stitches, because my mother was passed out. When my dad asked, "Are you of this world?" I vowed silently, "I'll show you," not knowing—how does a child know?—that I was setting out on a lonely path.

I loved mowing lawns as a kid and made money mowing for neighbors, including the one whose dog bit me. I was industrious and never minded hard physical labor. I proved that on the clean-up crew at boarding school and again on a cattle ranch in Wyoming one summer during college.

When visiting a hardware store with my dad, I saw a small riding mower and desperately wanted it to grow my business. I came home and wrote up a proposal, outlining for my dad how I could earn money with the mower to pay him back if he'd buy it for me. I slipped the business plan under his bedroom door. His answer was, "No." Later in life, he told me I almost won my first case.

More self-reliance.

Knife Edge IV

My father and brother used to be critical of me. My father didn't get me, and my brother was too much in his own head to enter mine. "You'll see," was all I ever got from him when I wondered what clever thing he was doing as the older of the two of us. In any outdoor events, I was always yelling, "Hey, Gard! Wait for me. . . ."

My mother, whose Danish maiden name is Sorensen, had hoped for a Sorena but got me.

I've had too much therapy to keep feeling sorry for myself. There were just inner voices I still had to face, and Pennsylvania became the place where I dealt with them. And that "I'll show you!" vow living in a deep, dark silence within me? It was like a mythical black stallion with an extraordinarily muscular build who, because of age and circumstances, had only partially retired from the track.

Pennsylvania is the halfway state on the AT. It is hard on the feet. It is also my home—the place to which I moved from suburban New York. My 75th birthday and then Pennsylvania were big milestones on the first half of the trail. Beacons lighting the way for my emotions. The state was also the dividing line between the unknown South and my home turf in the North. As I passed through Pennsylvania, I was time-traveling. Being on the trail was taking me into my past.

"Why'd you do that?" I heard my brother say.

"You should have gone this way."

"That was stupid."

I started hearing those stored inner voices from long ago. They surfaced against the backdrop of my father's judgment of me. My brother was criticizing my stepping on this stone instead of that one. Unbidden, the voices were there for many miles until something within quietly turned them aside.

I was being true to an ancient desire, put on my heart by something beyond myself, beyond my Connecticut family, beyond my work, and beyond my Pennsylvania family. It came from deep within, and I answered with an unadulterated will. I said "Yes" to me over all exterior demands, suggestions, and requirements. I set all the "musts" aside to answer. And it was good. It was right. It was more than right. It was ordained, and God had smiled on my desire many times already.

Maybe because of these out-of-reach reasons, I came to a point on the trail where I took charge of the voices that were haunting me, even from beyond the grave. Were these people actually looking down on me and seeing what I did? Did they see a near-fall because I misstepped? Did they know only what they could criticize?

I would turn those voices around. I gave my father and brother each a new mind, which became consciously aware of only positive moves. I spoke for them now, so that on my next step among the rocks they remarked,

"Good move!"

"Nice recovery!"

"Good choice!"

"I am in awe of what you are doing. You are a remarkable person, a truly remarkable human being."

"Congratulations!"

I hear only a faint echo of those earlier judgmental voices these days. The stronger voices are those I won for myself. The ones I commanded and authored. I don't need to think about the whys and wherefores of the darker times. The trail has become mine, leading me to my true self.

Knife Edge, Pennsylvania

Knife Edge V

I had passed over a knife edge in my mind. On the AT, a knife edge of stone was just ahead.

The second day out with JP, we found ourselves in a tall stand of trees by a stream, getting water, when Applejack showed up. He had introduced himself to me at the NOC in North Carolina after someone told him I'm from Lancaster. He comes from Columbia, 10 miles from my home.

He had gone off the trail to heal from shin splints and was now back. He moved out at such a pace that he finished 50 days ahead of us. In the Whites, he covered a distance in one day that took us three. I think his trail name should have been Jackrabbit.

Well, this kind soul reached the sharply angled slabs of rock, known as the Knife Edge, and waited. He wanted to be sure Theo and I would get across okay. We did. I won't forget the Knife Edge— nor Applejack's kindness.

All We Have Is Each Other

In a couple of days, Theo and I reached Palmerton, Pennsylvania, and another famous rock formation on the trail—Lehigh Gap. The hostel at Bert's Steakhouse was a cinder block garage out back. The shower and water supply were behind the restaurant next to metal, fire-escape stairs. In the morning when I called Theo from the shower area, he thought I was up those stairs. When I beckoned him down, he got his paw caught between the metal slats, but for- tunately his momentum was such that he didn't break anything. It did take a little jimmying and care to free him.

It was July 4th weekend, but Palmerton was like a ghost town, with Monday the actual holiday, the day we would do Lehigh Gap.

Rocks. Piled high one upon the other. Up and up and up. It was steepest at the top, and at one point I had to take Theo's pack off to help him up a particularly difficult section. I tried with only modest success to heave his pack up after him. It made it only partway. When I followed, I reached down with my trekking pole, hoping to hook it, but unfortunately I nudged it off a small ledge and it fell, just as a good-sized man and woman came along, causing me some concern for their safety.

Near the top of a steep climb out of Lehigh Gap, Pennsylvania

The guy retrieved Theo's pack and hoisted it up to me. To my "Thank you" he responded with a theme from the trail which I will never forget: "Hey! All we have up here is each other."

We weren't always on dangerous, steep terrain, but his comment fits all parts of the trail and life. He gave me back Theo's pack and wisdom to live by.

From Ridge to Rude

The trail on the ridge was long, straight, and interesting. A gentle breeze was blowing, causing the vegetation to dance in the muted light of an early summer mid-afternoon under a mildly overcast sky. On both sides of the thin brown path were little yellow flowers, Queen Anne's Lace, thistles, purple and white flowers, and large dandelions gone to seed but still intact. And all along the way were tall grasses. These hardiest of plants cover around a third of the earth—always beautiful and pervasive, whether short or tall, and, when tall, flourishing with a crowning stalk of seeds. Giving, generous, essential, sturdy, nourishing. Grass. In Africa, tall enough to hide an elephant, according to David Attenborough's *Planet Earth*. On this stretch of the AT, tall enough to hide Theo.

When rain began in the late afternoon, I set up the tent in a bed of ferns concealing a tangle of tiny thorns. We survived—better than we did the next night, which found us in a hostel sleeping on a garage floor. That was no problem, but the owner felt the need to prove to me, and especially to a young female hiker with a German shepherd, that he was the alpha dog with his two, huge, brown Doberman Pinschers. One kept picking a fight with the shepherd until I finally asked the owner to remove his own dog.

Because of bowel issues, dehydration, and related fatigue, I was thinking of taking a zero here. My doctor in Lancaster wanted me to stay off the trail until my diarrhea passed (pardon the expression), but I had to keep going (pardon me). There was no way I would put in another night at this "hostile."

Wind Gap

Our next stop was Wind Gap, where a family friend and her husband took us in for a couple of nights. I was treated royally the whole time. Good food, good drink, excellent quarters to myself, and WiFi to connect and write as time allowed. Our friend was more than just a good cook. Clearly she was very skilled and knowledgeable and pulled out all the stops for the hungry hiker as, I suspect, she always did for her hungry husband. Theo and I could not have been more comfortable.

Her husband informed me that the rocks on the AT in Pennsylvania were dropped during the Ice Age when the glaciers stopped here. The Appalachians are believed to be the oldest mountains on the planet and were once higher than the Rockies. For thousands of years, erosion from glaciers and weather has worn them down.

Pennsylvania's rocks are just an accident of Mother Nature's. It is her world—we are just visitors. The designers of the AT, Benton MacKaye and Myron Avery, in the early 20th century, envisioned a trail on the summits of the ancient mountains. That they happened to be rocky in Pennsylvania, so be it. I like knowing that Theo's and my footsteps added ever so slight an imprint on the geologic history of the trail.

Delaware Water Gap

We hiked from Wind Gap to the Delaware Water Gap, home to the Deer Head Inn, established in 1869, and one of the oldest jazz performance places in the country. We spent the night at Church of the Mountain, an Appalachian Trail thru-hikers' center supported by donations only.

After a good meal at the hangout spot in town, I headed for the porch of the Deer Head Inn for dessert. I returned for breakfast the next morning before crossing the very busy bridge into New Jersey.

Reservoir
HARTFORD

East Mountain State Forest

Martin Van Buren NHS

Great Barrington

Mt Everett
2602ft
793m

CONNECTICUT

Mt Everett State Reservation

Sages Ravine

Falls
Village

Mohawk State Forest

Housatonic State Forest
Housatonic Meadows State Park

Salisbury

Cornwall Bridge

WATERBURY

Macedonia Brook State Park

Kent

Hudson

River

Housatonic

River

NEW H

KINGSTON

Pawling

Lake Candlewood

Ashokan Reservoir

Vanderbilt Mansion NHS
Home of Franklin D. Roosevelt NHS
Eleanor Roosevelt NHS

POUGHKEEPSIE

Depot Hill State Forest

Weir Farm
NHS

BRIDGEPC

CONN.
N.Y.

NEW YORK

*Pepacton
Reservoir*

*Neversink
Reservoir*

Clarence Fahnestock
Memorial State Park

Hudson Highlands
State Park

STAMFORD

MIDDLETOWN

Bear Mountain–Harriman State Park

Delaware

River

Port Jervis

Unionville

NEW YORK
NEW JERSEY

NEW YOR

Upper Delaware Scenic
and Recreational River

Abram S. Hewitt State Forest

Wawayanda State Park

Vernon

High Point

High Point State Park

PATERSON

*Lake
Wallenpaupack*

Stokes State Forest

NEWARK

*Culvers
Gap*

Delaware Water
Gap NRA

SCRANTON

Mtn

Kittatinny

ELIZABETH

Delaware Water Gap

Worthington State Forest

NEW JERSEY

Stroudsburg

WILKES-BARRE

Wind Gap

EASTON

PENNSYLVANIA

TRENTON

BETHLEHEM

River

Lehigh Gap

ALLENTOWN

PENNSYLVANIA
NEW JERSEY

Hawk Mountain Sanctuary

Port Clinton

Hamburg

POTTSTOWN

PHILADELPHIA

Valley Forge
NHP

READING

Schuylkill

River

Delaware River

Hopewell
Furnace NHS

Susquehanna

River

WILMINGTON

NEW JERS

NEW JERSEY
72.1 Miles

N

Miles

0   10   20   30   40   50

NON

LANCASTER

CHAPTER 9

New Jersey

The Delaware

Theo led the way across the bridge over the wide expanse of the Delaware River. He was steady as he periodically took in the fact that the river and land were far below. I took some videos, primarily to capture the vast difference in pace as cars rushed by us, whiiizz-whiiizzzzz-roooooar-whiiizzzz-roar-whiiizzzzzz, in rapid succession. The Amish, Theo, and I were so much slower. Our pace revealed the grass, the flowers, the insects—the world that is always there beside the highways of our lives. You could sense the importance of the undertaking compelling each vehicle on its way. Our mission, by contrast, felt so simple. Compelling in its own way for sure, but generous with allowances for every single step, leaf, and flower along the way.

As it was when we arrived in Pennsylvania a month before, Theo crossed into the new state ahead of me. We had 895 miles left on our journey.

What did hiking the Appalachian Trail mean to Theo? How did he compute each additional day as we hiked? He had no sense whatsoever of how much longer we'd be out, or if we'd ever again be home. Was this life now? Was back home over? Was it a place at all?

Rocks, Bears, and Scenery

It is rumored that New Jersey is not much better than Pennsylvania rocks-wise. This proved to be true, at least at the start.

I had hiked 40 miles or so on the AT in New Jersey about 10 years before and recognized much of the terrain. New Jersey is reputed to have the highest bear population on the trail, and I did scare one who made a crashing commotion nearby.

Some of the scenery in New Jersey is spectacular. We were on a ridge under a high overcast. It was clear below and exhilarating with strong winds. It seemed you could just about see the curvature of the earth in all directions. Gliders and military jets entertained us for the better part of an hour before it was time to move on.

Just Another Hiker

We stayed at the Mohican Outdoor Center just off the trail. The price included breakfast. We were directed to a large building in the back. There was a big common area, a well-appointed kitchen, and halls to several rooms.

A middle-aged, weekend hiker was already set up for a stay. He had a good supply of groceries, which he was glad to share with me. We sat and chatted about our lives and the trail, and at one point I reflected, "I'm probably older than most of the hikers out here." Without hesitating he said, "Than ALL!" As the oldest, I guess I wasn't just another hiker!

After breakfast at the lodge, we were northbound once again. At lunch, I saw my roommate from the night before, and I ate while Theo made a rock look like a billowy collection of down feathers.

Beautiful views from Kittatinny Mountain, New Jersey

Almost In-Laws

After a night in the lap of luxury at Culver Lake, New Jersey, where we stayed with friends of my brother-in-law Shawn, we were back on the trail at 5:15 a.m. An hour and 15 minutes later, we stopped for breakfast and a leisurely, hour-long break.

By midday, we were at a pavilion high on a ridge in the north-west section of the state. I decided to call the parents of my youngest daughter's first fiancé. The romantic relationship was over, but not the friendship. Sure, I could stay with them—and they could see the pavilion from their house. I would hike down to High Point State Park, and they would meet me there.

I had the best time with them and the children still at home. Mom brought out an overwhelming supply of power bars for me. Dad, a cardiologist, gave me a pair of insoles which I cut to fit my boots. I ate extremely well and drank five or six 7-Ups.

Breakfast in the morning was over the top, and soon Theo and I were, too, as the next mountain claimed us on a misty, overcast day.

Wallkill Wildlife Refuge

At a viewing tower from which we could see nothing because of the mist, another hiker showed up with a very sweet red dog carrying red saddlebags. I would see them again.

Field- and road-walking brought us to the Wallkill Wildlife Refuge I'd hiked through before. As we approached the preserve, I noticed a deer in the distance off to my left, jumping high above the grass to get its bearings. I kept an eye on its antics until it disappeared in the high growth at the edge of the road. My eyes were glued to the spot where I imagined it would emerge and cross the road.

Deer on the run

As the video rolled, I saw a doe and fawn move carefully to the road and cross. I watched directly but kept the camera going. When Mama saw me, she let out a grunt, and she and fawn darted across the road and into the woods by the preserve. Unfortunately, I had let the camera droop, and I missed most of the crossing, but I had enough footage to extract some stills.

It took perhaps an hour to circumnavigate the preserve and return to the woods on the other side. Up a steep climb was a shelter which Theo and I had to ourselves. I hung my water filter bag so gravity could do its job and left it there for the night.

Red

The next day we came to a stream where a hiker was filling up. The red dog we'd seen was his. I decided to filter water as well. I looked in my backpack's outside pouch for my water filter bag, and it was not to be found. Where could it be?

Hermano, Red's owner, was happy to have me use his filter. I thanked him for his offer, knowing it was only a quick fix. What was I going to do going forward? Maybe just keep borrowing from other hikers.

I remembered then that I had left the bag hanging at the shelter—and that a woman I had met several days before was still there when we left. She had been sleeping in her tent, but if she'd used the privy, she would have gone by the shelter and might have seen my bag.

She was a little aloof when we first met, but warmer the next day. That time I had also started hiking before she did, and when she passed me at a good clip, I decided to give her the trail name Kick-Butt, which I reduced to KB.

Having again left KB at a shelter that morning, I thought she might come along soon. And, indeed, she did—with my water filter bag! Instead of the big squeeze I felt like giving her, I said a polite, fellow-hiker "Thank you!" Once again, my butt had been saved, this time by Kick-Butt.

I filtered while enjoying Red's company. There was a little pathos about him, which tended to widen the berth in my heart, but Theo was watching.

Apple Bag

The trail was pretty mild from here to the rather well-known board-walk over a vast swampland. I had been here before, as well. When

There was something about "Red"

it was time to camp, the only water was under a bridge with no other access. I had a thick plastic bag which had contained apples. I used it to carry excess water short distances and as Theo's water bowl. Its home was his saddlebags.

So to get to the water from the inaccessible stream, I tied a rope to the handles of the apple bag and put stones in the bottom so it would sink below the surface. Lower. Fill. Lift. Filter. I love making do.

Stratton Mtn
VERMONT MASSACHUSETTS
NATIONAL
eorge
MASSACHUSETTS
Glastenbury Mtn
3748ft
1142m
Harriman
Reservoir
Quabbin
Reservoir
FOREST
MASSACHUSETTS
CONNECTICUT
Bennington
Clarksburg State Forest
North Adams
HOLYOKE
Saratoga NHP
Mt Greylock
3491ft
1064m
SPRINGFIELD
Mt Greylock State Reservation
Cheshire
Dalton
PITTSFIELD
October Mountain State Forest
SCHENECTADY
TROY
Lee
Tyringham
Beartown State Forest
Barkhamsted
Reservoir
HARTFORD
ALBANY
River
East Mountain State Forest
MASSACHUSETTS
NEW YORK
Mt Everett
2602ft
793m
CONNECTICUT
Martin Van Buren NHS
Great Barrington
Mt Everett State Reservation
Sages Ravine
Falls
Village
Salisbury
Mohawk State Forest
Housatonic State Forest
Housatonic Meadows State Park
Cornwall Bridge
WATERBURY
Macedonia Brook State Park
Hudson River
Kent
Housatonic
River
NEW
KINGSTON
Pawling
Lake Candlewood
Ashokan Reservoir
Vanderbilt Mansion NHS
Home of Franklin D. Roosevelt NHS
Eleanor Roosevelt NHS
POUGHKEEPSIE
Depot Hill State Forest
Weir Farm
NHS
CONN.
N.Y.
BRIDG
River
Pepacton
Reservoir
NEW YORK
Neversink
Reservoir
Clarence Fahnestock
Memorial State Park
STAMFOR
Hudson Highlands
State Park
LONG
MIDDLETOWN
Bear Mountain–Harriman State Park
NEW YORK
NEW JERSEY
NEW YO
Delaware
Unionville
Abram S. Hewitt State Forest
Port Jervis
Wawayanda State Park
PATERSON
Upper Delaware Scenic
and Recreational River
River
High Point
Vernon
High Point State Park
NEWARK
Stokes State Forest
Lake
Wallenpaupack
Mtn
Culvers
Gap
Delaware Water
Gap NRA
ELIZABETH
SCRANTON
Kittatinny
Worthington State Forest
Delaware Water Gap
NEW JERSEY
Stroudsburg
WILKES-BARRE
Wind Gap
P
NEW YORK
89.8 Miles
N
EASTON
TRENTON
Miles
0   10   20   30   40   50
BETHLEHEM
PYLVANIA
JERSEY
River
ALLENTOWN

CHAPTER 10

New York

Feet

In the morning, I got my feet ready for another day on the trail. I was in the very same boots my feet had enjoyed at the start in Georgia. Now I was fighting my way back to that original comfort with everything at my disposal: toe spacers, moleskin spots on little toes to act as a buffer against the boot sides, and duct tape to minimize friction at the ball of the foot and the bottoms and tops of the toes. I was so desperate one night that I tried to create a mold around the outside surface of my right little toe with Super Glue. It wore off in no time.

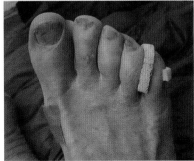

Feet were painful from Marion, Virginia, to Massachusetts

I even thought to make a little cast with a wide straw, but the toe didn't fit.

We were underway by 7:30 in the morning and soon crossed into New York, our ninth state. Although the AWOL profile was not intimidating, New York proved to be a difficult state with steep climbs up to sheer rock summits.

We emerged from the woods onto a parking area where a hot dog stand was just closing. I prevailed upon the woman to sell me a few, along with some sodas. An ice cream stand afterward was a delight for both me and Theo.

Hollie

We stayed in a shelter that night and then made our way to NY 17 and a reunion with my niece Hollie from Mamaroneck, New York, where we'd spend the night. On the hour-long drive south, I consumed a can of Sprite and almost another liter bottle, which I finished at her condo.

Hollie served me a magnificent meal of steak leftovers. I enjoyed every morsel, as did Theo who got the scraps.

My Thermarest pad had begun to leak air, happily only slowly. I tried to find the leak by inflating it and submerging it in Hollie's tub. I saw no bubbles. On our return to the trail, we stopped at an outfitter's along the way and attempted an exchange, but I was not happy with the selection. In Andover, Maine, I would receive a new one from the manufacturer at no charge.

Lemon Squeezer

Back in the woods, we hiked in the rain to a rock formation known as the Lemon Squeezer. There was no way Theo or I was going to get through this tight fit with our packs on. I took both off and hurled them up to a rock ledge overhead.

When we emerged, with packs back on, we were confronted immediately with a sheer rock face about 10 feet high. I pushed Theo up where he waited, probably with indifference, as I labored to gain his position. A tree was growing so close to the ledge I was on that I had to swing around it, precariously leaning out into space with 30 pounds on my back, and gravity lusting after me like a swamp alligator, to make my way to the top.

That night I met a couple of grey-bearded day-hikers at a shelter and felt I was in good company. A troop of Scouts camped nearby in the woods.

The Grand Lady

In the morning, I took a picture of my shelter floor mates still in their sleeping bags, bearded, barely breathing, and beautiful. Theo and I were underway by 7:00.

Sleeping beauties

It was a bright, sunny day, and the trail had several steep ups and downs. Seeing two trees growing right out of a boulder, I marveled at the tenacity of life! Perhaps my hike is a small way of exercising the I-WILL-LIVE instinct deep in our DNA.

On a ridge top we got our first view of the mighty Hudson River leading to my birthplace, the Statue of Liberty, and the ocean beyond. Liberty! What a word! What a blessing! We are fortunate far beyond our knowing.

President Reagan warned, "Freedom is never more than one generation away from extinction." We don't pass it to our children through our bloodstreams. It must be fought for, protected, and handed on for them to do the same, or one day we will spend our sunset years telling our children and our children's children what it was once like in the United States where people were free.

Down the river was the Grand Lady, torch held high. When I was 10, my parents took my brother and me into New York for the usual sights. At the Empire State Building we made a clay recording of "On Top of Old Smoky." Vinyl records were still in the future. Of course, we went to the Statue of Liberty and climbed the steps inside all the way to the crown—and then up into the torch—or so I thought. Google tells me the torch was closed in 1916 after the Germans exploded our ammunition nearby, causing shrapnel damage to the statue. I've enjoyed all these years thinking I went into the torch. Oh, well, "Just keep going."

After several difficult climbs and descents, we came to a suitable place to camp for the night not far from Bear Mountain Park. The area, lying in a depression between two large rock faces, had a slightly spooky feel, but we survived just fine.

The night before Bear Mountain, New York

Bear Mountain

In the morning we climbed steep stone steps up Bear Mountain, summited around 8:30, and headed for the observation tower. "Stay" prompted Theo to wait reluctantly at the door. Once back at ground level, I took a picture to the south with the faint New York City skyline visible just over the distant hills.

On a steep descent, we saw John and Laurie from the ATC!

They both remembered me and might have been a little surprised to see that I was still at it. It was Laurie who had commented about my weight loss: "Oh, you'll lose more weight in the Whites." It was good to reconnect.

Pavement Walking

Hessian Lake, on the east side of Bear Mountain, made me feel cooler. I had lunch at a café at the back of Bear Mountain Inn and returned to the park outside where I found a bench to work on my painful toes and left heel. Looking for the trail north, I walked around the entire lake on hard pavement with unhappy feet without success. When I finally found the trail, we descended to the bridge over the Hudson, 124 feet above sea level, the lowest point on the Appalachian Trail.

The river crossing brought me into my homeland. New York and its surroundings were the center of the universe in my adolescent mind. All other places in the country were just psychological concrete supports for Mecca. I was now close to Connecticut where I grew up; close to Rhinebeck, New York, where my parents moved when I was in prep school; close to riding school in New Canaan, to camps in Connecticut and New Hampshire, and to Mount Hermon and Yale.

Theo and I did some road-walking on the Hudson's east bank until the trail turned into the woods for a steep climb to a campsite under the trees at the top of the ridge.

The Appalachian Deli

By 8:10 the next morning, we were near Peekskill, New York, and emerged onto US 9 and NY 403 forming a V, making room for the Appalachian Deli where we stopped for breakfast. I ordered up a significant amount to eat, sitting at a high top with a big TV overhead. The only other table was occupied by two fully armed cops who looked like they could muscle their way through any conflict and pull any weapon in under a second.

As the TV overhead displayed a large image of candidate Trump, I engaged them in a little conversation.

"Hey, guys, I've been on the Appalachian Trail for months. Who's this guy Trump?"

Smiles. Brief conversation. A hint of, "We're friendly but not friends. We'll bow out now, thank you." Respectfully, I returned to my meal, finished before them, and went outside where I'd tied Theo to one of the tables.

There I met a young woman with a hard, red plastic, violin case attached to her backpack. A conversation piece for sure. A-Note was her trail name. She was a part of a clown troop that played in New York's Central Park.

Glenna

I was approaching the closest point on the trail to Danbury, Connecticut, the home of my brother's first wife, still sister-in-law to me. I had called ahead, and she was happy to have me recuperate at her home. She could tell I was exhausted and needed the rest. I had hoped to make another 30 miles or so before a pickup, but she convinced me now was the time. My drive may have been getting in the way of knowing what was best. I guess we all need a little encouragement from others now and then, as I did from Bonnie back at Port Clinton.

Glenna's and her husband Ed's home would become my home for four days. They gave me love, concern, admiration, and service, the healing balm I needed.

Glenna and I enjoyed a gin together most nights. Ed was away all but one on business. When home, he told me how much he respected what I was doing. It was clear he knew what it was, for he had hiked a good bit himself.

I examined my feet before going to bed and saw that my little toenails had all but given up. They had been squeezed into nonproduction while my toes looked like little blond sausages. I was not in pain for a few days because I was not walking over rough terrain in boots with 30 pounds on my back. I slept well, Theo on the floor in my room.

Doctors

Glenna took me to resupply and to doctor visits for my bowels and my feet. I begged the orthopedist to shoot my heel with cortisone so I could finish. He refused because he said it would destroy the fat in my heel. He did provide me with silicone gel heel pads which added weight to my boots. I would use them for a few hundred miles, and then remove them in favor of kneading my heel firmly every night, which eventually did the trick.

As for the bowels, the tests were all negative. I just had to tough it out.

First Birch Tree

On Tuesday, July 26th, we were back on the trail, northbound once again. We were only a few miles in when I saw my first white birch tree, a tree dear to my New England soul. "One could do worse than be a swinger of birches," wrote Robert Frost. They prompted thoughts of cooler weather, as did the more abundant, colorful leaves on the ground.

Bed-down was at Ralph's Peak Hikers' Cabin. Several hikers were set up in the shelter and in tents nearby. There was water at a pump, but filtering was recommended. We were near enough to a road that some ordered pizza to be delivered. I felt a little disconnected from the younger hikers there, so just went about my business and turned in.

A-Note

In the morning we went under the Taconic State Parkway, which I had traveled many times early in our marriage. The afternoon would take us over more ridges, eventually to meet up with A-Note again. She was standing on a rock with a small tree and a vast blue, green, and white view behind her. She was barefoot in a short navy blue skort and skimpy red-and-white striped top. And she was playing her violin!

A strange sight in the middle of the woods, perhaps, but interesting to say the least. She petted Theo as I took some pictures, and then I asked if she'd mind playing something which I would video. She obliged, tuned up, and played a slow rendition of "Danny Boy," exhibiting the skill of a beginner. She'd said she was a clown. The skill set might have fit the act, or was she just clowning with me the whole time? It didn't matter. A fun, young woman having a good time. I'm glad I met her.

Nuclear Lake

Five hours later I came to the ominous-sounding Nuclear Lake, so named because of an explosion at a chemical plant in 1972 which blasted an unspecified amount of bomb-grade plutonium across the lake and surrounding woods, according to Google. The lake has long been cleared of any concerns, and, I can tell you, the fish were happy.

A-Note was there when I arrived. Maybe she was more mysterious than I first thought. I had left her five hours earlier standing on a rock, her gear at her feet, violin in hand. I don't recall stopping to eat, going off the trail, or her passing me. She'd been swimming and was just leaving as I arrived. Hers was A-Note I never heard again.

Another hiker was sitting with his feet in the water. When I stepped in, small fish started nibbling at my toes. Nothing drastic but weird and uncomfortable. I'd learned some time before that, in some Asian countries, this is how they debride the feet of dead skin. I guess that's what the fish were after.

Notwithstanding the little nibblers, I stripped to my black undershorts, and in I went. My vigorous movements kept the fish at bay, and I emerged free of radiant illumination.

I dressed wet—who cared?—and carried on. Destination? The Telephone Pioneers Shelter—there's got to be a story there. My last picture of the day was at 8:20 as darkness filled the forest.

Dover Oak

At 6:05 the next morning I took a picture looking out of the shelter as Theo greeted the new day. Other hikers were also up and getting started. We were moving by 7:30 down a 500-foot slope to West Dover Road near Pawling, New York. Just across the road was the Dover Oak. Its girth of 20′ 4″ was 2′ 4″ greater than the Keffer Oak I had slept under on May 9th, Day 79. Each tree predated the American Revolution.

Greeting the day and smelling breakfasts

A slight climb up from the road led to a stretch of beautiful fields, followed by a large, deep swamp, which we traversed on an elaborate boardwalk. I wondered if Earl Shaffer, or other early AT hikers, ever had to deal with this kind of territory. Except for the most adventuresome, without the boardwalk, it seemed impassable.

At the far side were a railroad crossing and the Appalachian Trail Station where you could flag a train for a two-hour ride to New York City on a one-way ticket for about $30. I stuck to the trail, which passed a store with hiker supplies, and crossed more soft, green fields before re-entering the woods.

CHAPTER 11

Connecticut

Gateway to New England

At the New York-Connecticut border a sign welcomed us to the "Gateway to New England." I spent my grade school years in Connecticut. That made it home. I was back. We spent a rainy night under tall pines on the eastward-flowing Tenmile River just west of where it connects with the north-south Housatonic River.

In the morning we crossed the Tenmile and hiked north along the west bank of the famous Housatonic. The day got off to a misty, foggy start but gradually turned sunny as we hiked westward into the woods.

In time, we came to what AWOL describes as the "steep stone steps down to the Housatonic River." A misstep here could be very serious. There were enough hazards on the trail that, if they deserved mention, they were hazardous indeed.

Down at the riverside, the trail followed a gravel road for a long stretch. As night was falling, the road eventually came to an end at a large boulder, where I and a couple other hikers stopped to get out our headlamps for the 1.3 miles in dark woods.

I hiked this straight path at a fair clip but struggled with a film forming over my left eye after a bug flew into it. In addition, my

headlamp light was dim. The nighttime trek became rather precarious. I kept adjusting the headlamp and wiping my eye for temporary relief and modest clarity.

In this fashion, I made my way to the Stewart Hollow Brook Shelter, just off the riverside trail, and found a spot to pitch our tent a little removed from several others.

With difficulty, I pushed through an overgrown path down to the river for water, cooked, ate quietly, and turned in for the night.

Sharon

In the morning we were back along the Housatonic for an interesting, low-lying part of the adventure. The path was straight and long with occasional views into fields off to the left. Several were filled with Queen Anne's Lace.

When the trail turned away from the river, we had ups and downs, crossing swamps and streams to a short section of trail leading directly to West Cornwall Road. There, a distant relative picked me up for a night at her beautiful home in Sharon, Connecticut. She treated me to the finest Scotch, followed by an exquisite meal and a delicious night's sleep. The contrast between my cleanliness and that of her house cannot be overstated.

Breakfast would be whenever I liked, and we could then do whatever shopping I needed before she'd take me back to the trail.

Explosion

French toast started the new day. After resupplying, Theo and I were on the trail by 10:00. The climb out of the West Cornwall Road "gap" was immediately interesting with wet rock faces presenting the morning challenge. We crossed a gravel road and continued on, taking in glistening wet vegetation and silver-drop-studded spider webs.

Sometimes I was just grateful to be out on the trail when most of the world was involved with busy lives in busy cities. This was a private, away world, affording a sneak peek down into a valley, below the hills, under overcast skies. A moment of solitary, personal gratitude that would stick with me.

It must have been around 3:30 when I finally stopped for lunch at a spring just off the trail to the east. A woman stopped, refilled her water bottles, and left. I sat facing the spring as I ate, and, when finished, I got up to answer a call of nature. I climbed over the stone I had been sitting on and headed into the woods away from the spring—and that's when the explosion occurred.

Well, not really an explosion, but it might as well have been for the surprise it was.

I was instantly flat on the ground. My arms had gone out to break my fall, a reflex action involving no conscious awareness at all. This was the first time I tore the rotator cuff in my right shoulder.

I lay on the ground trying to figure out what had happened. I needed some time to compute, time to solve the mystery that had so flattened me.

Looking back toward the spring, I saw a strand of rusted barbed wire at shin height. I had stepped to within an inch of it. My next step caught the wire, and my hop to recover sent me to the ground.

WHAM!

Over and done.

Regroup.

The rusted barbed wire was virtually invisible a foot above the brown leaves. My right shin was a little bloodied from the barbs. Although my right shoulder had taken a serious jolt, I don't remember any serious pain or disability.

What do you do deep in the woods? You get yourself together and carry on. There is no other choice. And I wasn't so badly hurt that I needed an alternative. I packed up and headed north.

Still Small Voice

The whole day was grey and overcast with rain on and off. I have no recollection of my campsite that night, but I do have pictures that tell me I was stealth-camping in the wet forest.

In its strictest sense, stealth-camping means camping without fire, lights, or noise to avoid detection, at least if you're camping where the activity is not allowed. More loosely, it just means camping in the woods away from a campsite or shelter, which I did often.

Getting a little closer to New Hampshire, I made a note in AWOL:

> WHITES—the closer, the less fearsome.
> Distance magnifies reality.
> Face into fears.

To this, I added a quip by Mark Twain: "I've lived through some terrible things in my life, some of which actually happened."

It is the still small voice that leads aright. The persistent inner whisper I heard said, "Just keep going."

Mt Cube
2911ft
887m

Smarts Mtn
3240ft
988m

Newfound Lake

Laconia

Lyme

Moose Mtn

Hanover

NEW
HAMPSHIRE

CONCORD

HAVERHILL

Lebanon

Woodstock

Saint-Gaudens
NHS

*Sunapee
Lake*

MANCHESTER

NASHUA

LOWELL

BOS

les Newell
WMA

Marsh-Billings-
Rockefeller NHP

Kent
Pond

Sherburne Pass

Concord

Minute Ma

NAL
OREST
State Park

Killington Peak
4235ft
1290m

e State Forest

Rutland

Wallingford

GREEN

Hapgood State Forest

Manchester

MOUNTAIN

Brattleboro

KEENE

Stratton Mtn

NATIONAL

Glastenbury Mtn
3748ft
1142m

FOREST

*Harriman
Reservoir*

MASSACHUSETTS

WORCESTER

SPRINGFIELD

*Quabbin
Reservoir*

Bennington

Clarksburg State Forest
North Adams

Saratoga NHP

Mt Greylock
3491ft
1064m

Mt Greylock State Reservation
Cheshire

HOLYOKE

Dalton

PITTSFIELD

October Mountain State Forest

SCHENECTADY

TROY

Lee

Tyringham

ALBANY

Beartown State Forest

*Barkhamsted
Reservoir*

HARTFORD

East Mountain State Forest

Martin Van Buren NHS

Great Barrington

Mt Everett
2602ft
793m

CONNECTICUT

Mt Everett State Reservation
Sages Ravine

Falls
Village

Salisbury

Mohawk State Forest

Housatonic State Forest
Housatonic Meadows State Park

Cornwall Bridge

WATERBURY

Macedonia Brook State Park

Kent

Housatonic River

KINGSTON

Hudson River

Pawling

Lake Candlewood

NEW H

Ashokan Reservoir

Vanderbilt Mansion NHS
Home of Franklin D. Roosevelt NHS
Eleanor Roosevelt NHS

Depot Hill State Forest

POUGHKEEPSIE

CONN.
N.Y.

Weir Farm
NHS

BRIDGEPO

NEW YORK

Clarence Fahnestock
Memorial State Park

STAMFORD

Hudson Highlands
State Park

*Pepacton
Reservoir*

MASSACHUSETTS
90.5 Miles

N

Miles

0   10   20   30   40   50

ETOWN

Bear Mountain–Harriman State Park

NEW YORK
NEW JERSEY

NEW YOR

Unionville

Port Jervis

Vernon

Abram S. Hewitt State Forest

Wawayanda State Park

Upper Delaware Scenic

CHAPTER 12

Massachusetts

August

August 1st. We awoke to another wet day, and so it would be into the night. On our steady climb, I saw three young boys bounding downhill toward me as if they were on a mission of some kind. Theo, however, was cause for a pause.

They were running ahead of their dad, and I told them that when I saw him, I could tell him, "I never saw them," if that played into their game. Of course, they knew I wouldn't do that, but I enjoyed being part of their fun.

As we climbed to the 2,316-foot summit of Connecticut's Bear Mountain, the terrain gave

us a taste of the Whites and Maine. We were approaching the Connecticut-Massachusetts border and the Berkshires, where my brother had gone to school.

Sages Ravine

Scrub pines stood at the summit, and larger pines where we reentered the forest. The tall trees made it overcast and dark as we descended into a ravine. We were alone. It was a little eerie.

Somewhere in the descent we left Connecticut. Our first night in Massachusetts was at Sages Ravine Campsite at mile 1506.0.

I climbed up the hill from the stream running through the ravine and ran into my first Campsite Caretaker, who told me where I could camp. As with all the caretakers I would encounter in the northern reaches of the trail, she lived in the lap of luxury out in the

Hint of things to come

Sages Ravine — an eerie, lonely campsite

wilderness. She had a big, stand-up tent with cots, canvas chairs, and, I believe, a propane stove. Some caretakers would stay the whole summer, shifting with others for a break. She and her boyfriend were in this location for just a couple of days.

I went to the campsite we were assigned, took off my pack, retrieved my water gear, and headed back to the stream to fill up and filter. I had learned not to take off my boots or Theo's pack until I got water. I'd have him come with me and put full bottles of filtered water in his pouches to carry back to our tent site. I carried the extra.

As I filled the water bag, Theo waited on the split-log bridge we'd used to cross the ravine. He seemed a little forlorn, as if he, too, felt both the mood of the place, with its ever so slight air of uncertainty, and our loneliness, our complete isolation from the world. We were in the north woods—away, removed, lone hikers.

Finish Up

It was a different time from the early days on the trail. Here there was no bunching of hikers. Many had already conquered Katahdin and were on their way home. We'd carry on until it was our turn. We were getting closer to the home stretch, 10 states behind us and four to go—the most difficult part of the trail ahead. But that's just the way I wanted it—to finish going UP! I didn't want to float down-river and take the finish lying down. We had to climb. The end is UP—up there, ahead—at the end of perhaps the hardest climb on the trail. It had to be that way.

I set up the tent in the large open area on wet dirt and did the usual things before turning in, still sleeping on the pad with a slow leak, still thankful it was slow.

Pine Needles

August 2nd. I awoke with a slug, the slimy kind, making his way along the tent floor. I helped him to the door and got on with morning chores. It was slug weather outside, but there was no point in bothering about it. Just do what you do, I reminded myself, even if it is pouring buckets. Pack up and move on.

Mount Race was reputed to have good views. Clouds did break at times, revealing forests, farmers' fields, and a lake in the distance to the east. Theo seemed to enjoy the view as well when it opened up. In a way we were getting the best of all worlds, seeing above and below the clouds.

Just as we came to the end of the ridge, there was Outstanding, wearing sandals as she had when I first met her several states back. I would see her again at an unexpected rest stop a mile or so ahead. After a steep 600' climb up Mount Everett, who would have guessed what we saw? Trail Magic! Such a treat was customary in a field or along a road—but on a mountain top? This was truly magical. Summit Trail Magic!

Theo liked the views from Mount Race

After a modest treat, we continued our way north, down the far side of Mount Everett to the Hemlock Shelter at its base. On our descent, the clouds gave way to brilliant sunshine and vistas opened up all around. This was South Egremont, Massachusetts, home to Jug End Barn Ski Area in the early 1950s. I'd skied there as a boy, ascending the hill with a rope tow that lifted me off the ground in spots. The ski area no longer exists, and rope tows are a thing of the distant past.

As we descended farther into the valley, the sunlight became all the more brilliant. The sinking orb was low enough to stretch out my shadow the length of two football fields. When high in the sky it revealed my profile.

Back in the woods we were soon at a stealth campsite among the pines with a stream nearby for water. A thick bed of pine needles and water—open arms to the weary traveler. We were guaranteed a good night's sleep.

Feet

In the morning, I tended my feet as always. At night it was sheer joy
to bathe them in Johnson & Johnson's powder, as I did every sweaty
part of my body. I was liberal with it because it was worth it. And
if a whole bunch got in my sleeping bag, what could possibly be
wrong with that?

"Bathed" and comfortable in dry clothes, I had a good sleep.
Nearby on the tent floor were the wet, smelly pants and shirts ready
for morning.

My outer wool socks were soaked with sweat and water. The
inner white liners were filled with holes and were anything but
white. They were tube socks so I could rotate them to avoid my toes
pushing through holes which could cut or irritate them.

I applied duct tape, toe spacers, and moleskin. Then I put on
the liner tube socks carefully, so as not to loosen or dislodge the
moleskin tabs on the outside of my little toes. Finally, I put on the
outer Smartwool socks, preparing for the full-dress drill of the day.

Bogged Down

We had crossed a footbridge to get to our campsite in the pines
last night. This morning we passed over several more, and then
traversed a long boardwalk, as well as many boards suspended on
log supports over spongy earth and bogs of deep mud. We came to
more and more of these going north, some able to swallow a person
up like quicksand. I am grateful neither of us got bogged down in
one of these.

On The Long Trail in Vermont in 2010, Theo made his way
through many shallower bogs. Then, in the dark confines of a
shelter at night, with other hikers nearby, he would groom himself

endlessly. On our last night on the trail in August of 2010, on the south side of Camels Hump Mountain, we stayed in a shelter where there was a bevy of Girl Scouts, all of whom went crazy over Theo. That night many of us were on the bottom of two decks, packed in like sardines, when Theo, next to me, started slurping away at his dried bog boots.

"Theo! No!" I tried to whisper in a commanding voice.

Quiet. . .and then, "Slllluuuuurrrp, Sllllluuuuurrrp," again and again.

I'd poke and pull at his head in an attempt to dissuade him. My earplugs helped but, if any of the girls was not asleep, Theo probably kept them that way.

We were spared such nighttime grooming on the AT.

Slow Mass

At road crossings in Massachusetts there were bulletin boards with maps that served only to tell you how slow your progress was. Massachusetts was more like a roadblock than a meaningful state to traverse.

It was here that I first conceived the idea of hiking the entire Appalachian Trail. But now Massachusetts felt like a state I just had to get out of the way so I could get to the biggies up North. I arbitrarily include it as the last of the middle states instead of the first of the northern ones. The last three big ones were in a class by themselves. But Massachusetts isn't a middle or a northern state. It's a psychological bog without boards to get you through. The southern states were now a distant memory, the true middle states were also history, and the challenge of the northern three was out ahead. Massachusetts, sorry to say, even underfoot, was nowhere.

We came to a beautiful shade tree where we stopped for lunch. With lots of area between the road and a cornfield, we took the opportunity to dry out gear still soaked from Sages Ravine.

At some point we came to a large rock face overlooking a valley with a view westward to the Catskills in New York State. A handsome, bearded hiker was sitting on the rock, reading. In time he was joined by friends Brew, Dragon, and Danger. Tapeworm and Cake were nearby.

The trail took us down a gradual descent to woods where we would stealth-camp, again with water nearby.

View of the Catskills in New York

Jerusalem Road

We woke late. Theo lazed in the grass and leaves with his saddle-bags on, waiting for me to finish packing. Once underway, we were soon at MA 23, site of another map.

I called a hostel in Sheffield, Massachusetts, and was told they were full but we could tent in the back. It was cheaper, and we would have all the amenities of the house. We would be in good time to meet our ride at Jerusalem Road.

In the course of conversation with the son of the owner, I mentioned that I had gone to Mount Hermon School. He said that his mother had gone to Northfield, the sister school, but she was away taking care of her mother.

After dinner at a nearby restaurant, Theo and I had the back yard to ourselves for a peaceful night.

Dalton

A slow morning, followed by a 1¼-hour drive, and we were back on the trail at 2:15. It was a glorious, sunny, midsummer day. We hiked over fields and through woods to another stealth site with a rocks-in-the-bag water supply.

Before long we were down in the valley, heading for Dalton, Mass. We crossed railroad tracks into town and made our way down Main Street. I asked a woman walking in the opposite direction if she knew a place to stop for lunch. She pointed to a spot down Main Street, the way we were headed, and we each continued on our way.

In short order, I heard her running up behind me. She had turned around from her intended course to find me, because she realized the place she recommended was closed. That left me with a warm feeling of gratitude. I instantly made a friend I'll never see again.

I had lunch at the Dalton Restaurant, sitting by the window looking out on Main Street. I had begun to wonder if we were going to get to Katahdin in time. Tough states and tough mountains were ahead. As I sat in the restaurant, I divided the days left until October 10th (64) into the miles left according to AWOL (620.4). We would need to cover almost 10 miles per day to finish by that date. That pace was not going to be easy in the Whites and Maine. So we had to make tracks now and put miles in the bank.

If we did 12 miles in a given day, I circled a "2" in the AWOL margin for that day, indicating the number of miles above 10 we had covered. If we did 15 the next day, I circled "7," showing the total extra miles we were accumulating going forward. When my circled number got to 20, I knew we were two days ahead of schedule, and seven days ahead of October 15th, the closing date for Baxter State Park where Katahdin rose majestically. We could easily lose seven days in New Hampshire and Maine, so we had to keep up a good pace.

Feeling that I now had a handle on what we needed to do, I finished up at the restaurant and headed back to the trail. We soon came to a spring. It was a little after 6:00, so I looked for a campsite.

A perfect perch for the night

We had descended a small knoll to the stream, and on top was a delightful spot, just off the trail and under a few pines. It was a special place. We were in bed by "midnight."

Bushels of Corn

Leaving our private perch in the woods, we crossed the stream to a small climb before the descent to Cheshire, Massachusetts. Along the way we witnessed magnificent views west over the Cheshire Reservoir, with the town to the north. Farther on was Mount Greylock, the state's reigning monarch, stretching in her dark green cloak upward into a mantle of soft blue.

In time we left nature's canopy and emerged into the unguarded sunlight of town, where bright houses glistened against green lawns.

On the far side of Cheshire we were reminded of Mother Nature's generous gifts and those who tend her fruits. A farmer had cut a wide swath through a cornfield, just for hikers. How many bushels of corn were given up for this passage? Let a Thank You ring out to this farmer, and to all the people who opened their land to passing hikers. These landholders give to countless souls they rarely see who wend their way over their fields or lawns, as if to say, "Pass this way, my friend, and carry on for all the miles you will. 'This land is your land; this land is my land. . . . This land was made for you and me.'"

After the cornfield, open grasslands led to the woods at the foot of Mount Greylock. Step by step, we gained the summit with its tower and lodge, but this was the day we would meet son Soren and grandson Bergen near Williamstown, so we had to keep moving. From open lawns at the summit, I could see North Adams in the distance. Then we headed into the woods for a 3,000-foot descent.

Soren and Bergen

When hiking the AT, the purpose of a "down" is simply to get you to the base of the next "up." And so it was. There were two significant climbs during the Greylock descent. We arrived at the summit of the second around 7:20, as the sun was just beginning to set at the Massachusetts-New York border. Immediately after taking a photo, I saw a jogger heading southbound.

BERGEN!

What a thrill to see this vigorous, young man, my grandson, come to find me, not in a motel lobby but on the summit of a mountain. Five minutes later, his dad arrived with a backpack.

No planned meeting on the trail just happens. You look ahead three months, two months, one month, fine-tuning each time until you nail a date and make yourself keep it. This was one of those times.

"Let's meet at Bennington, Vermont, on August 1st."

"No, it won't be the 1st. What days have you told your work you won't be there? Okay. Let's make it Williamstown."

"Not going to make it on the 1st. It's looking like I can make it on the 8th. Okay?"

And then fine-tune further on the day: "Where?" We settled on Pattison Road, southeast of town, where they arrived early and sought me out on the trail.

"Where should we stay?" I'd given my son a suggestion in keeping with the kinds of places I had frequented on the trail. When Soren checked it out, he opted for finer fare and was happy to provide it. But I'm ahead of myself.

We reconnected at the mountain top and began the long plunge down into the valley. It seemed to go on forever, mostly with me in the lead. It was finishing a round trip for Soren and Bergen.

We spent a night in luxury with drinks and a meal to match. The trail isn't ALL rough. People think the AT thru-hiker disappears in the woods for the duration, never to see a shower, good food, or a bed until the other end. In fact, the best way to think of the real situation for a six-month trek is to consider 26 week-long hikes, each punctuated with a stop at a hostel or in town where there are all the amenities you can afford.

In my room, with all one could want on a business trip or the like, I felt almost claustrophobic, breathing in filtered air. It was also too much luxury for me. My body and mind had become attuned to the outdoors, to woods and leaves and a breeze. I wanted to consume the natural world and leave luxury to others. But I was not shy in accepting my fine son's generosity. I slept well.

Soren and son, Bergen, crossing into Vermont with me

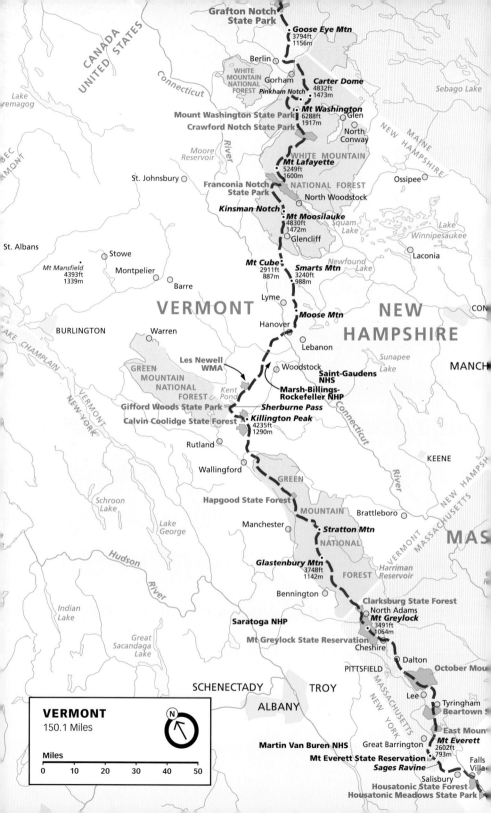

CHAPTER 13

Vermont

Slow Start — Fine Finish

We must have taken it slow and easy that first morning together, with a lazy breakfast at the hotel and then a drive to get my laundry done. We were not actually moving with packs on until nearly 2:00. We crossed the Hoosic River and headed into the woods bound for the MA/VT border some four miles away, gaining about 1,600 feet as we went.

Arriving at the final three states was sweet. My Massachusetts blues were history.

Our start was at the southern end of The Long Trail, which, for 105 miles, is also the Appalachian Trail. It was built between 1910 and 1930 and follows the Green Mountains 273 miles from the Massachusetts border to Canada.

Hiking for a couple hours over modest terrain, we came to the Seth Warner Shelter where we selected a campsite for our tents. Supper was preceded by a delicious amount of wine Bergen was good enough to carry.

Breakfast at the Blue Benn in Bennington, Vermont

All Wet

Morning greeted us with rain. We called to one another from our tents, Soren and Bergen in theirs, and I in mine with Theo in the back vestibule. We ate, packed up, and hit the trail, passing the shelter as we trekked back to our path northbound, deeper into the Green Mountain forests of Vermont. We were wet and happy.

The trail crossed a marshy area and streams and passed some ponds. At one point, Bergen, in the lead, followed a wide and obvious path over a collection of branches, and I just followed. No big deal, except I knew that a collection of branches means THE TRAIL DOES NOT GO THIS WAY, TURN HERE. Mindlessly, I stepped over them for a ¼-mile diversion. We paused. Debated. Turned back and found our way.

We stopped for a late lunch around 3:00. Everything was damp but edible. Back on track, we crossed more streams and walked by more ponds in a wet and wondrous world. Near 7:00, we found ourselves at an elevation of 2,500 feet with a view west toward a sunburst through clouds over distant hills. The final steps of our day took us down a steep and potentially dangerous 900-foot drop over rocks to VT 9, where we got a ride into town from the owner of a motel we had called.

We settled in two rooms and did laundry. The owner's son drove us to a place for supper, after which we slept well and long.

Blue Benn Diner — Farewell

We ate breakfast at a diner not far from our rooms. When a fellow next to me took a picture of a friend, I asked him if he'd mind taking one of the three musketeers. He obliged, for one of the best family shots from the trail.

Back at our rooms, it was pack-up and decision time. Would Ren and Bergen join me for more, or was this a good turnaround point? They decided to go home, while I would continue on my way, but first we had our poignant goodbye. Oh, how we long for connection. We were so glad to have been together, to have shared a meaningful experience. They had walked some of the trail. They knew now what I was about. By doing so, they gave me an I've-walked-in-your-shoes kind of love, which did not leave me.

The driver who took me to the trail took them south to their car, as Theo and I returned to the woods on foot.

Big-Face

August 11th. On our way, we saw Sphagnum! She had left the trail on June 6th at I-70 in Maryland and got back on there on July 7th. During her time off, she had white-water rafted in Colorado. The trail crosses I-70 at mile 1045.3, and I was seeing her again somewhere around mile 1616.0. That's 570.7 miles in 35 days, or 16.3 miles per day nonstop. She was one strong hiker!

It was getting dark as we approached the Goddard Shelter, so I used my headlamp for the final climb. Sphagnum kept going. Cranberry, whom I'd met earlier in the day, was from Switzerland and was delighted to find another Swiss at the shelter with whom she could speak her native language. I met Bluegrass and Big-Face. The latter I'd see for some miles to come. He was a nice enough guy but a little on the loosey-goosey side. Shirt off or on. Pants off (boxers remaining) or on.

Six of us shared the shelter that night.

Singin' In The Rain

In the morning we each got ready before setting out into the misty, mountainous day, continuing northward in a long, wet, green tunnel. Our only views were of colorful foliage—all kinds of growths, from leaves whose time was over, to exotic mushrooms and round leaves that astounded me in their varied colors.

Approaching noon, Theo and I found ourselves at the Kid Gore Shelter, along with Big-Face, Bluegrass, and another old coot, who had all stopped for lunch. Theo and I ate and moved on.

The clouds threatened most of the afternoon but held off, thankfully, until we finished a climb to Story Spring Shelter. I crawled inside and was soon joined by others. A spontaneous musical gathering rose up from the woods of Vermont that very wet afternoon. Outstanding was there, and another young woman, a middle-aged fellow, and a late-30s to early-40s guy with a banjo. We were singin' in the rain, and we were happy.

Would Theo and I stay or go? It was nearly 5:00 and really wet out there, but the rain had stopped. I decided we'd go.

En route, we came upon the first of many bogs which unavoidably blackened the bottom foot or two of my pant legs. It was a northern reality—you just accepted it. It was a whole lot better than a paved highway any day!

As night approached, Theo and I crossed a stream to a flat, wet campsite. We were alone. It was dark and damp. We stayed.

Stratton

In the morning, I crawled back into my hiking gear. The night before I had slithered out of my pants, folded the lower legs in on themselves, rolled the cleaner top of my pants over the bottom, and set them aside. In this fashion, the bog mud was contained.

Lots of bogs in the North

With my pants back on, we headed for Stratton Mountain, a steep, 1600-foot climb on a wet day, carrying wet gear. The appearance of sky and a tiny dwelling told me we had arrived at the summit.

The caretaker and his wife have lived in this 120-square-foot dwelling for over 34 years, from May to October. They are honorary, lifetime members of the Green Mountain Club, which was formed to create The Long Trail. It and the Appalachian Trail were dreamed up atop this mountain.

Happily, the clouds had lifted when we summited, permitting me to dry out our tent and affording a broad, 360° sweep of the mountains of southern Vermont.

We descended on the north side of Stratton without incident and arrived at the Stratton Pond Shelter around 4:30. Even though it was early, we decided to stay. At a little after 5:00, we were glad we had, as the heavens opened full bore. The shelter was full. Big-Face was there hanging around in his underwear again. When nature called during the rainstorm, he simply stood on the edge of the porch and added to the flood.

I met an ex-Marine here who had a chip on his shoulder about everything. It was F-this and F-that in a loud, sharp staccato. Nothing really suited him. The F-talk was so frequent, I got really tired of it. At one point I said, "I don't think you could put a sentence together without the F-word." He didn't respond. We heard a little less of it afterward, but it did not stop altogether.

Finally, I had to say more. "I think you care a lot and it's hard to show it."

He seemed to soften a little. "How do you know?" he asked.

"I just think you do."

We dropped it.

I ate supper at the porch table, loft overhead, packed up my stuff, and turned in. It was very dark, but for a few headlamps. The pelting, deafening rain had stopped, but earplugs still helped me sleep.

Ex-Marine

In the morning, Stratton Pond was swollen under low, grey clouds, and the trail was flooded in spots. The heavy rains filled the streams with tannins, causing them to look like thin, translucent molasses.

The clouds did not break until midafternoon, and then only slightly. We stopped at Spruce Peak Shelter for a rest around 1:30. F-Bomb was there. As irritated as I can get sometimes with human behavior (my own included), something in me liked this guy. While abrupt and rough and offensive, he was right out there. He held nothing back. You might disagree strongly with where he stood or how he told you, but you knew precisely where that was. Authentic obscenity perhaps, but that was a start. Something there begged to be ripped off and exposed—and yes, loved.

Green Mountain House

Mother Nature continued to paint and surprise us as we made our way to the road where we got a ride to Green Mountain House Hiker Hostel for the night. The website for this hostel reads:

> In 2008 we opened our home to long-distance hikers, giving them the opportunity to rest and resupply as they continue along Vermont's wilderness corridor.

The owners are Jeff and Regina Taussig, who list their off-season mailing address as Richfield, Ohio. In Vermont, they live in a small cottage on the property. They have given the entire large house over to hikers. It was immaculate. The rules are clearly stated and enforced. The amenities could not be better. We were in a home.

Theo and I were assigned to very pleasant quarters at the back of the property near a paddock. Our room had two double-decker bunks and was at the end of a horse barn.

The cloud-draped moon made nightfall at Green Mountain House magical. God was in heaven and, in that place, all felt right with the world. We had two very different and magnificent nighttime experiences back to back.

Bromley Day

After breakfast, I packed up a little hastily because I had opted for the first ride back to the trail. We were hiking before 8:00. This was Bromley Day.

Although I'd skied at Jug End Barn as a young boy, it wasn't until we started skiing at Big Bromley that I got proficient. It was a slope appropriately named The Lord's Prayer that got me started. The first time down took me a half-hour. The last time took less than 30 seconds. My family knew Bromley when Fred Pabst, Jr., son of the beer magnate, owned it. We skied there in the late '40s and early '50s. I was about to climb it for the first time.

Not far from the summit, I emerged onto one of the upper Bromley slopes. There is something particularly hard about climbing up a ski slope. You're out in the open on a rounded climb. No variations, no relief, no rocks or roots or changes in terrain to break up the sameness of the climb. Just a grassy slope, perhaps with a worn path. All uniform, open and up. Climb! Just climb!

At the top were the usual structures found on ski mountain summits. The deeply anchored support for the entire ski lift that pulled thousands of pounds of skiers and equipment, not to mention cable, from the bottom to the top for the next run.

Oh, what joy to dismount, slip off the lift's elevated platform, and glide down the open slope, yielding to gravity's cosmic tug down, down, down, checking her force now and then to regulate your speed or just for the thrill of playing with her as in a dance of delight, a couple swirling in time to the music of the mountain, the schuss and swish, white gown flaring out in puffs of powder, lost in the depths of her glistening garment, deep in a silent reverie of exhilaration and boundless joy.

We call it skiing.

Skiing is in the West blood. Adventure. Outside. Cold. Awake. Alert. Driven even through driving snows. My late brother left funds for kids near his home in the mountains of Arizona to learn to ski. He often skied close to 100 days per year. It was his life. At his memorial service I read a lengthy poem I'd written about him containing these lines:

Feel that wind in your face
Feel your hair blown back
The burning in your lungs
The strength in your legs

Blow gentle, breeze
As he passes by
Blow gentle if you will
For the one you thought you'd
   catch
Stands yet again atop the hill.

Son Soren and brother Gard skied expert slopes together

The Record

From my ski reverie, I turned my attention to the constant stretch of mountains to the north where the trail had been leading me ever since February 21st. It was time to descend the monument to my snow-filled youth. Time to leave the thoughts of the cold inheritance embedded in my DNA there on Big Bromley under happy, dreary-grey skies. There was something of home at the top of Bromley.

Our descent took about an hour and a half. At the base was Mad Tom Notch and gravel USFS 21. I stopped for lunch and noticed a van west on the road. Soon the occupants came over to me.

"Are you waiting for someone?" I asked.

"Yes. Someone who's trying to break the speed record."

Soon Karl Meltzer showed up, heading south. He stopped briefly. We exchanged a few words. His team fed and watered him, and he was off again in probably less than five minutes.

Theo was not impressed.

Karl had helped Scott Jurek break the record in 2015, and now Scott was helping Karl break his record. True competitors know that records are made to be broken.

It was our turn to push on toward our goals. We began to climb Styles Peak and then Peru Peak, both higher than Bromley. Near the base of Peru Peak was the Peru Peak Shelter which has a platform off to the side. I was tired enough that I took out my pad and fell asleep for a half-hour nap-and-go.

We carried on in northern territory, the land of lakes, bogs, and boards, until I took to the tent and Theo to the vestibule.

Rules

In the morning we faced a wet forest, a long section of gravel road, and then the woods again. At the Little Rock Pond, we came to a sign to HIKERS:

> To better manage and protect natural
> resources, the Green Mountain Club
> maintains a caretaker at: [four shelters listed].
> The overnight use fee is $5.00 per person.

We were now on the part of the trail where the lone, gorilla-in-the-woods mentality would have to submit to the need to deal with increased traffic. Natural resources are more limited here, and alpine ridges are covered with fragile vegetation. This is a totally different environment than the less traveled and more hearty terrain in the South.

We soon came alongside a stream some distance below us. Theo waited for me before crossing on a footbridge on our way to the Minerva Hinchey Shelter, a small structure buried in the woods not far from Rutland, Vermont, to the northwest, and Hanover, New Hampshire, to the northeast. I slept behind the shelter in my tent.

Hike-Out

The new day was misty, windy, and socked in, but in time the clouds parted and, to the east, I could see the Rutland Southern Vermont Regional Airport from a ridge.

After crossing a stream, we came to a Trail Magic set-up. It was 2:15 and a good place for a late lunch. The Trail Angel, who was absent at the moment, was a kind and poetic soul. S/He left us a hand-written note:

> TRAIL FAIRY is having a
> hard time right now keeping
> up with sodas. If you
> read this, Trail
> Fairy has added Magic
> into your step as
> you hike. . . . Hike out

"Trail Fairy" is what the Angel called her/his angelic self, but I suspect "Hike out" was the Angel's trail name.

We were in New England, a land of rocks and walls. Were these walls remnants of a time when the landscape was very different, when fields may have held animals, like the cows we had just passed, and then were abandoned to Mother Nature's prolific growth? Whom or what did the walls separate? Now they are beautiful and mysterious in their hard-won presence.

I sat for lunch on a little rise not far from the stream and Hike Out's magic and soon sensed the light saying it was time to move on.

New England is known for its stone walls

Trail Nap

We crossed a gravel road and found ourselves looking down on Cold River. A sunlit vista cheered the sleepy afternoon, but the trek down to river level was a bit uncertain as a weariness settled in. We were more alone than in the South, and the seasons were clearly moving on as we pushed farther and farther into the cold, northern wilderness—every day farther away from home and closer to heavy climbing, alone. We were three states from the finish with still many miles to go before claiming the ultimate goal.

Across the Cold River was a long, gradual climb just east of Sargent Brook, which lay far down a steep bank beside the trail. As we made our way through this steep pine forest, my body was approaching the no-go mode. I had no choice but to obey my own maxim: sometimes the fastest way forward is to stop.

As soon as I came to a mildly comfortable place to rest my bones, I did. To remember where and when, I took a selfie—I wasn't as asleep as I look. However, I did fade out enough to realize that I needed to give myself a good kick-start when I decided to rise under the load of my backpack, which had served as the back of my "recliner." Theo was quick to follow suit.

When we were ready to carry on, high above the river gorge, we pushed ourselves on to Upper Cold River Road. Two blazes told us to turn left at the road. A sign under the blazes told us we had only 500 miles left to Katahdin. The same amount we had hiked while traversing Grayson Highlands in Virginia.

When we turned westward, the late afternoon sun cast my shadow on the road we had traveled. Soon we were back in the woods, heading for Governor Clement Shelter at the foot of Little Killington where we spent the night.

Killington

We were back on the trail by 7:30, and, just under five hours later, we reached the Cooper Lodge Shelter below Killington Mountain summit. We left our packs in the stone building and headed up a steep and treacherous climb to the top. At many places, trees beside the boulder-strewn trail were essential handholds for safety.

There was fine dining at the summit lodge, with tables outside filled by patrons. As a service dog, Theo could join me inside. I chose a table by a window and asked Theo to stay as I got in line for my meal. The views from our table were glorious. Kids nearby came over, asking gently to pet Theo. "Sure!" One of the maintenance guys came over to chat with me as I was finishing up. He, too, appreciated Theo and how I handled him. I got the feeling we were welcome anytime.

I immediately began burning the calories from the good meal on the steep and dangerous descent. Extreme care was in order here, and in so many times yet to come. The descent off Katahdin would be one of the most treacherous.

Another Recognition

By 2:45, we were packed up and on our way. We were hiking along a section of the descent around 6:00, when three hikers came toward us, southbound. As the hiker in the front approached, he said to my complete surprise, "Are you Soren West?"

"Yes."

"I'm Patrick, Harry Hand's son." And then he explained.

Remember Will and Melanie south of Waynesboro, Pennsylvania? Melanie's uncle is Harry Hand's business partner. I used to live near all of them and knew them well. Through Melanie, Harry probably learned that I was thru-hiking the Appalachian Trail. When his son said he was going to thru-hike the AT southbound, Harry asked him to look for me.

Patrick thought, "I'm supposed to find Soren West on the 2,000-mile-long Appalachian Trail? Sure!"

Well, somewhere in Vermont, wouldn't you know, he ran into Count and Lavender. He told them about his father's bidding and they said, "We know Soren West! He has a white beard and is hiking northbound with his dog."

Go figure!

When Patrick saw me and Theo—Voila! So he asked.

And that would not be the last of Count and Lavender!

Sweet Pea

By 7:30 that evening, we were on a shuttle traveling 8½ miles down US 4 to Rutland, Vermont. I had prearranged a stay at The Yellow Deli, run by a Christian communal group called The Twelve Tribes. The Tribes had settled in many places. They worked hard and ran businesses as well as farms. They kept many rooms and amenities for thru-hikers, and the food at the Deli was phenomenal!

The hostel was behind and above the Deli. The fee was by donation with a $1.00 charge to wash laundry, and $1.00 to dry it.

I had my own private space at the back of a large L-shaped room. I laid out my stuff, plugged in the backup battery, and went to do my laundry where I had a delightful surprise.

"SWEET PEA!" I exclaimed in a paroxysm of sheer pleasure.

Her real trail name was Berdie, and she was hiking with an intelligent fellow named One-Mile. I had met them first at the hostel at Laughing Heart Lodge in Hot Springs, North Carolina. They went off trail at Erwin, Tennessee, to get married as prearranged. It was not a common occurrence to reconnect with someone after five months, so there was an extra surprise in our reunion.

I had given Berdie the name Sweet Pea. It reflected how I felt about her, a delightful red-headed, fair-skinned, young woman with dimples and a smile that didn't go away. Her hair had been long in North Carolina; now it was short. She was a delight.

I learned that she was also a no-nonsense hiker. Her quiet, inner fortitude was as gentle and compelling as her totally unassuming, peaceful, and kind personality. She was a quiet, upbeat, and happy presence with not a trace of giddiness. Seeing her was Trail Magic!

Yellow Deli

I greeted Theo around 8:30 the next morning and fed him, to the envy of another dog on the deck where Theo had slept. After breakfast I walked down the street to Walmart to resupply, then carried my bags back. In every town which hikers frequent, you'd see your comrades walking back from the favorite resupply spots with plastic bags in each hand, their contents destined to increase the weight of their backpacks.

The Yellow Deli was great, and the Tribe members did their Christian, communal, agrarian thing without pushing or prodding. They had chosen a way of life, and anyone could see and feel and

The Yellow Deli in Rutland, Vermont

interact with them as they wished. It was Friday, and every Saturday they had a dance and sharing time in the back area behind the public deli. They asked, "Will you be staying? You'd be most welcome to join us." I was inclined to stay had it not been for the miles we still had to go. Some hikers stayed and even joined their ranks. Sometimes a commonality of spirit becomes a match.

... have a nice and restful stay before you continue your hike! Please let us know if you have any needs. We'd love to see you reach your goal! Your friends of the 12 Tribes Community

Before heading downstairs for lunch, I took pictures to remember my time and Yellow Deli's kindness. F-Bomb was there, packed up and ready to go. I had lunch at the Deli, and Theo and I were on our way.

Tall Grasses

Returning to the trail was always evidence of a silent resolve. To keep going. Something within was more powerful than the persistent tug of gravity or the weekly whisper of wants and pleasures at a deli or pub. It was about the sparse way, the difficult climb, the moments of solitary survival—and the companionship of a canine. Something in this adventure was finer than the choicest cut of beef with the finest wine. For me, the substance in the struggle and the elixir of labored breath were the fairest fare from head to toe and sole to soul. To hike day after day was to live within a persistent YES to life and the immediate good of being—alive.

Tall grasses by the side of the road marked the great divide between the here of town and the there of the wilderness. Each step was not always dramatic, but every one of them was part of a continuing commitment. Oh, how blessed to have a goal—an out-there that draws you into itself.

It was a long, gradual climb up from Route 4 to the point where The Long Trail continued north and the Appalachian Trail turned east toward Hanover. I had come to this split on September 19, 2012, on a very wet and windy day when Theo and I finished The Long Trail from Canada to here.

Quimby

This time it was a sunny, bright day. I was tired, and Quimby Mountain was up ahead. Would I be able to climb with my fresh load of food? If overweight when leaving town, I'd find it within myself to manage. The pack that threatened to force me through the floorboards of my room, I was now hauling up a steep climb, and with energy to spare.

I began and kept on climbing, amazed at how I was able to push myself. Could I keep going to Stony Brook Shelter over three miles ahead? It was 8:00, and we'd been climbing for an hour. It was getting dark and we were nearing the summit. We camped just west of the trail. As I moved this or that branch, root, or stone to make way for the tent floor, Theo sat off in the woods taking stock of my efforts.

Flying Piglet

Breakfast was my favorite meal. As I ate my hot oatmeal loaded with extras, Starbuck's ground French Roast was brewing in extra-hot water. As I had coffee, Theo and I would occasionally share a pastry. I'd done nothing of the sort in my shake-down hikes, but, when you're in the woods for eight months, you need to pamper yourself a bit.

As mentioned before, Theo ate handsomely on the trail. At home he got breakfast only and a dog biscuit at night. On the trail he got double his breakfast amount both morning and night, and he shared my snacks.

We were on our way by 8:30 and stopped for water at a shallow stream lying deep in a V-shaped crevice of rock. In the South especially, hikers would use a leaf to create a tiny waterfall to fill a container at a shallow stream. I did the same many times but took to keeping a straw with my water filter for the same purpose.

As I was filling my water bag, along came three young women. In the course of our conversation, I learned that one of the girls, at age 12, believed she was the youngest hiker on the trail that year. And I believed I was the oldest.

Photo-op!

Flying Piglet was her trail name. She got that name because her brother, whom she had hiked with before, always thought she was too slow. So she picked up speed enough to warrant that name. The Piglet part I did not pursue.

After Piglet and her friends flew away, I ate lunch in the shade by the stream.

The Lookout

Not long after, we came to a ladder tied into a high rock cliff. It reminded me of September 15, 2012, on The Long Trail when it took Theo and me an hour to go 10 feet. Back then, I had to get Theo up a cliff that extended far and wide, both east and west from the trail. I eventually emptied his saddlebags and cinched them tightly around his chest and midriff. I affixed a long rope to a hook at the front of the handle on the top of the saddlebags and managed to climb high enough to get the rope around a sapling, and then back down, so I could pull on the rope with all my weight and hoist Theo by the handle at the same time. When I had done that, I tied the rope to a tree across a gully so Theo was suspended against the cliff wall. I climbed the ladder, and then climbed down to the sapling, where I pulled and called to Theo at the same time until. . .WE MADE IT!

This time I was able to find a way through the dense growth at the side of the rock face, where I forced my way through intertwined branches, clearing a path for both of us as I went.

Late in the day we came to The Lookout, a cozy cabin that seemed open to all. The mini-trek up the wide, steep, rutted path of dirt and stones was worth it. It sat high on a hill with a small deck on its roof. Three backpacks sat on a small porch. The interior was neat and clean, with a brick fireplace and steep narrow stairs up to a loft where the owners of the packs were enjoying the view.

We found a way around the ladder for Theo

What a great place to spend a year watching the seasons come and go with the sumptuous green of summer and the wicked white winds of winter. From a poem I wrote after visiting Peru:

> *The desert calls, the mountain top*
> *The jungle trail, the sea*
> *The cold that threatens blood to stop*
> *They're calling out to me.*

Something there is about the quickening chill of a frosty winter, but we weren't there yet.

We slept in a shelter that night, alone.

Headlamp

As we continued on through field and forest, the trail was just a dirt path. I had seen a female jogger coming southbound a few days before, and I saw a second one on this trek. There are quite a few fall road races in New England, and the joggers were in training.

At one point we seemed to be on a long section of abandoned road, bordered on the right by a wall I came to think of as The Great Wall of Vermont. The stones gathered for this wall, and their careful placement, produced a genuine work of art. Surely there was not the army of conscripted men to do the work as in ancient China—just incredibly hard-working farmers.

It was dark by 8:30, and I needed the headlamp which cast a narrow beam on the terrain ahead. I ended up following a rocky streambed until Theo and I both suspected we had turned wrong, and he found the trail!

We missed the turnoff to the shelter that night as well. I must have been focused on the trail ahead and walked right past the sign. I repeatedly looked up to shine my headlamp on the trees so I could

"The Great Wall of Vermont"

pick up the next blaze, and then looked down again to cast the beam on the trail.

In time, after ascending a hill and trekking through a lot of dense brush at the crest, I figured we must have hiked farther than the distance to the shelter. I certainly was not going to go back to look for it. We continued off the hilltop, down and into the woods, and soon decided to leave the trail and ascend a rise on the left to look for a spot flat enough for the tent. I found it—but we had no water. What little I had left would have to do.

I pitched, ate, and slept.

Rain and Shine

We wakened to a new day, which revealed a large pond just down the hill from our tent. I filled water bottles and had a good breakfast. As I was packing up, I heard the proverbial tree fall in the forest. It made a sound because I was there, sound being how the human mind interprets the vibrations sound waves make striking the mechanisms in the inner ear. Sound waves are the movements of a medium, like air, caused by an energy source like a falling tree. The waves are there if no one is present, but not sound without a mind and nervous system to interpret the vibrations made by the waves.

Or so I have argued in considering the classic question!

About 10 minutes on our way, we came to a freshly fallen tree. The dirt under the roots was fresh, and the leaves were lush and green. I suspect the rain caused the tree to fall by eroding the soil and softening the entire root ball.

Fifteen minutes later, we emerged from our night of rain, and sometimes dangerous, dark forest, to bright sunshine, white clouds, and blue sky. It was as if we had found the mouth of a cave after falling into the depths of the earth.

Emerging from the bowels of the earth

We passed maple trees tapped in the modern way. In the past, wooden, and then metal, buckets hung on the trees. Now plastic tubing was strung from tree to tree, downhill to a common collection point. I saw this arrangement frequently on The Long Trail. The general wisdom is that it takes 40 quarts of sap to make 1 quart of syrup. I would soon enjoy some through the generosity of a new acquaintance.

Farther on, we came to a rough-hewn bench in the sunlight. At mile 1736, it was well placed and inviting. Deeply carved in the backrest was:

> **VT RELAX AND ENJOY**

It was a fruitful day. At our first eye-on-the-sky surfacing, I had seen blackberries. At this second time in the sun, apples! I indulged both times.

West Hartford, VT

Soon we emerged onto a local road passing through West Hartford, Vermont. It crossed the White River and intersected VT 14, where the trail turned left past a country store with a lunch counter. I stopped and ate well, with Theo at my feet getting an occasional bite.

By 12:30, we were finished with road-walking and were in the woods for a nine-mile trek to Hanover, New Hampshire. In time, we came to a stream where there was enough sunlight and breeze to dry out our clothes and tent after our night in the rain. By 3:00 we had reached the highest elevation of our afternoon trek, with six miles to go. We would have to make tracks to meet Kevin and Susan, friends from Boston, who were driving three hours to join us in our adventure. As with other scheduled meetings, plans changed so we sent each other frequent updates and shifts in our arrival time and meeting place.

Bernie

After a long, fast-paced descent, we exited the wooded world in Norwich, Vermont, where there was a long, paved road downhill through a residential area, and then across the Connecticut River, the border between Vermont and New Hampshire.

To give you a sense of how disconnected I was from the concerns of everyday society, I saw a blue sign for BERNIE in a yard and figured this must be someone running for commissioner or some other local office—until it clicked—BERNIE! The presidential race! Ooooh, woods! I love the detachment you've given me!

Little did I know at the time that two nights hence I would be staying in the house where that sign was posted, and I would hear more there about Count and Lavender.

We crossed the river and hiked another quarter-mile to the square in Hanover where we would meet my friends. I called them when we got there. They were an hour out. We went to a Starbucks and let them know where they would find us.

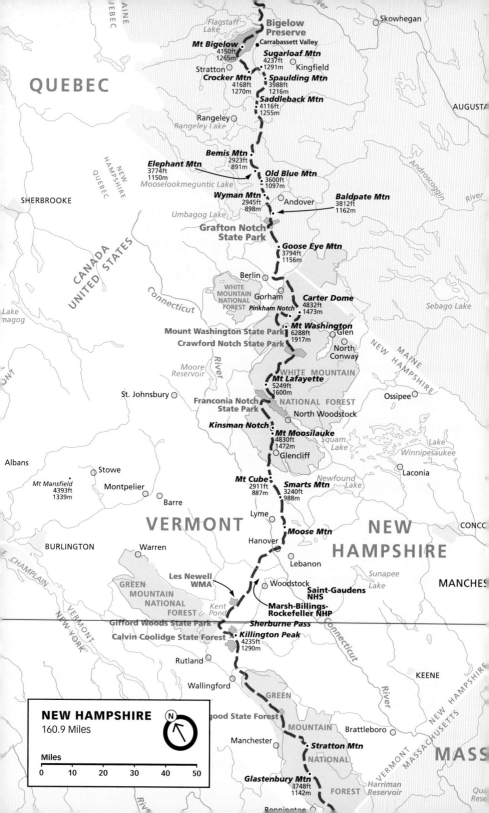

QUEBEC

Skowhegan

Flagstaff Lake

Bigelow Preserve

Mt Bigelow
4150ft
1265m

Carrabassett Valley

Sugarloaf Mtn
4237ft
1291m

Stratton

Kingfield

Crocker Mtn
4168ft
1270m

Spaulding Mtn
3988ft
1216m

AUGUSTA

Rangeley

Saddleback Mtn
4116ft
1255m

Rangeley Lake

Bemis Mtn
2923ft
891m

NEW HAMPSHIRE

QUEBEC

Elephant Mtn
3774ft
1150m

Old Blue Mtn
3600ft
1097m

Mooselookmeguntic Lake

SHERBROOKE

Wyman Mtn
2945ft
898m

Andover

Baldpate Mtn
3812ft
1162m

Androscoggin River

Umbagog Lake

Grafton Notch
State Park

Goose Eye Mtn
3794ft
1156m

CANADA
UNITED STATES

Berlin

Sebago Lake

WHITE MOUNTAIN NATIONAL FOREST

Gorham

Carter Dome
4832ft
1473m

Connecticut

Pinkham Notch

Mt Washington
6288ft
1917m

Glen

Lake nagog

Mount Washington State Park

Crawford Notch State Park

North Conway

NEW MAINE

NEW HAMPSHIRE

WHITE MOUNTAIN

Moore Reservoir

Mt Lafayette
5249ft
1600m

Ossipee

St. Johnsbury

River

NATIONAL FOREST

Franconia Notch
State Park

North Woodstock

Squam Lake

Kinsman Notch

Mt Moosilauke
4830ft
1472m

Lake Winnipesaukee

Glencliff

Albans

Stowe

Mt Cube
2911ft
887m

Smarts Mtn
3240ft
988m

Newfound Lake

Laconia

Mt Mansfield
4393ft
1339m

Montpelier

Lyme

Barre

Moose Mtn

VERMONT

Hanover

NEW

BURLINGTON

Warren

Lebanon

HAMPSHIRE

CONCC

Les Newell
WMA

Woodstock

Sunapee Lake

MANCHES

GREEN
MOUNTAIN
NATIONAL
FOREST

Kent Pond

Saint-Gaudens
NHS

Marsh-Billings-
Rockefeller NHP

Gifford Woods State Park

Sherburne Pass

Calvin Coolidge State Forest

Killington Peak
4235ft
1290m

Connecticut River

NEW YORK

VERMONT

Rutland

KEENE

Wallingford

GREEN

LAKE CHAMPLAIN

good State Forest

MOUNTAIN

Brattleboro

Manchester

NATIONAL

Stratton Mtn

VERMONT
MASSACHUSETTS
NEW HAMPSHIRE

MASS

Glastenbury Mtn
3748ft
1142m

FOREST

Harriman
Reservoir

Qu
Res

Bennington

CHAPTER 14

New Hampshire

Kevin and Susan

Kevin had been my classmate at Mount Hermon when I first decided to thru-hike the trail. He and his wife were extremely generous to me after their long trip from Boston to meet me on the trail. Kevin walked into Starbucks carrying a large sign mimicking Henry Morton Stanley upon locating David Livingstone in Africa.

Kevin and I had reconnected at our 40th class reunion. In another life, I hope to have the will and temperament to keep contacts alive the way Kevin does. He has been blessed with a gift in this regard, and many far and wide have been blessed in turn by his doing so.

Kevin and Susan took me to a hotel where kings were meant to stay. Theo and I had our own room where we felt like royalty. We had a great view and a well-appointed bathroom with a shower you didn't want to leave. There was a kitchenette with a refrigerator and, at the foot of the bed, a big TV which I never turned on.

Thoughtful Susan brought me a toothbrush, toothpaste, pants, shirt, underwear, snacks, bathing suit—you name it—anticipating my every need and beyond. It was more than I could use for an overnight and more than I could carry when headed back to the trail, if I could ever return after such treatment.

Supper. How to capture the luscious banquet coming my way as we drove to the restaurant where Kevin had made reservations? A couple of gins on the rocks with a shrimp cocktail started me off. Then clam chowder. I don't know if it was the relative proximity to the Atlantic Ocean, but I have never had clam chowder like that! I could have eaten four more servings.

Except that a medium-rare filet mignon, with a baked potato and a stupendous green vegetable, finished off with a fine Cabernet Sauvignon or two, was next on the menu. Talk about TRAIL MAGIC! I was transported! My hosts made certain there was no impediment to my pleasure. Notwithstanding my protestations about the expense, they did admit to being a little in awe about how much this depleted hiker could put away.

Food? Pleasure? Thy name is Hanover. There a restaurant feeds the gods, from whose plates I was privileged to eat!

If I am ever within 100 miles of Hanover, I'm going back to that restaurant—maybe 200.

Back in our room, Theo and I enjoyed the luxury, with our gear strewn about in some order for retrieval and packing in the morning.

Stone Age

Breakfast was self-serve at the hotel. Kevin wanted to swim and asked me along. I declined because of my appearance: emaciated, pale-skinned, wrinkly, old man. I didn't want to cause alarm or stares. I stayed with Susan, drank coffee, and chatted.

Kevin checked out and drove me to the town square. Then they were on their way, leaving me with memories of their extraordinary generosity. I watched them walk away until they were out of sight, grateful for how intimately they had connected to the health of my body, mind, and spirit.

After a time enjoying the sun in a park with Theo, I tied him to a bench next to my gear and went inside the Hanover Inn. I had stayed

there many years before. An amazing, thick, New Hampshire granite table stands in the lobby. I wonder how many workers were needed to place that gigantic piece of stone on a stack of 4x4s. I like a sturdy table that doesn't wobble. Here was one.

Canoe Club

I left the Inn, returned to Theo, and packed up. We made our way down North Main Street to look for a place to have lunch and tend to business. A fellow on the street recommended a place near the square where we could hang out.

The name of the place suggested it was too fancy for a hiker and his dog—the Canoe Club. I ventured in and explained my needs, including my service dog. They accommodated us, setting me up by a window on the street, next to a socket for charging as well. It couldn't have been better.

I had a good lunch and found a place back in Norwich to stay the night. The hostel owner would pick me up at a designated time. I worked out logistics for our next trek and wrote, Theo at my side. I made a short call to Bonnie to tell her what a wonderful time I had with Kevin and Susan, paid my tab, and went outside to await our ride.

Norwich Hostel

When we got to the hostel, it turned out to be where I had earlier noticed the BERNIE sign. About 10 other hikers were there. We all left our backpacks in the garage, along with our boots—and Theo.

We shared pasta around the table with the husband and wife owners. Wine, too. Then we gathered in the living room with the woman presiding. She told us a story, which she did with every group who stayed with them.

The owners knew someone who needed help, and they mentioned this concern to a couple they met. That couple enlisted friends to work together to provide the help that was needed. To pay this kindness forward, the hostel owners opened their home to hikers at no charge. She simply wanted to encourage all of us to pay forward the kindness and blessings we were receiving free of charge at their hostel.

And the couple who helped them? Count and Lavender! The same couple my son met in Vermont in 2015. The same couple who gave me Trail Magic on June 7th in Virginia. The very same couple who told Patrick Hand how to recognize me, as he did on the north side of Killington Mountain.

I have since seen Patrick's mom and dad, who told me he finished the trail in three months, averaging 25 miles per day at the end.

An absolutely extraordinary trek in my view! Just as remarkable as Count and Lavender figuring in my thru-hike at three significant times. Amazing!

Our accommodations were in the small basement where we slept on furniture and the floor, packed in like sardines. Getting to the bathroom at night was a real challenge.

Lou's

In the morning, I opted for an early lift into Hanover when the owner would be leaving for work. He dropped me off at the main intersection at 7:00. There was a café on the corner, but it lacked the good-breakfast feel. Someone recommended Lou's Bakery-Restaurant across the street. On our way there, I passed a man in his early 40s, sitting on a street-side bench. Inside I found a seat against the wall and sat facing the entrance. There were tables to my left by the windows and a vanishing row of tables to my right.

In short order the man I'd seen outside came over and asked if he could join me. I said, "Sure." He said, "I was sitting outside, and as you passed me with your dog, I said to myself 'If he goes into Lou's, I'm going to see if I can join him.'" I was glad he followed his nudge.

He knew Hanover and Lou's. He recommended pancakes with maple syrup. The waitress took our order and said we could have generic syrup or, for an extra $1.00, genuine Vermont maple syrup. I opted for the cheaper brand.

"No. Get him the real stuff—on me."

The Camera

We enjoyed our breakfast and some fascinating conversation—at least I did. My host, John Noerr, told me an intriguing story. He mentioned that he's an audiologist, and when I asked how he got into that field, he told me of a time he was hiking and found a digital camera in a stream. The camera was kaput, but the picture card was intact. He was able to read it and found many pictures of different locations and people. In some exotic fashion, he was able to determine the location of enough photos that he could estimate where the owner lived. A check of the story on the web tells me that he found two pictures with doors he was able to locate with Google maps. He eventually located the sister of the owner. His camera had been lost for three years.

How the camera led to audiology never surfaced. Perhaps my host realized he had a logical mind suitable for a science-oriented field.

My new and intriguing friend paid for my breakfast and, after my sincere thanks, we parted ways.

Entering DOC Territory

Outside, we continued our trek back to the woods, completing the 3.7 miles of road-walking, the longest on the AT. The first thru-hikers had a lot more.

Hanover is the home of Dartmouth College, which has a reputation of being not only academically demanding, but also challenging to the outdoor enthusiast. The Dartmouth Outing Club (DOC) manages a great deal of the Appalachian Trail in this vicinity and, according to a friend who graduated from there, also owns a good bit of the mountains, including some in the Whites, even Mount Washington at one time.

We made it to the Moose Mountain Shelter by nightfall and set up our tent near a few others. Morning revealed what was perhaps the least private privy on the trail, but no one was inclined to be intrusive. Mutual respect provided privacy enough.

The least private privy

Holt's Ledge Lunch

Noon found us at Holt's Ledge with "precipitous drop-off, views" (AWOL). I enjoyed my usual PB&J wrap, water with Crystal Light, and then light, easy-to-prepare ramen noodles. They are a staple on the trail. One young hiker planned to eat nothing else.

We camped at Lambert Ridge where it rained during the night.

Sweet Sunshine

The rain continued as we wakened, making for wet climbs all day. Almost unavoidable bogs, along with slippery rocks and steps, required careful maneuvering. By 10:30 we came to Smarts Mountain Fire Warden's Cabin right off the trail. Sweet Pea and One-Mile were inside. She made all the clouds go away, but we had just a "Hello" and then went back to the trail.

In an hour, we came to a bog I am very glad I did not step into. It was nearly as deep as the length of my entire trekking pole. Happily, Theo avoided it as well, though barely.

By 1:30 we were at Eastman Ledges in bright sunlight, and Theo and I were ready to dry out. I set the tent up in a small space between the rock ledge and some woods, positioned so that the sun and air could reach inside and out. I hung up my rain clothes as well, then had a second breakfast for lunch, including crushed donuts.

Don't step here

A 1500-foot descent took us to Brackett Brook, where Theo and I stealth-camped again. My last picture of the day, at 8:47, was of a rather bulbous spider of unknown name, nature, and venom. I urged him outside and turned in.

Carl

By 10:10, we crossed the gravel Cape Moonshine Road and headed back into the woods for the best Trail Magic of the entire AT. Ten minutes from the road, on the left side of the trail, was a fairly stout Trail Angel with wavy red hair, wearing glasses and a grey T-shirt. He had set up a large tarp as a slanted roof above tables, supplies, and a propane grill. On the ground, facing northbounders, was a sign made of sticks on a wood background. It was inviting, yet ominous:

WELCOME
TO THE
WHITES

This was a fuel stop for the struggles to come. It had only been about three hours since breakfast, but all intake is quickly burned when you're pushing mountainous miles behind you on foot.

"Take off your pack and have a seat."

I did.

"Would you like an omelet?"

"Sure."

"Six eggs okay?" He had served thru-hikers before.

"Sure."

"Now I don't have any ham. I ran out. But I have kielbasa, peppers, onions, and cheese. Would you like any of that in it?"

"Sure. All of it."

Trail Magic at the start of the Whites in New Hampshire

He loaded that omelet with so many goodies that the eggs were there just to bind everything else together.

As I thoroughly enjoyed every morsel of my second breakfast, I took in the surroundings and learned a little about my benefactor.

He had two large boxes, each containing five dozen eggs, purchased from Walmart for $4.50 each. I was thinking, there are some chickens out there that need to form a union.

He showed me claw marks where a bear tried to get to some food the Angel had hung in a tree supporting the tarp.

My benefactor was Carl. He is part Abenaki Indian and resides in Canada. He likes the Native American art of Robert Griffing and the books of Reverend Paul Stutzman, who thru-hiked the AT to deal with his grief after his wife died of breast cancer.

As I neared the bottom of the bowl, Carl asked, "Would you like some more?"

"Sure."

"Six eggs or three?"

I hesitated. There is no doubt whatsoever that I could have repeated my first course with ease.

"I think I'll do three this time."

I look back at pictures of Carl giving out—just plain giving—there in the middle of the woods with all his gear, all that he had to carry to this spot. I am impressed with his selfless beneficence and with the sacrifice of his time and energy for a hungry hiker who's out in the wilderness meeting Mother Nature on her terms. His goal, his ultimate prize, was not for himself. It was for all of us who enjoyed all that he freely gave. He was there to help us each on our way. He was a silent supporter, a balm in Gilead.

I stayed with Carl for a little more than an hour. Thoroughly refreshed with good food, coffee, and company, I thanked my host and headed northbound once again.

Slackpacking

Late in the afternoon, along came Sweet Pea! We talked until One-Mile showed up. Sweet Pea was the faster hiker. She quietly had what it took and just did it without a hint of complaint, ennui, boredom, exhaustion, or superiority. She was powered by a solid core of fuel, keeping her unruffled and very pleasant.

One-Mile arrived and urged Sweet Pea onward, southbound. They were slackpacking for a day, which meant they had to meet the hostel's shuttle driver at a designated road crossing at a specific time. They had left their gear at the hostel in the morning and were driven to a point about 20 miles north, carrying only their lunch in a daypack. They were now under the gun to meet their shuttle driver to get back to the hostel. The next day, they would get a ride to where they started their southbound slackpacking and continue northbound, fully loaded.

I had no desire to slackpack. Hiking north? Then stay north. Hiking the trail? Then hike the trail—and carry all your goods all the way.

Hikers Welcome Hostel

By day's end we were at Hikers Welcome Hostel, about a half-mile from the trail up a paved road. The female owner was tattooed and pierced many times. The hostel reflected her style. Each hostel on the trail has its own character, each a little off the beaten track, perhaps countercultural in its own way. Here there was a large area out back with benches and fire pits, a large stone "couch," outdoor sinks, laundry, and shower. In the house itself was the off-limits kitchen, common area, and upstairs sleeping quarters. The new bunkhouse was clean, neat, and unfinished—still without electricity.

Hikers Welcome Hostel

At supper, five or six hikers squeezed onto benches around a large table, next to a wall full of books and videos to watch on the TV at the far end.

Theo and I slept in the bunkhouse.

Moosilauke

For breakfast in the morning we had pancakes and eggs. Now that I'm back home, and steeped more and more in social shenanigans, I'm drawn again to the unadorned life of the trail. It grips my reclusive psyche like quicksand. Pancakes at a T-shaped table, no tablecloths, no fancy forks or tidy decor, no spotless trousers or hands fit to take the queen's. Just a table, chair, plate, pancake, fork, coffee, and an uncomplicated gratitude for the goodness of the earth.

We ate, packed, and left. It took 12 minutes to return to the trail. This was Moosilauke Day! The first biggie of the Whites.

Until that first step, the Whites loomed as a behemoth in my untethered, limitless imagination. But once we got underway, the mountains became real, solid, apparent, present, doable. I just took the next step, as carefully as necessary, and then the next. . . . They were smack in front of me. I could hike them. I was DOING IT!

Moosilauke did not require climbing on all fours, not on the south side at least. But there were difficult sections strewn with rocks for long stretches. As we approached the tree line, where the trees look like shrubs, the trail is a beaten path with rocks jutting out. I had to plant each step carefully, lest I ended up with a severely twisted ankle.

The summit was grass and rocks. Like many hikers, I took cover from the blustery weather while eating lunch. Theo took a rest and then rose, nose pointed into the wind, ready to go.

Theo, ready to roll

We continued along the broad sweep of the crest until we entered the forest of stunted growth, descending over the rocky, treacherous trail. Every step had to be extremely well calculated under a very well-balanced load. A misstep could prove quite serious, if not fatal. I was not alone in that assessment.

For 1,000 feet the steep trail follows the Beaver Brook Cascades, whose rushing waters fill the forest with their inevitability, persistence, majesty, drama, and intense chorus of sound, never letting you forget that they are in charge and you are a mere visitor. This is their forest. Humans proceed at their own risk.

The descent seemed easy for Theo. Although he would fall off a short cliff and down a hole among boulders before we finished, he managed the Moosilauke descent the way he did the rock slabs before Four Pines Hostel—piece-a-cake.

Carefully placed wooden steps are bolted into the sheer rock face, but hikers still need to use extreme care. A slip

Moosilauke cascades descending 1000 feet

or trip here could have drastic consequences. When I reached the bottom, in the dark, I saw this sign for those climbing up the north side:

> THIS TRAIL IS
> EXTREMELY TOUGH.
> IF YOU LACK EXPERIENCE
> PLEASE USE ANOTHER
> TRAIL. TAKE SPECIAL
> CARE AT THE CASCADES TO
> AVOID TRAGIC RESULTS.

NOW they tell me. I knew to take extreme care, yet a sign with the same message belongs at the top, too. Descending is always more treacherous than climbing. When you climb, you face into the mountain and can use both your arms and your feet and legs. Your toes lead, and they bend and shape to the trail or rock surface. Any tendency to fall would be forward into the mountain, which is closer to your face, the steeper the climb. Your next move is right in front of you.

Not so on the descent. Then you face out into space. Your heel leads and does not bend. It must find at least a lip to support it. You do not want to lean back because you're afraid of your forward movement, nor do you want to lean too far out into vacant space, risking a tumble onto the land which falls away from you far below.

Sign or not, the reputation of the trail ahead reaches the thru-hiker long in advance. The nature of this descent is well advertised. Nonetheless, I am most certainly glad that Theo and I avoided "tragic results."

When we reached the bottom, I was ready to turn in. Including our lunch break at the summit, it had taken us 11 hours to do Moosilauke, up and down.

Kinsman Notch

August 29th, and I was up by 6:45. The day before we had done 9.1 miles—the first day under 10 for some time. I had lost .9 miles on Moosilauke Day, but, by the end of today, I would have the most miles in the bank account I was ever able to accumulate: 30.2.

Soon we came to Kinsman Notch and NH 112. The bulletin board at the highway trailhead was the first one I saw that included French in its pronouncements. This, of course, was for Canadians coming south to hike in the Whites.

I had arranged to meet son Christopher (46) and grandsons Thomas (17) and Isaac (9) at the end of the day at I 93, some 16.3 miles ahead. But this was not to be.

Kinsman Notch does not get the attention it deserves in AWOL or in AT lore. There are many steep and difficult climbs that no one mentions. There are also a lot of rocks and boulders to climb. Days later someone agreed with me that Kinsman Notch was tough!

As we climbed toward the East Peak summit of Mount Wolf, we saw our first college group on the AT. They were from Dartmouth. We would see several more from Dartmouth, Tufts, Bates, and even a high school group from near Boston as we continued northward. In the fall, many schools and colleges use treks in the wilderness as icebreakers for making friends and as a proving ground for establishing the can-do attitude needed for much of college life.

Near the summit of Mount Wolf, bright sunlight struck the mountains under a low ceiling of light-grey clouds. At times they seemed

ominous. Under those clouds was Franconia Ridge where I had first climbed a portion of the Appalachian Trail as a 12-year-old. The most extraordinary event on the entire trail was awaiting me on that ridge.

Before I reached the beautiful mountains I'd just seen below the clouds, I needed to focus on summiting Kinsman itself. The trail was steep and rocky, and it was getting dark. My original goal was to make it to I 93 that day, but as time moved on, it was clear that wasn't going to happen. My next best option, other than stealth-camping somehow in the dense forest, was to get to the Kinsman Pond Shelter.

I kept following the trail—up, then down—then, "Where the bleep am I?"

I had been calling Christopher to change my ETA, and then finally to tell him that it would be tomorrow before I'd meet him. I had gotten lost and actually summited Kinsman more than once. The views were becoming all too familiar. I stood on what I believed was a portion of the trail on the north side of the mountain, examining small trees that I thought I had seen before, wondering if I should head back up or continue down. It seemed I had already

been down this trail, but that led me in a circle. Not knowing for sure where I was, I made the best choice I could and decided I was going down, hoping I would come to a path that continued down.

It was dark, and I had no indication of where the Kinsman Pond Shelter might be. I checked my phone to find my location on Google Maps via GPS, hopeful that would give me some clues.

Happily, the map included the Kinsman Pond Shelter on the east side of the pond near the base of the mountain. That was off in the woods to my right, which meant I was on the west side of the pond. I would continue to the north end of the pond, then make my way around to the east side, hopefully ending up at the shelter.

Soon I had the good fortune of meeting the shelter caretaker who said I was on the right track. She was rather serious about her job and said, "I'll show you to the tent sites. You'll have to sleep there because dogs are not allowed in the shelters."

I was not in a compliant state of mind. It was late, dark, and I had gotten lost. I was about as immovable as the steep, rocky mountain I had just climbed twice.

"No dogs in the shelter! That's ridiculous! We're sleeping in the shelter."

Instead of further unkind and rude remarks, I pulled out the clincher. "He's a service dog."

She led us to the shelter in silence. It was a large, sturdy structure of heavy, stripped logs. Theo and I had it to ourselves. After my ordeal on Kinsman, I was very ready to do the usual and turn in.

The Hut System

The next morning, Theo and I ate breakfast and then set out toward our goal: Franconia Notch. We were about to see our first of many huts, famous in the Whites. In time, I would understand the hut system and how it worked. For now, it was still wrapped in mystery, as it had been even from my planning stage before we began hiking.

The huts are notoriously expensive and get booked early. Some thru-hikers book the huts before they start and, if necessary, hitch-hike forward to keep their reservations. They would then return to the place they hitchhiked from and resume their hike.

If you are a thru-hiker and do not reserve a place in the huts, you might get lucky and do a work-for-stay. For that, there is no fee. You do the assigned work, most likely in the dining room or kitchen, get some good leftover food after work, and bed down on the dining room floor once it is vacated and cleaned.

There are conditions for doing a work-for-stay, however: 1) Arrive after dark; 2) There has to be enough work; and 3) Leave before breakfast.

The management at each hut has its own character. Some huts stick to the rules while others tweak or ignore them.

I had the impression there were few if any campsites in the Whites. The winds could be so fierce it would be difficult to survive out in a tent anyway. So hiking through the Whites seemed to mean:

- There are no shelters.
- You can't tent.
- The weather can blow you off the mountain, so don't stealth-camp.
- Camping above the tree line is not permitted (and very dangerous).
- If you're lucky, you might be able to do a work-for-stay in a hut.

You would hope for such good luck because it costs $150 per night for paying guests, and for good reasons. The huts are well made, country cottages built high in the mountains. They are run by volunteers who bring their own belongings on foot, along with supplies for the lodge. The food is good and the accommodations superb-country. The volunteers work 11 days, including taking four trips to resupply, and then have three days off. Helicopters bring in supplies at the beginning of the season and remove items as needed during it.

Well, no matter the mystery, rumors, or facts, and hoping for good luck, we just kept going.

First Hut

We first encountered the Lonesome Lake Hut, which was hardly inviting. The small staff kept to themselves. No, "Hi! Welcome to Lonesome Lake Hut." So I looked around, took a few pictures, saw Lonesome Lake out a window to the north, and then we were on our way. This was not Carl's WELCOME TO THE WHITES.

The lake itself was, indeed, majestically lonely in its frosty-cold depths and isolated mountain setting.

Lonesome Lake Hut

Christopher, Thomas, Isaac

As we turned back into the wooded wonder of the wilderness, it was a mere 1½ hours until Theo would find comfort in the back of Christopher's mini Subaru SUV, while I embraced my son and grandsons who had driven at least nine hours to meet us here.

They had reserved a small cabin at the Indian Head Resort a mile or two south on I 93. We pulled into the cabin parking area, and I unloaded and stripped for the shower as they all went to inquire about mealtime.

As we planned this get-together, we made many adjustments, deciding finally that we would hike to Crawford Notch, 27.7 miles over some of the most difficult sections of the trail to date. I was wiped from the Kinsman experience, but a zero was out of the question.

The boys and I would grab lunch at the Resort while Christopher took his car to our endpoint and got a cab ride back. That took a little over an hour.

Theo was used to the "back" seat

Liberty Spring Campsite

When Christopher returned, we put our packs in the cab and headed for the trail. By 3:30, we were back where the trail crosses I 93 and on our way up the rocky Liberty Spring Trail to the campsite of that name, 2.6 miles ahead. There were campsites in the Whites after all. In three hours we reached our destination and registered with the caretaker. Tent platforms were built over the rough terrain. Christopher and the boys shared a four-person tent they had gotten when they joined me on some of my shakedown hikes. We set up, ate, and turned in.

Franconia Ridge

August 31st. We were on the move by 8:00, with a steep climb to waken us fully, followed by a descent, and then a swing upward to

Little Haystack summit. From there we went farther up to Mount Lincoln, Franconia Ridge, and Mount Lafayette. Then it was on to the Franconia Ridge Trail, and, farther along, the Garfield Ridge Trail.

Our climbs were steep and challenging. Theo watched over us from a perch more easily won by his four legs. But you love what

A superior climber

demands much of you. The more you give and survive, knowing you have given your all, the more you love what has required that effort. You hike to do it, and you hike to have done it, to reap its great reward.

And there was a great reward indeed on Franconia Ridge where mountains, wind, and clouds made Mother Nature ever so present. I turned my face into the wind and looked west into the weather where clouds were opening and closing, and I never felt so free!

In 1956, two years after I hiked in The White Mountains of New Hampshire. the idea of a thru-hike was planted within me. Sixty years later, I was back. The weather on the Ridge was spectacular. Mist and clouds formed and separated, came and went again and again, opening up views and shutting them off in a fantastic weather show, the wind howling all the while. Something in me came uncorked, and I howled back at Mother Nature with a primitive cry from deep within. I faced her head-on and relished the encounter. My grandson Thomas captured a moment of that sublime connection, with Theo at my feet, the two of us touching the heart and core of what our adventure was all about.

This moment was the epitome of our entire undertaking, from conception to completion. It was the focal point of every step, every wound, and every ethereal wisp of wonder and awe. It was as though I was face to face with the Creator, and perhaps, like Jacob, wrestling with him in a way that evoked unrestrained approval and boundless joy in each of us.

While up here in the wind, Christopher asked me, "Dad, what has been the most impressive moment on the trail so far?"

He barely finished his question before I answered, "This one!"

My grandson took some video of my Native American war whoop, the cry of my soul in touch with the natural order, but the video got lost or erased somehow. No matter. The moment dwells deep within me and will never leave. It was my nonverbal, vocal expression of primal oneness with creation in all its manifestations.

We in the West are most often too self-conscious to express that connection with reality deep within.

Oooh, how we connected that day!

Theo

Good Theo deserves a page all to himself for his regal and attentive bearing on this day. On the day we met, we owned each other's heart before either of us took another breath.

I have known many dogs over the years, but I have never known a dog like this one. I was bitten by a dog as a boy, so I know that they can be unpredictable and that they are not people. They are dogs. And while I am surely alpha dog to Theo, I do not lose sight of the fact that there is a canine brain in that handsome skull. He loves me, but his primary concerns are: 1) Do you have food? 2) Are you going to scratch me?

One wonders, nonetheless, what he would do if I were injured or attacked by an animal. There are tales of dogs doing heroic things to save their masters. Would Theo? Whenever I fell, he just waited for me to get up. No matter how hard the fall, he would just lie down until the ordeal was over.

He would always check on me, however. Was it because he knew he needed me in order to eat, or because he cared about me? I like to think he cared and wanted to be sure I was okay.

Theo was magnificent as we moved along this misty ridge. I never felt closer to a canine. He was a four-legged, furry expression of my heart and soul. I don't know exactly how, but, in some way, this animal entered my psyche and fixed himself there. It happened the moment I saw him as a pup, and now, on Franconia Ridge, our bond was acted out most dramatically in splendor beyond words. We were together, totally dependent on one another for life at the banquet table of creation. We were one in rain and wind, under misty-blue skies. Dog and master. Master and dog. Totally trusting in this airy happiness.

We hiked over Lafayette and on to Garfield Pond. We found a clearing in the woods where we set up our tents for the night.

September

September 1st. We were packed up and ready to go by 7:45. We were on top of the world with views in all directions. At the Galehead Hut we stopped for a lunch of weak, leftover potato soup and bread. Our goal was the Zealand Hut, but we were so taken with views that our resolve evaporated.

To the west, clouds hung over Franconia Ridge, fracturing the sun's rays. I gestured in happy, silent reverence toward this place that had lived in the recesses of my mind for so many years as a powerful, moving force and, just the day before, had welcomed me back in a grand display.

A few hours later we were on South Twin with views to the east over mountains catching the sun's broken rays. We could not rush. We were in church.

As we descended from the ethereal heights into the dark, we were impressed with the clear night sky and brilliant pinholes in the canopy of heaven—so much so that we stopped mid-trail and lay down, headlamps off to marvel and feel small.

With our heads in the heavens, our feet on the ground were not going to make our goal. We'd descend and see how far we got. Hiking in the narrow beam of my headlamp, I slipped forward into my downhill trekking pole planted in the ground and broke the bottom telescoping section. But I managed fine with the uneven poles.

Isaac, Christopher (pointing), and Thomas on South Twin

Perhaps in an hour or so, it would be time to stop. We scoured the woods on both sides of the trail for a spot to pitch our tents. Not getting to the hut made Christopher and the boys one supper short, but I had enough food for all of us. Before bed, Theo engaged in some leisure activity—"I think I'll chew some sticks." Surely he was

just operating on an instinct to keep his jaws, teeth, and gums strong and healthy, but it's fun to imagine him thinking about these things.

It was 11:00 by the time we turned in.

Crawford Notch

Indulge me

We were on the move by 7:30 and at the Zealand Falls Hut by a little before 9:00. Relieved of his pack, Theo wormed his way into the affections of a young hiker.

On South Twin Summit we saw a helicopter disappear over the edge of the mountain down to Galehead Hut. At Zealand Falls Hut, despite its windstorms as we watched, a helicopter was able to come and go three times. It landed or hovered, making deliveries with a cable suspended from the craft. It was exhilarating to witness so much aeronautical engineering knowhow and mechanical force at work.

The goal for the day was Crawford Notch where Christopher had left his car. We passed a stream that he and his boys could not resist. I could and moved on at a good clip for a long haul. Nonetheless, soon after I arrived at the car, Thomas showed up.

My hiking companions changed their clothes discreetly behind the car, packed up, and prepared for the long ride home. Theo and I squeezed in for a ride to lunch at a pub-restaurant on the west side of the highway. I made reservations for the night and, after lunch, Christopher drove me to my motel before our usual bittersweet goodbye.

I had a good meal up the hill from the motel and returned to my buddy in the room. His needs were as much a part of my routines as my own. As my family has long observed, we're littermates after all. I think I am more familiar with his face now than I am my own.

Webster

In the morning, with some coming and going at the mercy of travelers in vehicles, I managed to get my trekking pole fixed, with the charge picked up by Leki, the manufacturer. Then it was thumb-out for our ride back to Crawford Notch.

The climb up from the Notch was difficult, especially on Mount Webster as the sun rested on the summits to the west. I took a selfie with the sun behind me. When my son Soren saw it, he said, "POW—that's my father!" He was seeing the essence of the man who has tried to fulfill his responsibilities in life, including his commitment to his wife and family, but has always had a wild streak that lay dormant for decades.

Not so for my brother who was drawn away from our alcoholic parents, and the social norms of the East, to the Rockies in the West. The "White Knight" stayed home to do the "right" things.

A heavenly moment on Webster as the sun was setting

My wife and I have sought counsel from many knowledgeable people over the years. One of them said, "You can depend upon it; you are being drawn with mathematical certainty to the things you need for your own healing."

My brother was drawn to the mountains and then to the deserts of Arizona for rehab. The mountains called, but alcohol almost took him. It was at a desert campfire that he was able to remember the time he was ready to kill our father for his cruelty to our mother. Recalling that sobered him up for the rest of his life. Perhaps my lack of memory here means I have more mountains to climb, a summit to gain where I can see all of the past and release it into the heavens, "as far as the east is from the west." Thank God for Theo whose companionship was encouragement enough for me to head to the mountains.

After straddling a wide vertical crevice so I could boost Theo up, and then climb up myself, we came to a small clearing to the right of the trail. It was a pine grove just large enough for the tent. We had a happy time of self-fulfillment on Webster's summit, all to ourselves.

Lakes of the Clouds Hut

We left Webster for Jackson, and then the Lakes of the Clouds Hut at the base of Mount Washington. Some hikers at Jackson offered to take our picture with Mount Washington in the distance behind us.

At Lakes of the Clouds Hut, for $10.00, thru-hikers could stay in "The Dungeon" at the bottom, back right, outside corner of the structure. It was a cold, dank room that would have been fine, but I decided to try a work-for-stay. We got there an hour before sunset. One-Mile and Sweet Pea were there, already signed up and waiting for guests to finish dinner so they could do their work, eat, and turn in.

I arranged for the same.

After the guests ate, my job was to scrape years of blackened food off large aluminum pans, rinse bowls and cooking utensils in large sinks, and then set them aside to dry.

I slept on the dining room floor while Theo slept outside.

On Jackson with Washington behind us in the distance

Washington to Madison

We were up and out before 6:00 and hiking by 6:20 with a plan to have breakfast on Washington's summit. A sign reading STOP reminded us of the truth about Mount Washington. The weather on September 1, 2017, proves the point. Snow fell as temperatures plummeted to 25° and winds climbed to 94 mph.

We hiked past the lakes and climbed the 1½ miles to the summit. Although there was the odd patch of grass to satisfy Theo, rocks would be our fare for days to come. Although the ascent was steep, the weather was perfect—brisk and clear.

Theo looking super-handsome in rare grass on Washington

Mount Washington had loomed in the back of my mind ever since I was the 12-year-old camper hiking Franconia Ridge. Fellow campers had climbed it on another trek, but I had not. This day I would slay the dragon on my way to the mountainous monarch farther north.

I had my photo taken at the summit and then sat at a table in the morning sun where the first Cog Railway of the day was soon to arrive. One of the passengers was an Asian man. He and his friends came over to me and asked lots of questions, fascinated by what I was doing.

One of them wanted his picture taken with me. I gladly obliged and, after my breakfast and moment of international fame, I packed up and got on with our day in the Whites.

The trail took us west of the first peak after Mount Washington, then east of Mount Jefferson and Mount Adams, and on to the Madison Hut, where I planned to do another work-for-stay. It had been a long day, my first over nothing but boulders. The hut was a welcome sight when it finally came into view in a notch below the Madison summit. I took our packs off and went inside.

"I'd like to do a work-for-stay."

"Sorry. That's only for those arriving after dark."

"Okay, I'll go away and come back after dark."

"It doesn't work that way. If it's still light out, we expect you to keep hiking."

Pause. Regroup. Reconsider. Figure. Plan.

"We can give you some bread."

"Thank you."

Find a place to tent nearby or climb Madison?

I chose to climb. I'd had a little rest just chatting with "Sorry." I stuffed the generous supply of bread Sorry had torn off a large round loaf into the top pouch of my backpack, swung the pack over my right shoulder in my usual way, saddled up Theo, and off we went.

Rocks. Steep. Climb. Sun sinking behind us in the West.

Before long I saw a handsome hiker, with a hat that reminded me of *The Man from Snowy River*, walking southbound.

"Where are you headed?" he asked.

"The first place I can pitch my tent."

"There's a spot just over the summit that might do."

I thanked him and continued climbing.

The sun was hugging the horizon as we arrived at the summit where the views were spectacular. There was, indeed, just enough room for a single tent. Only a mound of rocks was closer to God. I pitched, ate, and turned in.

Sunset on Madison

Pinkham Notch

It was still dark when heavy winds caused my tent walls to flap vigorously, to the point that some of my stakes were pulled out of the ground. I crawled out in a blustery, thick mist and took heavy stones off a nearby cairn to put on the stakes once I had replaced them.

Staked out again, I crawled back into the tent out of the raging damp mist, and then back into my sleeping bag. My earplugs muffled the heavy flapping sounds enough that I did drift off.

There was a little light in the sky when the ongoing wind and heavy mist, making their way into the tent, were enough for me to know that my best bet was to get off the mountain.

"We're not eating now, Buddy—we're getting down below as soon as possible."

I packed up everything while still inside the tent, and then packed the tent in the blowing mist. We moved out and down—and down—and down—an interminable descent over wet boulders, some slippery with algae.

The morning was thick with mist and a powerful but muted sun. We had started down a little after 6:00, and at 7:45 we stopped for breakfast. I created a seat for myself on a patch of wet grass, using my yellow, heavy canvas, bear bag, which I had purchased in Damascus, Virginia, and my Crocs as a cushion at my back.

After breakfast we came to forests with forgiving dirt underfoot. Theo remained ever the loving and faithful companion, the leaf that never ceased floating in the sweet mountain breeze of my soul. He just hovered there, as certain as I was that he was where he belonged.

In time we came to the Tuckerman Ravine Trail which we followed for a short stretch to Pinkham Notch. It was only 4:45, so we had time to chat and leisurely figure out our next steps.

There was a Visitors Center with an extensive porch where several fellow hikers hung out. Younger ones gathered to shoot the breeze, play a game or two, and indulge in a peaceful sing-along.

Brother Blood came over to record an interview with me on his phone. He wanted to know what had gotten me out on the trail. What was my story? He assured me he would follow up with me after we completed the hike. It was a brief contact, but not more. Others really wanted to hear my story as well but never pursued it. Another person was going to do a series of podcasts. It didn't happen. John Noerr from Hanover was going to contact a local TV channel to run a video of a talk I gave. That didn't happen either. Perhaps some of them will come upon this book and learn here what they had hoped to hear for themselves.

Some of the hikers were talking about getting a shuttle to a Twelve Tribes place in Lancaster, New Hampshire. I decided to tag along. It was not a tent-here night, nor a time to carry on. Wildcat Mountain and Carter Dome were ahead. Both were reputed to be difficult climbs. A little downtime suited me well.

   We arrived in Lancaster at 7:35 after an hour-long drive. I asked for a group picture. As I review it now, I am impressed with how old the white-haired guy looks. At the time I felt like I fit right in. But looking at the group photo today, I experience a flash of fleeting objectivity. Clearly I had some deep-seated, yet beneficial, denial going on!

   The Twelve Tribes storefront in Lancaster, New Hampshire, was called Simon the Tanner. The Tribes seemed to be welcomed wherever they located. Frequently, if not always, they ran an organic farm or two just outside of town.

   Because I had a dog, I was going to be housed in a shed down by the Israel River. There was a bathroom and shower for me nearby in a large storage space, which had electricity to charge my battery. The shed was made of 2x4s and plywood, but it sufficed.

   I left Theo settled in at the shed and headed for JL Sullivan's Irish Pub. I found a seat at the counter and enjoyed a Beefeaters on the rocks, followed by two bowls of some awesome chowder and a beer. One of my barmates was from Lancaster, Pennsylvania, so we compared notes.

   Well-fed and content, I returned to my loyal companion who was waiting for me. My gear told him this was our home for now and that I'd be back.

Lancaster

This would be a day in town. It was another misty morning with a quiet, low-lying fog. I was told that every morning started this way in Lancaster, and that it would burn off. It did. I had breakfast in town and returned to our abode.

As I walked across the lawn toward the shed, Theo appeared in the door. Did he smell me from that far away? Did he hear me? As soon as I entered, he made his way back to his comfort zone and lay down.

As the sun burned through the fog, I took all our gear, which was still soaked from Madison's mist, and spread it out on the lawn by a grove of beautiful white birch trees.

I had many things to get done today: retrieve my battery charging over by the shower, do laundry, resupply, blog, write emails, and pay bills online with my tablet. The gear dried quickly in the sun and faint breeze. I put it back in the shed before heading into town for lunch, writing, and planning logistics at the Lancaster House of Pizza.

Later I resupplied at the Family Dollar Store north of town, went to my first movie since before starting the trail, returned to Sullivan's, and then went back to the shed and my companion.

Aliens Aloft

By 9:30 the next morning we were back at Pinkham Notch, and at 9:45 we were on the Lost Pond section of the AT, heading up Wildcat Mountain. It was a difficult climb that seemed to go on and on, up and over one knoll, just to begin all over again with another. At one point, we encountered a couple of southbound hikers. Thinking we must be near the top, I asked "How much farther?" They said we had an hour or more of difficult trail.

It is so gratifying now to get the aerial view from Google. While I was in the Whites, I had no idea what I was approaching next. I just knew they were mountains—and I had no idea as I climbed Wildcat and looked out across the highway, that I was seeing the sweep of mountains at the top of Huntington Ravine: Washington, Jefferson, Adams, and Madison. Now with an aerial view, I feel like an eagle soaring above the land I walked.

We came at last to the unglamorous summit of Wildcat Mountain where humankind's machinery dominated the scene.

We cannot have the repeated thrill of the schuss and swish, the dance of delight, the exhilaration and boundless joy of surrender to gravity in the art of skiing without the assistance of machinery. For sure, the purist can carry his boards up alpine slopes and ride the avalanche-prone snows to the start of another climb. Maybe that's the way it should be, but we accommodate. We cannot turn left and right at the same time. We cannot both stay home and go abroad. We adjust.

Ski lift on Carter looking like a UFO

Theo and I crossed the torn land past the hut, the propane tanks, the lift, all the residue of aliens who must have visited from another world a long time ago and left. Theo seemed to understand that something was amiss. It was 3:30, and we had been climbing the three miles from Pinkham Notch for the last 5¾ hours.

Happy Hour

We left the torn-up slope and moved back into the woods as mist and fog from the south moved in. The descent was steep, and, with the weather and the advancing season, it was getting dark.

"Sojo!" came from the woods to my right. I looked, and there was a young woman I had met on the trail before. She was convivial with fellow hikers. She liked staying up late and chatting, singing, telling stories, and laughing. I think her trail name began with a K, so I'll call her K.

She was sharing her tent with some guy, or vice versa, but they were together.

"Come join us!"

It was getting dark and I was ready to set up for the night.

"They're expecting 75-mph winds. You may want to look for a safe place to set up your tent."

I went past them and found an area I could clear next to the root-ball of a fallen tree. I looked up and scanned for "widowmakers" (branches which could fall and kill you). The site seemed okay.

The forest was dense and roots plentiful, so it was a bit of an ordeal setting up the tent's floor and guys in a suitable way, but in time I managed. As I was finishing, K asked, "You wanna join us?"

They had started a fire, somehow contained, in the dense woods. They were a little like rebel hikers—well, maybe they were just younger and had more energy for waywardness. A little more like party animals than this old codger.

"Sure! I'll just finish setting up my tent."

I made my way over and around underbrush and pushed through to their cozy campsite. Their tent was off to my left as I approached. I sat by the fire and got comfortable.

"Would you like some vodka?" K asked.

"Sure!"

She poured me some and asked, "Would you like some smoked salmon?"

"Are you sure?"

"Yeah, we have enough. Would you like some crackers?"

"Wow! How cool is this! Thanks!"

I couldn't have been happier to have friends like these two kind souls who invited me into their world to enjoy what is surely the most memorable, thick-in-the-wilderness, happy hour a person could possibly have. The vodka and hors d'oeuvres hit the spot. I'm not sure I even cooked that night. I didn't have enough to put me under, but the delightful time by the fire, with a little warmth going down with the taste of crackers and smoked salmon—well, that eclipsed any other memories of that night.

Mount Hight

We never got the 75 mph winds.

I was out and moving around camp by 7:30. My comrades were still in their tent. By the time I finished eating and packing up, however, they were gone. They were fast hikers. A few times before, K had left a site after me and whizzed by me hours later and disappeared. I remember that on Webster, and so it was here.

As I left, I took a picture, as I often did, of the flattened earth where I had slept.

The fire was well out, but we failed to "leave no trace" or, as the French sign read, "*ne laissez pas de traces*." Some places a firepit can be left—certainly at a shelter—but here in the middle of the forest where the best of all, post-hike, late night events took place, they shouldn't be. Our mistake. I should have made good.

We came to a pond on our descent, the first of many ponds and lakes we would see going deeper into the wilderness on our way to Katahdin. It was beautiful. The whole world was aglow from atop Mount Hight with its stunning 360° mountain views.

As I summited, along came a couple southbound. We chatted. They were husband and wife and came from Barrow, Alaska, to hike the Whites.

On Mount Hight with Washington behind my trekking poles

"Barrow!" I exclaimed, adding, "I'm from Lancaster, Pennsylvania." One year, we had so little snow that I looked up people in Barrow just to talk about snow. "How did you end up there?" I asked.

The man said he wanted to get to know the native Inuit culture firsthand. They were retired teachers and free to move there. I admired their goal and willingness to endure the environment.

I asked if they minded if I took their picture.

"Not at all."

When I finished, they asked if I'd like them to take a picture of me with my dog, as happened often. "Sure."

They took several of me looking like I owned the world with my loyal canine at my feet.

As these good folks headed south, I took one last picture of them framed in the panorama of the Whites' tallest domes and then left my perch at the top of the world to continue north.

My new friends and I have since exchanged emails. They've sent me pictures of seals, snow, and moonlit nights.

At the next shelter, several hikers in their 20s were established already. We greeted each other with modest grunts as we went about our business. We were coming to the end of the Whites and would soon enter Maine, the last state. We were veterans, but it wasn't yet time for excitement. We still had a lot to accomplish out ahead. That evening most of us were eager to just do the usual—turn in and get up early to carry on with the mission.

Gorham

Saturday, September 10th, took us over Mount Moriah and on to Gorham, New Hampshire, at the north end of the Whites. We were only 16½ miles away from the Maine border.

I didn't think of the Maine border as a great milestone at the time. Borders were markers of progress for sure, but the trail didn't

"Wise old man in the mountain" — Washington in the distance

change, not that next step, at least. A weathered wooden sign on a tree probably noted the border. The GA/NC sign was the first, but then there were so many more, small punctuations in the steady, daily theme of hiking the trail north to Katahdin, that they no longer stood out. We knew what we needed to do: just keep going.

This was not Georgia. It was not the Shenandoah. Not Pennsylvania, nor any of the other states. This was New Hampshire and the north country, its own world, challenging and exhilarating.

As we climbed Moriah we could see the Carters, Wildcat, Adams, and Madison to the south and west. I could locate Mount Washington in the distance with its summit-hugging clouds. We looked back at the majesty of the mountains we had climbed. A cloud over the Madison summit marked where the winds almost did us in.

A group of men and women, one with a head of thick, white hair, passed us on the ascent. A younger woman in the group was a real dog person, and Theo knew it. I admired that older hiker as I came to difficult, rocky climbs that she had obviously managed.

Soon we crossed Rattle River, and not long after that we came to US 2. The White Mountains Lodge & Hostel, a large, white, clapboard house, sat up on the left side of the highway. I entered through the garage where there were many packs, boots, poles, and gear strewn about on the floor. I found a place for my gear, took off my boots, and headed into the lodge. The place was full and run by very hiker-savvy people.

Folks were ordering food for delivery. I put in my order and joined others for a trek to Shelburne to resupply. After supper, Theo stayed the night in the garage with me overhead.

Two happy creatures in my shadow

Moose Droppings

Breakfast, included, was specially made Belgian waffles and plenty of coffee—self-help. It was a well-run hostel. Because it was raining, no one moved—except Theo and me. I knew we had to; I wanted to keep my appointment with Katahdin.

The trail was straight out the door and across US 2. Several hikers were watching from the drive as I left with my best friend

at my side. We followed the road over a bridge, up a slight grade, and then left onto a dirt road until we came to a sign for the Centennial Trail (AT), leading into the woods to the right. The rain was picking up as we began to climb. In short order, I met Happy Feet walking southbound. Her motto was "Christmas at Springer." What lay ahead of her was all that we had just done—to the mile. And all that she had done was ahead of us. So it is when NOBOs and SOBOs meet. We are the reciprocal of each other, with an instant bond of compassion and admiration.

The foliage, as always, was all the more brilliant because of the rain. The mosses and fungi were white and puffy and different than I'd seen before. Not at all like the green string balls of fungus that we saw freestanding along the trail in the South. These in the North were not loose but fixed in large beds found often on open sheets of rock that crowned so many of the northern summits.

The day was bracketed by two major climbs. By midday, the rain cleared, and the sky turned blue and white, affording wonderful views to the west. A series of descents would soon bring us to Page Pond, where we were peaceful and alone. I spotted moose droppings where we camped, but I figured he'd done his business already and would probably not return. It was a cozy campsite by a beautiful and ready source of water. I filled, filtered, ate, and turned in.

We had a good night.

Camping on Page Pond, mile 1899, just south of Maine border

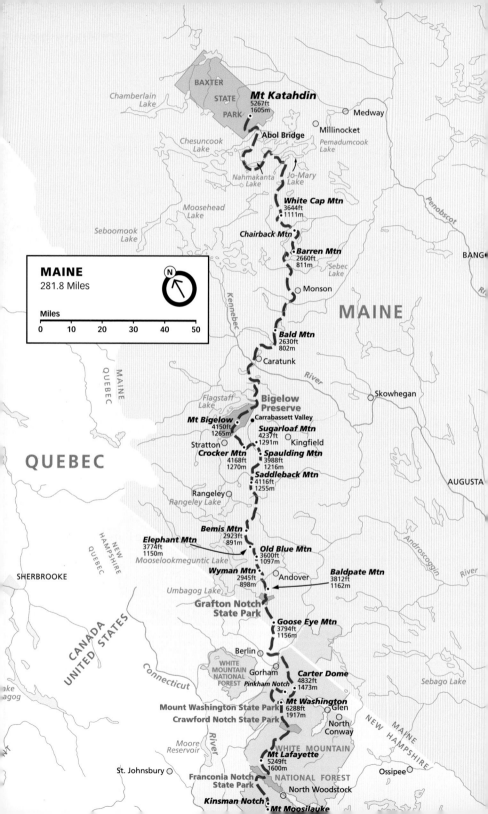

CHAPTER 15

Maine

Skywalkers

Since our daily treks in the Whites were always under 10 miles, my mileage bank account dropped from a high of 30.2 to -5.7. I was eating into my five-day buffer. I would drop further to -84.5 by the time we got to Monson, Maine, almost 8½ days behind schedule. From Monson, we had only the 100-mile wilderness, followed by the 10-mile trek into Katahdin, and then the Goddess herself left to manage. I decided to quit counting.

Today we crossed into our final state—a big day. First, we found ourselves in a sea of mountains on a trail whose name bore the ominous-sounding "Mahoosuc." We traversed high plateaus, and then marshes and bogs on narrow boardwalks, happily without incident.

Google again provides perspective on that day's location. Imagine living life at all times with God's view of your every move. It is a divine gift to be able to orient our mountain-high adventure now and see where our six legs had taken us.

I wondered when we'd come upon our first view of Katahdin. According to AWOL, we would see it from 72 miles away, on the north side of White Cap Mountain in the 100-mile wilderness.

Every footstep on the whole trail, and especially where we were, was memorable. It was as if we were tiptoeing on colorful clouds in an ethereal dream. A glorious light illuminated this walk in the sky. At the same time, the hike was getting exceedingly long, and the terrain was challenging with the end still out of sight.

Deserted

Brush and bogs and mountaintops. That's how Maine begins. She is a wonderland of natural phenomena, not a part of most people's daily fare. A forest ranger's perhaps, but certainly not a city-dweller's.

Why do we hike? Why do we go into the wilderness?

For the challenge.

To build stories.

To be close to home.

In the wild, I feel something of the reverence that Saint Pope John Paul II exhibited when he descended from his aircraft, knelt down, and kissed the ground. I do not fear death, the time when I am to be embraced by the cold earth. I come from her, and to her I am happy to return. I am now and ever will be a sojourner in eternity, no matter where my atoms go from here. I pray only that the spirit I leave behind—the memory of me—bless those in whom it lives.

Within an hour of leaving camp, I could see the west peak of Goose Eye Mountain with its rock dome. We were skirting the tree line, in and out of woods, and crossing many bogs and marshlands where grasses prevailed. We also had some steep climbs that caused Theo to wonder about his ability and mine.

The Goose Eye summit was off the trail to the left. I decided to divert and have an early lunch there. It wasn't long before a young woman showed up and joined me. She was doing the 100 highest peaks in New England and had already done Katahdin, including the Knife Edge Trail, which she recommended. The Knife Edge Trail

Theo looking up and looking down

was not for the faint of heart. I wondered if I could possibly conclude with that daring descent.

Where would the Knife Edge take me? There were ways to manage. But clearly, the Knife Edge should not be taken lightly. It was well named, dropping off precipitously on both sides.

The mystique of the Knife Edge Trail was part of the lore about Baxter State Park and Katahdin. AWOL shows trails and names on paper, but what would the boots-on-the-ground experience be in the complex and carefully managed State Park? Apparently the 100-mile wilderness led to Abol Bridge but what was Abol Bridge? The name took on a life of its own. And then there was The Birches Lean-tos & Campsite and Katahdin Stream Campground (KSC) at the base of the mountain's south side. How were they related, and why were the campsites so limited? AWOL notes "thru-hikers only; $10PP pay at KSC ranger station or info board (9.1S)." 9.1 south from where?

It all seemed so controlled and strict after days in God's wilderness. And then there was the matter of the closing date at Baxter State Park. What closed? Did Katahdin close? Could I climb Katahdin after Baxter closed? In time I learned that "closing" means you cannot camp in the Park. You can get a ride to Katahdin. Climb. Descend. And leave. But Katahdin, too, can be closed on account of weather. It was all so iffy.

And if I took the Knife Edge Trail down the north side of the mountain, how would I get back to the south end for my gear, which I'd leave in favor of a daypack borrowed from KSC? The Knife Edge could be deadly. Should I even think of walking it with a dog? What about high winds? My endless questions could only be answered by getting there.

My lunch companion on Goose Eye summit had a sandwich wrapped in foil with a logo, suggesting she was a day hiker who had recently purchased her meal. She also had no overnight gear with her. She ate and moved on. She had come after we did and left before us. Theo and I were not under her do-it-in-a-day pressure. We finished our lunch and were alone again. That was the usual order of our days. People came and left like winged creatures. Here, then gone.

It was time to head to Goose Eye Mountain's east peak. In the distance we saw the path forward, resembling the spine of a blue whale just breaking the surface of the deep.

As we made our way north, we knew that somewhere up ahead, over one of the summits, was the infamous Mahoosuc Notch. It lay out there as if in wait, like a troll under a bridge. But the Notch was inanimate, passive, unaware of our coming, and it would not know when we had passed.

It was almost 5:00 when we arrived at Full Goose Shelter and Campsite. No one was there, and no one would come. We were again alone in the Maine wilderness, facing the most difficult mile of the entire Appalachian Trail the next day. It felt like this place had seen more active days and more people in the weeks gone by. Now it was deserted, the long summer season over.

I pitched our tent on a platform, ate, and turned in. The moon shone bright that night.

Mahoosuc Notch

The sun shone bright upon our new day. We ate and headed for the Notch, its mystery soon to vanish. "Do not do it alone, and do not

do it in the rain" was the advice of those who had gone before. We would do both. No one else was around, and it would start to rain partway through.

We faced a climb as we left our lonely outpost and summitted under a vast overcast sky before moving down into the Notch. Theo

A dignified canine before our ordeal

was calm, alert, knowing, and trusting.

We descended into the woods on our way to the long, rock-filled crevice. Some of the way was steep, and soon high dirt and stone walls closed in upon us, leading into the Notch. Inevitably we came to a raucous jumble of monster boulders that seemed to have tumbled down from higher ground until they became locked in place by gravity, their own mass, and whatever was immovable below. Each had found its eternal destiny, and, if we wished to pass, we would have to do so on their terms. There was no give—none!

I was saddened to learn that, ahead of us, a 78-year-old hiker had made it here from Georgia, intent, of course, on Katahdin. He slipped somewhere, dislocating his shoulder. His friends carried his gear and somehow got him out of the Notch, and then up the notoriously long, steep, slippery rockface called The Arm, which follows. After that they hiked four miles to ME 26 at Grafton Notch, where they got a ride to a hospital. His hike was over.

Because of this tragedy, I became the oldest hiker to finish in 2016, but not without a deep sadness for a fellow hiker I never met.

There were many places where I had to help Theo up, over, or under boulders. More than once I had to take our packs off and crawl through on my belly, pulling the packs behind me. There were many

In the hole— reminiscent of
Devil's Gulch in Vermont in 2010

Sojo on the edge

Opposite page:
An arrow shows the way

places one could fall and be very seriously hurt. Theo fell into a hole reminiscent of Devil's Gulch. I climbed in and got him out.

At some points I had to step into air, trusting that I would make it over an abyss to the next foothold or tiny ledge or dirt mound, which I hoped would be secure enough to hold me. Sometimes all I could do was grab for a branch, which I hoped would not give way or be too slippery. Or I would hold onto a sapling overhanging the way forward, and swing from one foothold to the next, trusting momentum to carry me, my pack, and poles to a secure place. Poles were a great help with stability, but they could definitely get in the way of an awkward maneuver.

Happily, Theo was able to squeeze through places I was not and had more options with four legs than I did. He had proved his prowess at Devil's Gulch on our first shakedown hike in July 2010. Now as I was focused on surviving a delicate sequence of moves, he was

proving it again and again. There were times, however, that he seemed stumped by his surroundings, scanning left and right for a way forward.

Mahoosuc Notch was anything but a smooth path. This was most certainly not the South or even the middle states. Not even Pennsylvania came close to the Notch! Somewhere during our ordeal, it occurred to me, "This must be where Adam and Eve sinned, and Mother Nature lost it." It seemed as if we'd come to a place on the planet where nature had no concern for humans at all. A doorway to another world.

After a long time in the boulder-strewn mile, we saw a couple of SOBO hikers. Thinking we must be getting near the end, I asked, "Do we have much farther to go?"

"You're about halfway."

We had only one choice—just one!—keep going.

We did, and came at last to the northern end of Mahoosuc Notch. The famous mile of boulders had taken us 4½ hours.

It was raining. The Arm was out ahead. Should we keep hiking or call it a day? It was only 1:00. Our miles bank was at -19.5. At a nearby campsite, four fellow hikers were running through the same debate I was having with myself.

I decided to stay. They did, too.

Completely at Home

Our long time in camp was comfortable and relaxing. We had been through quite an ordeal, so it was helpful to have some downtime to regroup before tackling The Arm. Maybe tomorrow would dawn sunny and bright.

I spent the whole afternoon and evening in the tent, sitting on my inflated sleeping pad folded up against my backpack, which I'd leaned against the back trekking-pole tent support. I had a very comfortable chair. The weather was cool enough for my down booties. There I sat most of the afternoon, sewing up holes in my pants and going over AWOL to plan the stops ahead.

I had not had to tend my feet for weeks. God smiled on me so many times on the trail: weather, extraordinary encounters (another one coming), and feet, while bad for over 1,000 miles, were doing just fine in the Whites and thereafter. Somewhere in northern Massachusetts I stopped the daily duct-tape-spacers-and-moleskin routine. The left heel plantar fasciitis also had cleared up because of my repeated kneading night after night.

I was completely at home in our portable digs, and Theo wanted to be at home there, too. I let him in and got him comfortable.

Before long, it was time to prepare supper. Time, too, to feed Theo, eat, brush teeth, and turn in. We were now north of the Notch and ready to face The Arm.

The Arm

Soon after our start the next morning, we faced a steep climb over boulders. As we neared The Arm, Theo was up ahead, as on most all of our climbs. He looked particularly bright, knowing, and maybe a little superior as he gazed out into space, seemingly over my right shoulder.

Does he possess the character and thought I attribute to him? Does he strike poses only out of mindless instinct, or is he communicating something of what I see in his stance and expression? Is there a conscious mind intending to communicate, or primarily a package of hormones working outside of intentionality?

The Arm was a sheer rockface, which, at times, seemed to flow down the mountain as if once molten in earth's history. Gripping saplings on either side was essential for safety.

At the summit we once again became sunlit skywalkers among white puffs of clouds hugging nearby peaks. Close to the top I met my campsite companions. We were all doing well.

Old Speck Mountain

We passed Speck Pond on our way to a very steep climb. At the start, Theo needed a boost. He tried valiantly but couldn't make it, so he stood poised as if saying, "I can't quite make this one, Boss." On the way to Old Speck Mountain, the going was very steep, and the rockface, thankfully, quite rough. I needed every tiny nub of rock to interact with the still-deep tread of my boots to resist the powerful tug of gravity.

Somewhere at a suitable elevation, I called for a shuttle and made reservations at Pine Ellis Lodging in Andover, Maine, for the night. I did my best to estimate when we would be at ME 26 in Grafton Notch, having verified that I would have no cell service when we got farther down the mountain.

We continued our four-mile descent, with me mentally mouthing the first of many mantras that would help get me through some very difficult times in Maine. Looking forward to getting off my feet and sitting in a comfortable car seat, I hiked to a silent rhythm that assured me there was a reward out ahead:

> IT . . . IS . . . NOT . . . HERE
> BUT . . . IT . . . WILL . . . COME
>
> IT . . . IS . . . NOT . . . HERE
> BUT . . . IT . . . WILL . . . COME

. . . and so on, step by step, to the foot of the mountain. Aloud, it made a comforting, self-generated, resonant, verbal cadence that gently urged me forward with a promise of satisfaction at last. It occupied my mind as only words and voice can, transporting me, to some degree, beyond my physical and psychological weariness.

At last we did come to the parking area at ME 26. A van was sitting there with an elderly woman behind the wheel. She got out and introduced herself as Gloria.

We were later than expected and I apologized. Being off schedule was not uncommon, so she was prepared, trusting we'd show up at last.

I put my gear in the back of the van and called Theo to pile in. He had gotten well used to riding in the back of such vehicles. I sat in the passenger seat next to Gloria. You'd have to hike through Mahoosuc Notch, up The Arm and Old Speck Mountain, then down again to know how completely amazing it was to settle into a seat contoured to your every weary muscle. I luxuriated in the comfort as we drove the 20 miles to Andover along country roads, winding through deciduous forests just beginning to turn colorful.

A Tug of Sadness

The North. Lonely. Beautiful. Getting colder. Days becoming shorter. Leaves turning and beginning to fall.

Deep inside I felt a light, inner tug of sadness. I had started months before in a land that was not familiar, among people I didn't know, who, in a narrow sense, were not "my" people. But with a larger view, they most definitely were, and every step in the Deep South made them only more so.

Now I was far north, above the New England I grew up in. I was going to finish about 45 miles north of Montreal.

Foreign start, familiar middle, foreign finish. I knew all this before I began, but now I was living it out and approaching the end of my mission.

Notwithstanding any difficulty, I NEVER really thought of quitting. It was all part of the deal. I wouldn't have it any other way. The only premature end to my hiking the AT would be a body that had simply stopped and could not go another step.

As we drove to Andover. I mentioned the injured 78-year-old hiker I'd heard about.

"I drove him to the hospital," Gloria said. Now I was closer to the tragedy. I imagined the difficult, disappointing ride after so many painful miles hiking out.

Gloria drove around town to show me the lay of the land. Andover General Store on the corner opened at 6:00. Mill's Market, a little friendlier, with more for resupply, was about 50 yards south. The Little Red Hen, for the best and only breakfast in town, was across from Mill's and served a weekly, all-you-can-eat, Italian buffet to boot. I'm sure I'm part Italian. It's in the Irish, English, Scottish, and Danish mix somewhere—gotta be!

I would be staying with Theo at a cabin by the Ellis River. Gloria drove us the few miles to the campground and pointed out the common area with a bathroom and shower, and then walked with us to the cabin. She showed me up a few stairs, in through the screened porch, and into the single room with the bed on the left. There was electricity to charge my battery. It was a little chilly, so I was glad to have a heavy blanket, but not so cold that Theo shivered. We had a good night in an otherwise deserted camp.

Nostalgia

Gloria had taken my laundry, saying she would deliver it to me in the morning. And there it was! I left some items in the cabin that I wouldn't need on the next leg north, and we were picked up for the ride into town. We would hike over Bald Pate West and East, stay at Frye Notch Lean-to, and then hike out to East B Hill Road for a ride back to Andover.

Before departing, I took a picture of my left elbow, which I injured on a fall coming down a rocky descent from Old Speck Mountain. There was a steep step down onto a wet rock. It was the only way to go. My foot slipped, and down I went, landing hard on that elbow. I was happy to see that I wasn't hurt worse.

It's often hard to tell if you're going to slip or not. The stone that took me down I deemed rough enough to provide a grip. Wrong. With over 5,000,000 steps, you have many different surfaces to negotiate, and many are surprisingly slippery: dry leaves on rocks or firm, dry ground, a slick root, a wet board or log, a wet rock, frost or ice. Often such a surface was your only choice.

Falls happen because of slips, of course. But also from sinister little things jutting out of the ground, or that are just plain invisible under leaves or other debris. A tiny nub of a tiny stump, a little rock, an invisible root, a root loop, a stick under one foot which raises the other end to catch the other foot coming forward, a stub of a ground-level bush catching the loop of your boot laces.

If it can happen, it *will* happen in 5,000,000 steps. If each step was a word in a book, the book would be over 18,000 pages. Some of those steps caused me painful feet in the middle states. And I was hearing less well, I suspect from the frequent elevation changes, precipitating a natural aging process. But neither the falls, nor the feet, nor the hearing loss, nor the tooth or shoulder injury (coming up), could dampen my joy in thru-hiking the AT at 75. What a gift to have the health to do such a thing, and to be at a stage in life when I know nothing is forever and, at the same time, everything is.

Bald Pate

It was a little after 11:00 as we entered the woods on a sun-filled day. Round leaves turning endless colors were strewn beside the trail like rose petals for a bride. There was much underfoot to demand attention, while overhead, contrails accompanied our peaceful pace in the dappled woods. It was not often that I was reminded of my undertaking with Theo by such a dramatic contrast. The brilliant,

Study in contrasts: their pace and ours

streaked sky and the demanding terrain brought our disparate experiences together for a time, in a moment of quiet beauty.

We climbed past more brilliant foliage and fungi to the crest of Bald Pate West Peak, where we had a perfect view of Bald Pate East Peak and the bogs in between. If there is any soil between two peaks, it is the runoff from both that overloads the soil with moisture. What a recipe for a bog!

We had a steep descent by ladder before we got to bogland, after which we climbed again. A notice at the trailhead reads:

> USE CAUTION WHEN CROSSING BALD PATE IN BAD WEATHER. THE SUMMIT IS COMPLETELY EXPOSED AND INCLUDES BARE, SMOOTH LEDGES THAT CAN BECOME SLIPPERY WHEN WET AND VERY HAZARDOUS WHEN ICY OR SNOW-COVERED. DO NOT ATTEMPT TO CROSS OVER THE EXPOSED AREAS DURING AN ELECTRICAL STORM.

Our trek over Bald Pate proved the merit of these warnings, even though we could not have had better weather. Going from West Peak to East Peak was typical of so many of the climbs in the North. It wasn't like the South, where you'd go from summit to valley, and then back up. Here you climbed up and stayed up for a good while, descending significantly steep drops but not down to a valley floor, just down a dip in the mountain range and then back up. Here we went from one bald pate to another.

So many of the mountain tops from New York north were rock-faced. Certainly that was true of the Pates. A bald pate is a bald head. And bald they were! The balds in the South were covered with soil and grass but bald for lack of trees.

The views we enjoyed at the top were again breathtaking, as the sun, low at 5:30, cast long shadows. We saw lakes to the north, and our second line of wind turbines to the east. The Maine Appalachian Trail Club worked hard to eliminate, or lessen, the impact on the Appalachian Trail "view shed" by the unnatural turbines. There was give and take on both sides, and they clearly reached an agreement.

At 6:00, Theo stood statuesque in the late sun against a blue sky, looking back from where he'd come. From our high perch, we continued over rocky mounds and down a rope-assist ladder to the Frye Notch Lean-to.

One awesome canine under clouds that mirror his stance

Andover

The next morning, as planned, we hiked out to East B Hill Road for our ride back to Andover. En route, we came upon a trail maintainer putting in his final weekend for the season, and, by 12:45 we were in Gloria's van. The leaves were beginning to foretell the beauty I would see farther north as the season advanced. By 1:30 we were back at Pine Ellis Lodge where I got some good news. We could stay in the bunkhouse at the back of the Lodge, and my Cascade Designs package arrived.

It was time to replace my leaking Thermarest pad. Cascade Designs sent me a new ProLite Regular sleeping pad at no cost to me—a thru-hiker benefit.

I retrieved my gear from the cabin and settled into the bunkhouse which Theo and I had to ourselves. Mid-afternoon found me back in the deserted town, having lunch on the porch of the Little Red Hen with an India Pale Ale from the Baxter Brewing Co. The ale probably softened my outlook on life as the sunny afternoon felt like a reward for the efforts that brought me to this moment.

Back in Andover for a second time, I was beginning to feel like a local. But I was only a sojourner who adopted the town and made it home for a couple of days.

There's a little bit of Andover in my soul. A residue of the rather laidback people, the more quiet life, the down-home, know-everyone feeling. Old-shoe folk hung out at Mill's Market around a long rectangular table with old newspapers and magazines scattered about. They talked only occasionally, probably about a tractor part or a cake that fell on the floor. A slightly more vibrant group ate at the Little Red Hen where the waitresses were no-nonsense, savvy, and pleasant. I'll never forget this little Maine town where I stayed a couple of days.

Back at the Lodge I opened my new, bright orange ProLite Regular pad and packed my muted red one for return shipment. And then I was off to the all-you-can-eat Italian buffet. There was never a question that this hiker, who has been known to rescue a pasta noodle from the garbage disposal, would leave town without a meal there! I did not go home hungry my last night in Andover.

Little Red Hen

The next morning, after getting myself ready to hike, I went to the Little Red Hen one more time. I joined three fellow hikers in their 20s who stayed with their prior conversation. I excused myself and went to the next booth, explaining that I needed to tend to some emails and make a call. I checked in with Bonnie, who assuaged a little of my loneliness from the sparse, colder north, where the sun, like the hikers already finished, was moving farther south on the horizon.

I got a ride back to East B Hill Road and bid farewell to Andover, a sweet, dry, sunny spot in my journey.

At 8:30 Theo and I began Day 211 of our trek, a day that would take us into the last of the eight AWOL sections I had created before we headed to Gainesville, Georgia, back in February. We had a steady climb to a mounding summit, which led to a steep descent to Sawyer Brook Campsite for our next night on the trail.

Bed by Boughs

We were underway by 8:00 the next morning with Moody and Old Blue mountains ahead of us. A 1,200-foot climb was followed by a 2.8-mile, 2,200-foot climb.

As the day wore on, we descended into Unnamed Gap. The name reminded me of a sign I once saw: DISREGARD THIS SIGN. And of an email I once sent a friend, kidding, "Let me know if you don't get this."

It was wet and getting dark, and I was ready to pack it in. At a turn-off for water, I found just enough room for the floor of our tent if I could tie its guys onto branches or logs beside the very small clearing. It worked.

I got water in the dark and returned without incident. We did the usual and turned in.

Providence

We had a ripply, up-and-down day ahead with a monster bog on the way, eventually crowning at Bemis Mountain with great views. As we climbed, we saw awesome lakes surrounding the mountain: Upper Richardson and Mooselookmeguntic, Abenaki Indian for

Mooselookmeguntic Lake from ME 17

"moose feeding place." Farther north was Rangeley Lake, which we couldn't yet see.

We stopped at the Bemis Mountain Lean-to to get water. It was down a deep hole. I reached for a branch as I stepped on another, which instantly gave way. I fell hard against a rock, landing on my left hip. It was startling, but my sufficient bone density saved the day without a serious mishap.

Not long after the lean-to, we found ourselves on the Bemis summit, heading to the far side. As we began our descent, a tall, strawberry-blond woman came by and, like nearly all females, stopped to admire Theo. We continued our descent to Bemis Road to a campsite in a sparsely wooded area. It was drizzling, but a young couple was eating at a table undisturbed. They were just relaxing in the wilderness for a few days and took what they got, rain or shine.

I set up our tent in a small open area beyond their site.

A Double-Digit Day

In the morning we had a steep climb in glorious sunshine up to ME 17. I relaxed on a bench on the near side of the highway, drinking in the 180° distant views to the northwest. Mountains to the left and Mooselookmeguntic Lake to the right dominated the scene. Out of sight, off to the right, lay the town of Rangeley on the northeast end of Rangeley Lake.

We had climbs from ME 17 north, but nothing dramatic on this sunny, warm day with a little breeze. The trail went past Long Pond and then Sabbath Day Pond, where I stopped for lunch at a small picnic table right on the narrow beach looking out over the shallow water. I thought I'd risk a skinny dip. I wasn't worried about being embarrassed. I was sure that if any thru-hikers came by, no matter their gender, they wouldn't be either. Other hikers, maybe. But thru-hikers, no. I dipped, dried, ate, and left.

We had not hiked 10 miles or more per day since August 29th, 23 days ago. The terrain today did not have a lot of ups and downs, and I felt we could pick up speed. Invigorated from my swim, I was ready to make tracks.

I got my stride and moved right along, confident that this was going to be a double-digit day. It was a cheer, a motivating fly-wheel driving my rapid pace:

> A DOUBLE-DIGIT DAY!
> A DOUBLE-DIGIT DAY!
> A DOUBLE-DIGIT DAY!

I was repeating those syllables like the punctuations of a powerful piston driving me forward, and then—WHAM!

I was eating a large tree root before I knew what happened. I rose slowly and realized I had hurt myself. Now on my feet, I noted that my lower front teeth were butting up against my left incisor, which had been pushed in. I took a napkin from my pocket and patted my mouth. Blood. Both my upper and lower lips were cut.

I had tripped over something in the trail with my right foot, and I went down. I was moving forward at such a pace that I couldn't stop myself. No stumbling forward; no getting my feet under me. I was face down in an instant.

I'm sure my right arm broke my fall. The involuntary action of my reflexes had acted without me thinking. I'm sure that without those reflexes, I would have been hurt more; worse still if I'd hit a rock.

I was not in pain. Something significant happened, so we'd deal with it. I got up and kept hiking. The usual routine—keep going.

My best bet would have been to get into Rangeley by nightfall and tend to the tooth in the morning. But in an hour or so, Theo and I came to a campsite on a pond where someone had cut a lot of wood and piled it. It was a little after 5:00. We could get water from a piped spring, so we stayed the night there.

I texted my oral-maxillofacial-surgeon brother-in-law in Reading, Pennsylvania, and attached some pictures of my mouth. I thought I had fractured the jaw bone at the left incisor's root and asked if he could recommend a dentist in Rangeley, Maine.

Coverage was spotty, but we were able to communicate briefly. He said I'd be fine with a general dentist, but he didn't know any in Rangeley.

It wasn't a problem. I'd sleep and deal with the dentist issue in the morning. We were 4.8 miles from the highway that went into Rangeley. We could probably get into town before lunch.

It was not a double-digit day.

Little Swift River Pond, 4.8 miles from the road to Rangeley

Rangeley

At 6:42 on September 22, the sun shone brightly through my translucent tent. I felt compelled to go to the water's edge to capture the black silhouette of shoreline trees rising up into the shimmering sky above and sinking into their reflections below. They looked like feathers on two arrows merging at the far end of the lake in a vanishing bull's-eye.

At breakfast, as on the night before, I managed to chew carefully, never fully occluding my molars. After eating, I searched "dentist in Rangeley, Maine." There was one. I put the phone on Speaker and held it as far over my head as possible to reach a signal. When the dentist answered, I told him what happened and asked, "Is there any chance you'd be able to see me today?"

"Well, if you can get here by 2:00 I can. I'll be closing then."

I arranged for a shuttle pickup at 12:00 noon, explaining my need. The driver said he'd be there. Theo and I boogied, but not enough to trip again!

The driver knew where the dentist's office was and took me right there. It looked deserted. I asked the driver to hold while I checked. The receptionist and dentist were in with no one waiting. All was well.

While I waited, I found the magazine of the Aircraft Owners and Pilots Association. The dentist and I had something in common.

He came to take me back. I mentioned the magazine.

"Oh, yeah. You a pilot?"

"Yes, but I don't fly anymore," I told him.

An X-ray of my tooth showed it was dislodged from the bone. He gave me a local anesthetic, then stood behind me, wrapping both his forearms around my neck. He stuck the gloved index fingers of both hands in my mouth, with one finger on the tooth, and the other helping to push the top finger up into my skull. It was so hard to accomplish, that he took a breath and repositioned his fingers. His whole upper body was hell-bent on forcing the tooth back into its socket.

Pop! In it went! I guess it took about as much force to get it back in as it did to knock it out.

Once the tooth was in place, the dentist squeezed the upper jaw in around the tooth to reduce the fracture. He told me not to bite on it for several weeks. I asked if pain would be my guide. He said yes.

I was imagining a charge anywhere from $500 to $1,500. I thanked the dentist, who, by the way, appreciated that looking at acoustical ceiling tiles is not the most entertaining view when you're spending time in a dentist's chair. Since his office sat on a hill overlooking Rangeley Lake, he had mounted a long mirror on the ceiling so a patient could see the lake behind him. Beautiful!

The pleasant receptionist texted me a digital image of the X-ray at my request and presented me with the office bill: $99.00!

Something that could have been so very bad was entirely tolerable. I had no pain to speak of in my mouth, tooth, jaw, or wallet. The tooth area was sensitive for over a month afterward but, hey, that was not a problem.

From the side porch of the dentist's office, where I had tied up Theo, I called the Rangeley Inn just down the hill. They had a place in an annex building out back for Theo and me. It wasn't cheap, but I decided to treat myself.

Our room was luxurious with a sliding glass door out to a small deck in the back, overlooking a large lawn and Haley Pond. Theo was quick to adapt, rolling on his back, chest and legs in the air.

I stopped at a laundromat a short way back up the hill, visited an outfitter, and decided to try Sarge's Sports Pub and Grub right across from the Inn for supper. Theo was an instant hit with my fellow patrons. I ordered soup and a sandwich and, of course, a beer or two.

Theo chillin'

As I sat eating, a woman I had met at the top of Bemis Mountain came over to talk. I loved reconnecting with hikers I'd seen earlier on the trail. I told her about my fall the day before. She pointed to two big eggs on her forehead and remarked, "We all fall."

Her trail name was Prov for Providence. She told me that our meeting on Bemis meant a lot to her. She'd been feeling down and a little sorry for herself and, when she saw me, many years older than she, with Theo, making our way, it gave her a boost. It was good to see her again.

Back in the room, I repaired gaping holes in Theo's saddlebags. Between our shakedown hikes and the AT, they had lasted through many scrapes in over 2,400 miles. I used several big safety pins in my repair kit to fasten thick, black duct tape over the holes. The fix got us through and is still holding strong.

With my chores done and dinner in my belly, I fed Theo on the back deck and relaxed there for a while before turning in.

The Inn and Farmhouse

September 23rd. I went to the Inn for breakfast in the dining room with the other house guests. It was a nice spread with plenty of everything. I sat at a table by myself and noted a handsome couple at a corner table by the window. They each seemed to be in their own worlds, reading and just being quiet. The woman was tall and attractive; the gentleman probably her height but not extra tall for a man. He had a grey beard. Both of them seemed a little reserved.

Our paths didn't cross, and I didn't force them to. We were all enjoying the quiet.

One pricey night at the Inn was enough, so I arranged to stay at The Farmhouse, a hostel up the hill. I would call for a ride when I was ready. Meanwhile, I had some things to do online, so I got permission to occupy a corner of the room by the fireplace and come and go as I needed for a few hours.

After lunch at Sarge's, I worked until 5:30, then called The Farmhouse for a ride. The hostel was full. I was invited to hang out with the family around the large kitchen if I wanted, and then sit at the dining room table for supper. It was pasta, served from a large pot in the kitchen. These were laid-back folks. A little messy. A little dirt under the fingernails. So what's not to love?

Theo and I had adequate private quarters in the basement where we slept well.

Lost

Next morning we were back on the trail by 10:15. A sign read:

    1.8 MILES TO PIAZZA ROCK.

Another for Saddleback Mountain read:

> DO NOT BEGIN FROM THIS POINT LATER
> THAN NOON. THE ROUND TRIP TO THE
> SUMMIT IS 7.8 ROUGH MILES.

These were signs for day-hikers. Thru-hikers just kept going.

Back in Georgia on Day 4, I had met Andrea and Optimistic Dreamer. OD was a Yo-Yo, one who hikes one direction and turns around to hike back. He had started at Katahdin and was almost finished with the return trip, hiking in memory of his dad, son, and two little brothers. He got as far as Piazza Rock where he twisted his ankle and had to quit. These so-close and so-sad stories broke my heart.

Optimistic Dreamer (OD), hiking with a purpose

We passed three ponds on the way to the 2,500-foot summit of Saddleback where we could see several lakes—Rangeley, Mooselookmeguntic, and Saddleback—in the sun with clouds gathered overhead. Nature was almost overwhelming my spirit. It bombarded my soul with gut-wrenching views, while hinting of certain bleakness farther north. A subtle sadness was settling in. I was paying a price but none too great for the gain. I would persist through the darkening, colder days that were in the offing.

Lakes from Saddleback Mountain: Mooselookmeguntic (distant), Rangeley (closer), and Saddleback (to the right)

My right arm, which helped to break my jaw-fracturing fall, was now almost useless. It had spared me a worse fate than resetting a tooth and socket. But muscles in my rotator cuff, which I first tore by tripping over barbed wire, had torn again, and the shoulder joint was very weak. I ran my right trekking pole through the shoulder strap on the right side of my pack and used it as a sling.

Gone was the hard-driving, double-pole assist, so critical to the steep, dirt climbs in the South. I'd be one-poling it from here on and using more and more of my thinner and thinner legs. But we had a job to do, and we were going to get it done.

After Saddleback came The Horn. Getting there meant a 500-foot descent, followed by a 500-foot climb to the summit. Darkness was falling by the time we were descending on the north side. I saw my way forward only in the small circle of light from my headlamp. I focused on not falling again, only occasionally looking up to check for blazes or important signs. Happily I did not miss the sign for Redington Stream Campsite: "water 0.2W on side trail" (AWOL).

We turned off the trail, and I unloaded my gear at the first campsite on the right. It was pitch-black and we were alone. I told Theo to stay as I took the side trail deeper into the woods away from the AT to find water.

The forest was very thick, as suggested by the schematic of the campsite. Water was at the far back. The trail was crisscrossed by intricate root systems and not very clear. I came to what looked like a fork in the path and opted to go right. I followed what I thought was a trail for a little while, and then realized I was bushwhacking. I was not going to find water tonight and decided to head back to camp. I tried to reverse my steps, but, after a short distance, there was nothing discernible to guide me.

I took out my compass, working on the assumption that the AT ran due north/south, but did it? The trail zigzagged all over the place, even heading due south for miles sometimes. I decided I couldn't trust the compass and stood still, considering my situation for a brief time.

I remembered the tale of Inchworm, a 66-year-old hiker who had gotten lost near here three years before. She was found two years and three months later, in her tent, a journal by her side. I didn't panic but was a little wary. And then all came clear to me: "THEO! THEO!"

Tiny, gold-white, iridescent marbles came bobbing eerily toward me, suspended in the deep dark of night.

"BACK! BACK!"

And back he went. As it turned out, he led me in the direction I would have walked, but that's easy to say now. Then it was dark, the forest was thick, and the direction unclear. If I were ever to venture off on an uncertain mission in strange territory in the dark again, I would take a compass reading before setting out.

We were without water and without supper. But all was well.

Inchworm

Today would be a short day. Up Saddleback Junior in heavy winds and down to a stealth camp on the east side of the trail. My sideways beard, and my nearly horizontal trekking pole—suspended from a nail on a signpost at the summit—tell the force of the wind. We

passed Poplar Ridge Lean-to at around 11:30, a little over a half-mile from where Inchworm was found on October 11, 2015. A Google search reveals that she was Geraldine Largay who was last seen at the Poplar Ridge Lean-to on July 22, 2013. Her last journal entry, on August 18, 2013, reads:

> When you find my body, please call my husband George and my daughter Kerry. It will be the greatest kindness for them to know that I am dead where you found me--no matter how many years from now. Please find it in your heart to mail the contents of this bag to one of them.

Her husband George called her "The Love of my life" adding:

> She loved camping. She loved outdoors. The ultimate hike for someone who really loves hiking

> as she does is the Appalachian Trail. . . . I'm. . . reminding myself that she was absolutely where she wanted to be, doing absolutely what she wanted to be doing with every fiber of her being. . . .
>
> She would want this to help inspire somebody who's maybe on the sidelines, and never thought about doing something like this at age 66, almost 67, to not hold back, just to really. . .go for it. . . . Because she embraced life, and she would want anyone who reads about this to—that this would serve as a reason to do it, or to do something else that they were thinking about, versus to sit on the sidelines and play safe.

Lonely Mountain Night

September 26th—another 2,500-foot day up Spaulding Mountain. Some say southern Maine is tougher than the Whites. It is at least as hard. Even when not climbing, there were endless rocks and roots.

After my fall south of Rangeley, I was very concerned about having another one. I did fall again, with another face plant against a log. My left cheek hit, but not hard. I got up and proceeded with greater vigilance.

I remember in the South, as I crossed an area of small rocks jutting out of the ground, I warned myself to stay awake and not get into a hiking trance, to be aware of every step. Now with a nearly useless right arm, I slowly recited a mantra for miles on end:

> DEAR GOD, PLEASE KEEP ME ALERT
> AND KEEP ME SAFE

> DEAR GOD, PLEASE KEEP ME ALERT
> AND KEEP ME SAFE

Mile after mile, I walked to this prayer, elevating my level of consciousness while heightening my senses and my physical and spiritual awareness.

Another chant was shorter but effective:

> THERE IS NO RUSH
> THERE IS NO RUSH

My slow delivery, out loud or internal, reinforced the point and drove it home to my feet.

A couple came up behind me. It was the reserved couple from breakfast at the Rangeley Inn — Highway80 and Lady Slipper. They came from Virginia for a break in the wilderness.

By 3:00 we had come to the Spaulding Mountain Lean-to, where we stopped for lunch, and I saw my first sign giving times for the Kennebec River Ferry. Hikers were urged to cross in a volunteer's canoe because the river was wide and fast moving. Water was released daily from a dam upstream, taking two to three hours to reach the AT crossing. People have died here.

Highway80 and Lady Slipper showing typical gender response to Theo

This was north country, and we were getting deeper and deeper into it.

After lunch, the climb was steep and the descent even more so. It was getting dark earlier and earlier. I saw a tent pitched just off the rail on the right side. Highway80 and Lady Slipper were tucked in for the night.

"Join us," Highway80 said.

"Thanks. But I think I'll move on."

They were day-hikers out for a brief time. They had each other and would be heading home soon. I'd been out seven months and had more than a month to go. I had to keep moving.

It was probably less than an hour later when, still on the descent, I decided to stealth-camp in a small clearing just off the trail on the right.

I called home and got a bit emotional. I was lonely trekking farther north—the shorter days, the sense that most thru-hikers were finished, the extended time and effort to achieve my goal. It seemed the hiking would never cease. Yet the finish was a given, no matter how long it took. I may have made a few such phone calls, but something totally off the charts was in store because of the sound of my voice and the loneliness I couldn't hide.

Sugarloaf Descent — River Lunch

At 8:00, my tent was still set up on this foggy day. But by 8:30, I was at the magic point where the Appalachian Trail was first completed on August 14, 1937, by the Maine Civil Conservation Corps (CCC). For hikers, it was like joining the first transcontinental railroad at Promontory Summit, Utah, on May 10, 1869. This spot was the culmination of a momentous achievement that took 12 years to complete. Benton

MacKaye's vision, while sitting atop a tree on Stratton Mountain in Vermont in July of 1900, had become a reality by 1937.

The descent from Sugarloaf was steep on a wet, rock-strewn trail through glistening fall colors. It was 12:30 when we reached bottom and stopped by a river for lunch under a sky beginning to clear. We basked in the emerging sun and took our ease until 2:00. A little farther down the trail, we set up camp for an early night.

Steep descent off Sugarloaf Mountain

Stratton

In the morning, we were again fogged in. That weather persisted as we climbed South Crocker Mountain and then Crocker Mountain. We "dined" at the summit before working our way down through the early afternoon as the sun broke through the bank of clouds.

The long descent down to ME 27 took us to mile 2,000, and then on to a shuttle ride into Stratton, Maine, where we stayed at a hostel connected to the Stratton Motel. I had a reticent roommate in his 60s.

I settled in and then went to The White Wolf Inn and Restaurant two doors down from the Motel. I had two bowls of exquisite clam chowder, followed by a meal as good. My time in the White Wolf was relaxed pleasure. If I'm ever in Stratton, Maine, again, I'm dining there.

Back at the hostel, I got my bearings for our next trek and what I needed to resupply in the morning.

Horns Pond

On waking, I found a spot for breakfast, did laundry, resupplied, packed, and hit the trail. Steep climbs in beautiful weather were up ahead. In the photo of Theo at the peak south of Horns Pond, I noticed that the hair between his toes, normally long, was well trimmed, as I'm sure was true of his claws. Many rocks over many months provided daily pedicures.

Beauty surrounded us as the setting sun shone upon the far side of the pond and the twin peaks above. It felt like we were in a place never seen before, our own private Shangri-La.

A steep descent brought us to the water's edge on our way to the Horns Pond camping site. There were signs of a caretaker, but none was around. I set up the tent in an open area and, as we settled in, a

The Horns and Horns Pond as the sun is setting

large group of high school kids from the Maine coast came by and set up farther into the woods. Before long, they returned, surrounding Theo with love and affection, causing him a great deal of stress which he endured as calmly as possible.

I got water from the pond, prepared supper, and turned in for a peaceful night. We would awake to climb the Horns, Bigelow, and Avery, surrounded by breathtaking scenery, and then descend into Safford Notch to sleep again.

A high school group from the Maine coast enjoy Theo

Impossible

October 1st. This day will blow me away! We were underway around 8:00, up a gentle rise to another ridge north of Bigelow Mountain, on the way to Little Bigelow. As we climbed up from Safford Notch, we were surrounded by those round leaves in colors glorious and confounding. How does the same plant turn so many different colors? Is it the soil? Some variation in chemical makeup? The slant of the sun? Regardless, we were greeted by a color guard on both sides.

As we neared the summit of Little Bigelow, Flagstaff Lake came into view under a high ceiling of grey clouds that would last all day. Then we were off the peaks and back in the forest. Around 1:00, we came to a sign for the Little Bigelow Lean-to 100 yards off the trail. I decided it was time for lunch.

Other hikers were there, pretty much packed to go. We chatted for a while with some banter and laughter, and then they left. A couple of trail maintainers remained for a short while for more conversation.

When they left, Theo and I were alone again. I was seated at the left side of the shelter opening, my feet dangling from the elevated floor as I reached for my pack.

As I pulled out some food, I turned forward, and my peripheral vision picked up a form to my right. I looked over, unable to adjust to what was before me. My brain simply could not compute what I was seeing. For a split second I actually believed I was encountering an apparition. I held my head in disbelief. Then my brain turned on the afterburners and acknowledged what was standing in front of me in the Maine wilderness, off the trail by 100 yards—my 34-year-old son Nathan!

Expletives rose up from my core: "What the bleep?" And "Holy bleep!" I repeated each more than once, incredulity supplying the emphasis.

My brain is laying rubber and my conscious mind is fishtailing

Theo was ecstatic at seeing another member of his pack! Nathan obliged him with attention, bowing low and exclaiming the dear canine's name again and again.

How to convey this moment? I had hiked 2,016.2 miles to this place. My family had met me along the way at predetermined spots for preplanned hikes. I had last left family members at Crawford Notch on Friday, September 2nd, a month before. Since then, Theo and I were heading deeper and deeper into the Maine wilderness each day, farther and farther north. . . alone.

Theo with a member of his pack

I guess one is never too far away to connect with loved ones. One is never so lost in a wilderness as not to be found. The bond of love is strong and enduring, and ever so sweet and warm.

He didn't say so, but I'm sure that in one of my phone

calls Nathan felt my loneliness in this final, later-than-expected stretch. The seasons were changing, and I was getting more and more tired and farther and farther from home. He wanted to come and support me and give me a serious boost. He blasted me into space!

My GPS pins on the map each night enabled him to figure out my pace. From that he could determine where I'd be on a particular date and time. He used some of his many credit card bonus miles to fly from Philadelphia to Bangor, Maine, rented a car, and drove to a point north of where I'd be on the trail at the time of his arrival. He would hike south until he saw me, and we would hike together back to his car.

But I was not on the trail! I was at the Little Bigelow Lean-to. He could have gone right by me, and we might never have connected. But he heard me laugh from 100 yards away through the woods, and he knew he was close to his mark. He waited until I was alone, and then made his way to the lean-to. VOILA! AMAZING!

Jerome Brook

Nathan brought a daypack, and, as he took pictures at the northeast finger of Flagstaff Lake, he carried a sweater and jacket over his arm.

We hiked together a few miles, crossed Long Falls Dam Road, and camped at Jerome Brook, where we had a handy water supply. For sleeping, Nathan had only warm clothes and boots. He knew he was going to be out only one night and figured he'd survive, cold or not. I had an extra section of foam pad for his hips.

Something struck Nathan funny as I was getting water from the brook—I don't remember what it was—but I was reminded of his subtle sense of humor, which has kept our entire family entertained for years. He has a fine grasp of cultural idiosyncrasies, including the internationally sophisticated and the down-home, Lancaster County rural. He can juxtapose the one with the other in a totally flat, deadpan delivery that conceals the humor until the last word.

We ate and turned in for a passable night, sharing the ample space in my tent.

I Better Turn Back

Sunday, October 2nd. From my ad hoc journal:

> Why do mountains hurt? What depth do they tug
> at, deeper than they rise? What is their song? What
> did the Sirens sing to Ulysses? Their song is heard,
> too, in mountain heights where winds whip through
> trees, gnawing at the heart of him who would be
> gone.

Waving good-bye meant I was alone for sure until the finish

We both made it through the night. Nate braved the discomforts of the cold and hard earth, sleeping some. It was part of what he was willing to endure to comfort his dad, who was winding down his months-long wilderness trek into the far north. I will never forget his love and kindness. I know from deep within, in a voice clear as a bell, that love and kindness are all that really matter.

We hiked a short distance before Nathan needed to return to his car and his responsibilities as a teacher of advanced Spanish and French in a private school in eastern Pennsylvania.

"I better turn back," he said.

We stopped. We hugged and started walking in opposite directions. Then we both stopped, turned, and waved. I watched him go as he turned a few more times to wave, distant now, bending below branches to be seen, and then he was gone.

Pierce Pond

The waters of West Carry Pond were grey under an overcast sky, evoking the mystery of a long, dark, barren winter coming. I've always loved the winter, "the cold that threatens blood to stop," the warmth of the hearth with a wood fire blazing. And I still do.

Theo and I spent the night on a knoll uphill from the Pierce Pond Lean-to where we could hear some hikers conversing quietly. I went straight downhill from our spot for water and returned to the routines of camp.

Kennebec River

It was a four-mile, gentle, downward slope to the Kennebec River, where there was a sign warning against fording especially because of the water released each morning at 10:30 far upstream and out of sight. I was riverside at 9:10 but was not inclined to risk it. Besides, it would be a fun canoe ride across the river, if only I could find the volunteer paddler.

I saw no ferry by the warning sign so headed upstream. The trail seemed to follow an old roadbed that turned away from the river. Soon there was a trail that left the road and was more in line with the river. Perhaps the ferry was upstream. I saw no signs or directions anywhere.

Not far up along the river, in frustration I yelled out, "Where's the ferry? Where the heck is the ferry?" I don't think I yelled obscenities, but there were a few brewing in the tension between what was surely near but nowhere in sight.

I heard a faint voice saying something. It seemed to be coming from across the river, so I scoured the distant shore for some sign of life. I saw a hand waving and a man walking toward a canoe. My captain was hanging out at his port on the eastern bank of the river.

I walked back to where the dirt road arrived at the river's edge and made my way along a rocky shore to the point where the good volunteer had beached his canoe. There were only rocks. Nothing to indicate that this is where the ferry stops.

I was confused by the total absence of direction on the west bank but, hey, you can't get angry with a volunteer who will transport you over dangerous waters at no charge. He proffered a release for my signature and gave me a life jacket. We loaded into the canoe according to his instructions and were off. Theo seemed to enjoy walking on water.

Caratunk

The east shore was my canoe captain's headquarters. He pointed me to the path that led to the road which would take me into town, where I'd find a free phone to call for a shuttle. En route, I passed a Trump supporter sitting on his porch. We said "Hello" with brief conversation, and I moved on. At the free phone I found the number for the Sterling Inn, recommended by a hiker a couple of hundred miles back. My ride was there in short order.

I settled in, which included plugging in, and went downstairs to get the lay of the land. There was a resupply room in the back where I scoped out what I might purchase before departure. I enjoyed watching lumber trucks head south, loaded with their harvest.

The Inn's owner drove me to Northern Outdoors Adventure Resort for some good food, then came to get me when I finished. Theo and I slept well.

The Far North

After a self-service breakfast, I selected the items I wanted from the store, paid up, packed up, and got a ride back to the trail where we began hiking at 9:30.

We were now north of the Kennebec River, another milestone. We'd survived the South, pushed through the middle states, crossed the mighty Hudson, the Connecticut River, and the Whites. We had survived the Carters, Wildcat, Mahoosuc Notch, Saddleback, Poplar Ridge, the Horns, Spaulding, the Sugarloaf descent, the Crockers, a dislocated tooth, a useless right arm, the Bigelows, and the Kennebec River. We were coming into the home stretch.

We climbed Pleasant Pond Mountain, took in the views, and descended to a stream at the south end of Moxie Pond. The woods alone know where we were and where we slept that night.

New England Morning

My first picture leaving no-memory camp at 9:00 is of a colorful swath of deciduous leaves amidst pines. Then a dirt road lined with brilliant fall colors at the edge of a vaporous, sunlit pond evoked memories of my New England prep school days and white clapboard villages muted in early morning mist. I felt a gentle sadness as the vibrant summer days were slipping away.

We left the south end of Moxie Pond behind and pushed on through the technicolored forest for the mountain heights of Moxie Bald, which was bald indeed. After lunch, eaten as I leaned comfortably against a smooth ledge of stone, we met a fellow with three bear-hunting dogs in tow on our descent. The dogs were sweet-looking, with instincts harnessed to their master's purpose by antenna-rigged GPS devices. Nature had given them powerful bodies driven by scent, and their master was using them.

Closing In

October 6th was a long, flat stretch. I heard a lot of talk about the character of the trail all along the way, and coming to the finish was no exception.

"After the Bigelows it's smooth sailing. You can really make time," someone said.

"There's a long, flat section, but also a lot of rocks and roots," said another.

There was some truth to all of it, but you never know until your boots do.

The trail now was not too rocky or full of roots, and it was a gorgeous day! There were a couple of fords with strung cables, which I hardly needed because of the recent dry weather.

That night we stealth-camped just off the trail, alone again, which had become normal. There were no more hiker bubbles. No more youthful chatter or bravado at shelters or hostels. No more anticipation of the long road ahead. And the many mysteries of the trail were now whittled down to two: the 100-mile wilderness and Katahdin.

Maybe a third mystery was the town with the musical-sounding name of Monson, the last taste of civilization on the trail. Just 100 miles to the north reigned the Queen Herself. All around the Monarch, sub-mysteries flourished: Abol Bridge, Baxter, Knife Edge, Millinocket, the closing date, the weather. We had made our way through the endless forest, and soon it would be time to slay the Wilderness Dragon and lay it at the feet of Her Majesty's Throne. This was the price to behold Her Crown of Sunny Gold or Misty Silver, depending on the whim of the incomparable Queen Mother—Nature Herself!

Monson

October 7th. We will reach Monson, Maine, today. The 100-mile wilderness and Katahdin are all that are left. It would be 20 days, however, before we would finish.

It was another sunny day with an easy trail underfoot, and we were soon at ME 15, about three miles from Monson to the east and 12 miles from Greenville to the west.

I'd arranged for a shuttle from Shaw's Hostel in Monson to pick me up. Shaw's is the oldest hostel on the trail in continuous operation—over 40 years now. It is owned by Jarrod and Kimberly Hester from Florida, who thru-hiked in 2008 with the trail names Poet and Hippie-Chick, which, of course, have stuck. Why would you go by anything else among trail folk?

I settled in and walked the quarter-mile to town for supper at Spring Creek Bar-B-Q, a favorite hangout for some of the 685 residents of the town and surrounding area.

Yes, they have IPA beer. Its name—Smiling Irish Bastard. I put in my order at the bar and took the misfit to a table near the door, along with a sandwich, and enjoyed relaxing at the last civilization on the trail.

It was back to the hostel for bed and a hospital visit in the morning.

Greenville

Shaw's breakfast is famous, standard, and essentially all you can eat: fried eggs, hash browns, and blueberry pancakes—as many as you'd like—with plenty of maple syrup. And, of course, orange juice and coffee.

All Shaw's breakfasts end with a cairn of progressively smaller pancakes piled high. A taker can volunteer to down the stack to fill whatever crevice might remain in the gut.

Fed well, I needed to tend to my shoulder, which had been getting increasingly hot, swollen, and painful. My right arm had been unusable since Rangeley. I wanted to have it aspirated so I could get back on the trail the next day.

Poet drove me into Greenville where a doctor looked at my shoulder and agreed that it did, indeed, need to be aspirated. The bursa was inflamed with extra fluid that had to be removed by needle and syringe. Problem: the fine doctor had not aspirated a joint in years, and the person who could do it would not be in until Monday.

"Do you want to give it a try?" I asked.

"No," was his expected answer.

Friday, Saturday, Sunday, and then Monday. I wouldn't be in the wilderness until late Monday at the earliest. So near but getting farther. All along the trail in the North I had been mulling the big questions: "Would I get to Katahdin before they closed the mountain? What governs when they close it? Can they stop you from going up? Surely the weather can. Do they close Baxter State Park, which surrounds Katahdin, or just the mountain, or just the park?"

Now the question was more immediate: Would I get to Katahdin?

A Confessed Hiker

I left the hospital and walked the mile into town, musing about my situation. I saw a woman tending some plants by a sign that read, Holy Family Catholic Church. I hadn't been to church since I started hiking, except for Mass in Middletown, Virginia, over my birthday. All days were the same. Hikers' office hours are all day, every day.

Sojourner's soul journey needed some attention. I was a weary hiker nearing the end of my ordeal, but now the finish was in jeopardy. I had covered a great distance, making it fiercely cruel to imagine that I would not finish. On the one hand, it seemed inevitable that I would finish. On the other hand, a little gnat of uncertainty was caught in my beard and I could not ignore it. I crossed the street and asked the woman, "Can you tell me what time confessions are?"

"3:00-4:00," she said.

Confessions in the Catholic Church are almost always on Saturday afternoons and Sunday before Masses. It would do me good to go.

As it got closer to lunchtime, I walked back past a finger of the lake and on to the Stress Free Moose Pub & Café. A crowd waited outside in the sunlight to be seated. As time dragged on, I questioned the accuracy of the name of the place.

At last I was ushered in to a table in a corner near a middle-aged couple. I ordered a beer and a delightful sandwich and soon got into conversation with my neighbors. They were very kind and friendly and interested in what I was doing. They bought me a beer. It was a pleasant, Saturday kind of exchange.

Waiting and eating at the pub filled the time until confession. I walked back to the church just as the priest was finishing up. I asked if he could hear my confession. He obliged.

Father, I'm thru-hiking the Appalachian Trail, and I am weary and injured. A doctor is going to aspirate my right shoulder on Monday. I just want to finish.

That was the essence of my confession. I just needed to have someone hear me say that, someone who cared for the soul within. I needed to be on my knees, so to speak, and state my desire and the real circumstances of my life. He heard my full confession, gave me absolution, blessed me, and sent me on my way.

It was helpful to hear myself articulate simply and directly where I was and what I wanted. It was straightforward and beautiful in its stark accuracy. I had laid the foundation for finishing the trail. I had stood at the doorstep of eternity and spoken my mind. My desire was not frivolous. It was not haphazard. It was not spur of the moment. It was deeply rooted. Fundamental. Longstanding. Spiritual. Ordained. A sure thing. It would come to pass.

Getting Ready

I called for the shuttle. Hippie-Chick was my driver.

Back at the hostel, I found Bill Bryson's *A Walk in the Woods* on the bookshelf. I did a quick read of it for the second time. I experienced the book differently now that I was a veteran. I would finish the book on Sunday.

I looked over the supplies in the hostel's barn, figuring out what we would need, including all the food for Theo and me until the finish. It is recommended that you not enter the 100-mile wilderness without at least 10 days' worth of food. Some can do the distance in five days. I figured we would be very close to 10 days, so would need all the food recommended.

Shaw's offers a food-drop partway through the wilderness. They would meet you at one of a few dirt roads into lumber camps. You would give them your best guess as to arrival time and update them en route. They supplied a large plastic bucket for you to fill with what you'd need. Our bucket had provisions for both me and Theo and was so full that I had to tape the lid shut.

That evening I went back to the Bar-B-Q for more time with the Irishman and good grub.

ATC Prep

I spent all of Sunday, October 9, waiting. I finished re-reading *A Walk in the Woods*. I would be back on the trail tomorrow.

The charm of the unconventional

In the afternoon, I went to the ATC Conservancy at Monson's Visitor Center. Theo came in, and we waited our turn. Patty Harding was a big help with the mysteries of Katahdin—the do's, don't's, and maybe's. We chatted outside afterward as she lit up her slender pipe. Puffing, and sporting a long braid of white hair over her shoulder, she is a north-woods beauty!

This is the New England feel I grew up with. As I read Emerson, Thoreau, Hawthorne, and Melville in school, something in them resonated with me—a common substance, maybe bacteria from the same soil coursing through our veins and living in our guts. New England said something about who they were, who my father was, and who I was and am. There's a West family strain that has been nourished on the cold, frozen earth of the North, the hard winters of New England.

The ATC issued my Baxter State Park permit, the first year they were required. The Park Rangers are charged with keeping the land "forever wild" as demanded in Governor Baxter's will. The officials take their jobs very seriously and do not favor large and sometimes destructive groups climbing Katahdin, nor do they permit alcohol or partying on the mountain.

Nonetheless, some have been so exuberant in reaching the summit that they are, sadly, mindless of these restrictions.

After a lazy day, I had another meal at the Bar-B-Q, tended to our resupply, and turned in.

Ex-Aspirating

On Monday, October 10, I was back in Greenville for a 9:00 appointment with the doctor who would aspirate my right shoulder. The needle was long—a little uncomfortable but nothing bad. He withdrew 45 ccs of cloudy fluid from my shoulder. Because of its opacity, he sent it off to a lab for analysis. Infection is serious business regardless, and I had had a partial knee replacement. A foreign substance in the body is notorious for attracting infection. Kevin, who met me in Hanover, had had "a total knee" and got a small cut on his toe, which became infected. He almost died from sepsis and had to have another total knee replacement. So it was nothing to take lightly.

As I walked back to town, I came to an American Legion building with a sign welcoming strangers to come in and enjoy donuts and coffee. "Why not?" I thought but found the door locked. Someone inside heard me and let me in. The three or so veterans inside were slowly closing up shop, but they were in no rush and showed me where to help myself. I sat with them to enjoy my treat. They were quiet but friendly.

I told them I was staying at Shaw's Hostel and was finishing a thru-hike of the Appalachian Trail. When I was done and set out to walk again, one of the fellows offered to drive me to Monson. His generosity saved me time and the money I would have paid for the shuttle. It was nice to get the financial and very friendly break from my final Trail Angel!

The day was absolutely spectacular. Neither water, sky, clouds, nor trees could have been more crisp and glorious. This bearded hiker? Well, he was a little weary.

After supper, I turned in and fell sound asleep, ready to hit the trail in the morning. And then, **KNOCK! KNOCK! KNOCK!**

"The hospital called. They want you to come in right away."

"Okay."

I got up and got ready to go in. The hostel hosts would take care of Theo, so I brought them his food. They were dog-friendly, with a slow moving, long-haired, black and white mutt of their own. I knew Theo wouldn't go anywhere without me, especially as long as my gear and my smells were still at Shaw's.

IV Drip

Monday, October 10, Patient Day 1. In the hospital I was told that the fluid from the bursa showed signs of infection, and they wanted me on an IV drip immediately.

A nurse tried to put the IV in my left hand but gave up after two tries. I was nothing but bones, muscle, and skin with veins popping out all over. Another nurse with a little more experience got the job done, and the drip started.

I adjusted to my private hospital room and drifted off in time.

Awaiting Lab Results

Tuesday, October 11, Patient Day 2. I was "enjoying" my hospital breakfast at 7:30 when the aspirating doctor came in to check on me. He expected results later in the day or tomorrow.

I had a quiet confidence that everything was going to be all right and that I would leave the hospital and finish the trail in time, even though it was only four days from Baxter Park's usual closing time. I had confirmed with Patty at the ATC in Monson that the closing had been officially extended to October 22nd, 11 days away. The timing seemed too good not to be just right for our finish.

I called Bonnie and gave her the scoop.

I watched some TV and sat on my duff propped up in bed as one bag after another dripped into my vein.

Many of the doctors at this hospital did not live in Greenville but came from Bangor. Delivering the best of medicine here in the North required providers to travel.

Lunch. Supper. Day 2 in Charles A. Dean Memorial Hospital, Greenville, Maine.

I Think We Should Operate

Wednesday, October 12, Patient Day 3. After breakfast the doctor came in to discuss my case. During the night he had been thinking about my shoulder and thought he should operate. He wanted to remove the bursa and clean out the shoulder joint to be sure there was no infection remaining. I was disinclined but discussed the situation with him at length.

I called Bonnie and an orthopedist friend at home whose specialty was the shoulder and asked him what he thought.

"I think you should have the surgery," he said.

"Is it true that infection in the shoulder joint is extremely painful?" I asked.

"Yes."

I was not convinced surgery was necessary.

After lunch, the doctor came back. "In order to schedule the surgery, we will have to coordinate with the anesthesiologists, and they are not available until tomorrow."

He gave me more time to think about it. I considered my friend's advice, and when the doc came back, I said, "Okay. Let's do the surgery. What will I be like post-op?"

"You'll be in a sling for six weeks."

"I can't do that."

I Reasoned

More time passed. When he checked again, I told him I was not going to have the surgery for three reasons:

- I feel better ever since you aspirated my arm.
- If I had infection in the joint, I would be in excruciating pain, and I'm not.
- If I had infection in my bloodstream, I would have an elevated temperature and I don't.

He did not refute anything I said, but he did caution me about the rigors of the trail and the need for frequent rescues. He sent in an EMT to talk with me about his many rescues and to try to convince me that I should not continue.

We had a private conversation, and I reasoned with him the same way I had with the doctor. He got it entirely. He was all in.

I was going to finish!

Severe Clear

Thursday, October 13, Patient Day 4. I was watching the weather on TV, and the forecast for Maine was what pilots call "severe clear."

Often pilots will receive a warning of "severe thunderstorms en route," but when the weather couldn't be better, a traffic controller might say, "severe clear." That was the report for northern Maine for the next three days: a high-pressure system with warm temperatures and nothing but clear skies and sunshine.

We were coming into the last half of October in the far North. Katahdin was 13 feet shy of a mile high. Anything could happen, and I didn't want to risk not finishing. I would leave the hospital and head for Katahdin. The 100-mile wilderness could wait.

Since I declined the surgery, I could be discharged.

Abol Bridge

I called Shaw's for a shuttle, had breakfast, and got ready for a noon pickup.

Back at the hostel, Theo seemed content and greeted me with a wagging tail as if I'd just been down the hall to the bathroom. He had been happy.

Poet and Hippie-Chick were leaving to visit friends to the south, but a would-be thru-hiker was helping them out and could shuttle me to Abol Bridge when I was ready. The assistant, who was in his 20s and had met Poet and Hippie-Chick the year before, had gotten hooked on trail life. He was a serious-minded and helpful person with long, dark hair in dreads. I liked him. He had to do a run or two, after which he could drive me the 100 miles north to Abol Bridge.

I double-checked our food bucket and packed for Katahdin. We were in the homestretch. We had rounded 3rd and were beginning our slide to the plate. We were bound for the foot of Maine's lonely, highest peak, the reigning Monarch of the North.

We were on the road by early afternoon. It was a beautiful, promising fall day. By 4:00, I had set up camp on the Penobscot

River about 10 miles south of the Great Lady. Theo and I walked to the point where the AT meets the Golden Road over the Penobscot River. This dirt logging road was the northern end of the 100-mile wilderness—where we would end our hike many days hence. We had skipped the wilderness to summit Katahdin while the weather was good. We would return to the beginning of the wilderness later and hike to this point: OUR FINISH!

I took pictures of the Mighty Monarch from the river at different points. She stands there, speechless, silent, supreme, an honorable, immovable majesty, demanding homage with not a word or gesture.

The Mighty Monarch in her splendor

Something inside me bowed to her, but, though we doted on her, it is she who serves. Her promise is immutable, sublime, sure. She is completely reliable. From high above, her quiet invitation is unmistakable. Come.

For over 2,000 miles, in all four seasons, I had come.

It was a lonely night on the Penobscot. Just the usual stuff before bed. Alone. Late in the hiking season, but still going.

A long time ago, an unspoken contract I made with nature, and the vision and handiwork of the many humans who built the trail, brought me here. Something that happened when I was 12 had captured my heart, had sunk into my soul, and I had no choice but to obey its command. It was as irresistible as the Monarch's whisper.

Base of Katahdin

One goal for the new day. Get to Katahdin Stream Campground, also known as The Birches, at the foot of the mountain. It was one of the three days for which the weather forecast in the hospital predicted warm, sunny, and clear.

Being somewhat of a purist, after packing up in the morning, I took Theo to the point we had visited the night before. We hiked from there into Katahdin, just as if we had finished the 100-mile wilderness and continued on. Instead, we had the detour and delay in Greenville at the hospital. If Theo and I were to reach Katahdin's summit before it and the Park closed, we had to do it now. The 100-mile wilderness would come later.

As the profile in AWOL makes clear, the hike to the base of Katahdin is without climbs. It is as if the earth pushed up this lonely mountain of boulders and then collapsed for miles around from the effort.

The trek is not without its challenges, however. There are risky river crossings, and rocks and roots for sure, but it was a lovely day with a single goal: the foot of Katahdin. A sign made it clear that no domestic animals were allowed in the park. But Theo was a service dog and he could not be refused. I had long been grateful for the advice I'd received to register him.

Signs near the start of the trail warn that advance reservations are required at The Birches for hikers who have hiked a minimum of 100 miles (for example, the wilderness). I did not have reservations and had not hiked the wilderness. I had no choice but to risk it. It was late in the season; maybe they'd cut me some slack.

After a colorful hike, we arrived at the campsite at 2:15 and crossed a footbridge to the ranger station to register. Inside I learned about the daypack routine. You could bring your backpack to the ranger station and leave it on the porch, no matter the hour of your departure. Daypacks were provided in a bin. You could help yourself and return it when you came back.

I was told there wasn't any separate sleeping site left for me, but I could see if I could share the site of another hiker (as on Memorial Day in the Shenandoah when I met Echo). Back across the footbridge was a pavilion. A female hiker was set up nearby for the night. She said it was fine with her if we camped in her area. I found a spot on the other side of the pavilion, closer to the road leading to the trail up Katahdin. I pitched and got the lay of the land.

When suppertime came, I cooked and ate in the pavilion. Apart from requesting her permission to share her spot, I didn't see my tent-site mate again.

As my day was drawing to a close, a ranger stopped to say that my dog should be on a leash. But he didn't force the point. He did, however, all but beg me not to take Theo up Katahdin. He spoke of moose stomping on dogs and of dogs falling and breaking legs.

He was doing his job, but I doubted he had ever thru-hiked. I didn't feel superior, but I carried a resolve that had only thickened as the days and months wore on. Theo was my hiking companion. I couldn't imagine finishing this adventure without him. We would have to assume the risks. I didn't argue with the young ranger, but respected his points and remained silent. In time he went on his way. I set my phone alarm for 3:00 a.m. and crawled in for the night.

Katahdin

October 15 is the day Baxter usually closes, and camping in the park after that date is not permitted.

Theo and I were up at 3:00 and hiking by 4:30 on the 15th. I had exchanged what I had hauled from Georgia for a daypack. We would reach the summit and be back down by day's end. I would get my gear when we returned. Our shuttle would meet us at Abol Campground at the base of the very steep Abol Trail at 5:30 and drive us back to The Birches and then back to Shaw's.

Over 100 lakes can be viewed from Katahdin

It was still dark as we headed into the woods. An ominous sign read:

YOU ARE ENTERING MAINE'S LARGEST WILDERNESS

- YOUR SAFETY IS YOUR RESPONSIBILITY.

- SET A TURNAROUND TIME AND STICK TO IT.

- YOUR DESTINATION IS YOUR SAFE RETURN TO THE TRAILHEAD.

- RESCUERS CAN BE MANY HOURS IN ARRIVING.

The doctor had tried to dissuade me because of the stories that prompted this sign. I did not disrespect him. I did not discount him. But something inside me would not be dissuaded. I didn't think that I was being bullheaded. I was operating on another plane. Not superior. Ordained.

My certainty did not rise to the level of "Get thee behind me, Satan," but it was along that path. It was fueled by a similar energy. It came from another realm than the one my fine doctor inhabited. No judgment. A different drummer.

As we emerged from the woods on the way to our royal audience with Katahdin, the sun began to shine upon Her Majesty. Steep climbs beginning at the base brought us out of the shadows and into the bright light of day, illuminating the regal scene. Mountains leading to the Queen seemed to bow before her. The sky above crowned her in glory. Hundreds of lakes were like goblets of wine pressed out through the ages to pay her homage and nourish her spirit.

To climb this mile-high mountain of geologic history under a clear sky was a gift beyond telling. I also know, deep in my soul, that had our climb been in the deepest mist or coldest frost, or the firmament's deluge, I would have bowed as deeply to "Greatest Mountain." For that she was, standing alone in Maine's northern wilderness, miles from civilization. Hers was the crown thru-hikers sought for their efforts. A room full of earthly diadems could not mean more than touching the sign at her summit. It was as if Mother Mary herself placed her tender hand on the cheeks of all who finish, in reverence for their deed and the ancient goal that prompted it.

At a few places en route to the summit, I had to hoist my canine. At one in particular, I got out rope from Theo's saddlebags and looped it around a hook of rebar. Then I tried to boost him up as I had in Vermont four years before, pulling and lifting at the same time. I wasn't sure we'd succeed. It even occurred to me that I might have to turn around. But the thought entered my mind as only the

Theo ready for more steep climbing

vaguest possibility, something so remote that it couldn't possibly come to pass.

Soon Mark, a young, very fit hiker, came by. He climbed to the top of the ledge to which I was trying to lift Theo. He knelt as I lifted Theo in his pack as high as I could. From his knees, Mark reached toward the dog, almost to the point of falling off. When he got hold of the handle at the top of Theo's saddlebags, he hoisted him up with gentle strength, admirable to see.

Farther up the trail, after Mark had disappeared, I once again needed assistance with my buddy. This time a middle-aged hiker named Bill helped me out.

Hey! All we have up here is each other.

After we emerged from the woods, we had over three hours of steep climbing until we reached more moderate terrain nearer our goal. It was 10:30, six hours since we left camp. We still had more than an hour before we'd reach the summit and the iconic sign. I knew the summit was up there above the massive, sloping mountainside of nothing but large stones.

As always, even with the summit in view. . .just keep going. . . until gradually. . .step after rocky step. . .I saw about 30 to 40 people at the summit. They were milling about as if waiting for a vision, a visitation from the spirit that had moved them for months on end to this place.

The day was breathtaking, as was the accomplishment of each thru-hiker who made it here. No one had champagne that I saw, but it wasn't necessary. The air, the day, the place were intoxicating enough. Spirits soared as we each had our obligatory picture taken at the KATAHDIN sign.

Theo and I were not finished. We had the 100-mile wilderness to go. Nonetheless, it was a grand occasion to embrace the mountain who had called to us from so far away. Over the course of the trail, we had climbed the equivalent of 16 ascents up Everest from sea level, and our effort had brought us closer to heaven than we had ever been before. Katahdin had kept her promise and we had kept ours.

Bill took pictures of Theo and me at Greatest Mountain's summit. I could not raise my right arm over my head. But more important, Theo was at my side. He stood by me in total silence, with, I suspect, not a single word on his mind. He took every step to get there without complaint, and getting there was my goal, not his. With his saddlebags carrying some of my load, he was a silent servant, devoted to the one he followed. I was deeply humbled by this unfathomable animal bond, silent, serene, and steadfast beyond words.

My view of the Knife Edge Trail on the north side of the mountain easily confirmed my prior decision that this was not the trail for a one-armed, 75-year-old hiker with a dog, whose ride was meeting him on the south side. The Abol Trail would be challenging enough.

After pictures, we ate lunch and headed back down. It had taken us 7½ hours to summit, and it was now after noon. By 12:30 we would have only five hours to meet our driver at the Abol Campground.

Knife Edge on the north side of Katahdin

The descent down the Abol Trail was not as long as our climb, but it was very steep. Some of the trail passes through scrub brush in sandy soil. Recent rerouting caused sand to spread out over the rocks, making them extra slippery and treacherous some of the way.

The forest of glorious colors below was our destination. When we got to the base, we had perhaps a mile through woods to the campground. We arrived promptly at 5:30. As

A steep and, at times, slippery descent on the Abol Trail

we walked through the area looking for our driver, he was walking in the opposite direction looking for us. In our search, we passed a ranger without comment.

The shuttle took us to The Birches where I delivered my day-pack, picked up my backpack, and loaded it in the van.

Then a ranger approached to talk to me about Theo. "He's supposed to be on a leash."

The ranger at Abol Campground had called ahead to alert him to a dog off-leash. I had no answer and no defense. The life-threatening descent was behind us. A leash there could have been deadly for one or both of us.

"Let me see his service dog registration."

I showed it to him. He went to his vehicle and checked something about the organization that issued the card. I suspect he was wise to the ease of such registrations. He asked me why he was a service dog; I told him about my knee surgery. He asked to see my driver's license. It was getting late.

As the ranger was writing my ticket, our driver was getting eager to get underway. No one, I had learned, wants to drive through the Maine woods after dark. Moose are big, hard to see, and can step out onto a road anywhere. To hit one can be fatal for animal and driver.

"Officer. My driver is eager to get started because of moose and driving after dark."

In short order, he gave me a citation. A $250.00 fine for having Theo off-leash. I pocketed the paper work, swallowed the bitter taste ending my time in Baxter State Park, loaded my co-conspirator into the back of the van, and climbed into the passenger's seat for the three-hour, dark ride back to the hostel.

Zero at Shaw's

That Sunday, October 16, I decided to take a zero before heading into the 100-mile wilderness. I needed to regroup after the hospital and Katahdin. Nothing would stop me now from finishing. We had accomplished the northern terminus of the Appalachian Trail. We were home free—sort of.

I spent the day relaxing and getting ready for the final push. When nighttime came, I went to the Lakeside House for supper. The bar at the back was crowded and noisy and didn't suit my quiet frame of mind so I sat in the front. I had a good meal and headed back to the hostel for my final night under roof.

Into the Wilderness

Monday morning, October 17, I enjoyed my fourth and final breakfast at Shaw's, my last home-cooked meal before finishing the trail. I figured we would need the food-drop at Jo-Mary Road, 58.5 miles into the wilderness, so I planned to call from White Cap Mountain to say when I'd be there. I would also call Bonnie from that spot to give her an update on our progress so she could arrange her flight and car rental to meet us.

Heading into the wilderness was hard at this point. I didn't dread it, but I had little to no excitement about disappearing into the woods for what surely would be a 10-day, lonely ordeal, likely to turn wet and cold. Time, loneliness, and the effort to finish weighed heavily on my spirit.

Theo and I entered the woods in the morning and began hiking. For 25 miles leading to Barren Mountain, the trail had a sawtooth profile, up and down many mounds. Barren itself was a reputed "tough climb." Slowly we made our way over a rustling gold and pale green carpet, running like a ribbon through a fantasy land with brilliant colors held aloft in cool, liquid sunlight by thin grey trunks.

Stop and See

On Wilderness Day 2 we continued climbing over larger mounds, with the same wonderland of gold and soft green colors overhead and underfoot. The views were serene and undulating, as if the earth were calling out to the weary:

> STOP AND SEE
> BREATHE AND LIVE
> THE REIGN OF GLORY IS BEFORE YOU

Every step through this fantasyland took us deeper into the wilderness, farther and farther from the warmth and security of human connection, closer and closer to what would be our last steps.

Patty Harding at the Monson Visitor Center had told me that the only thing she had trouble with in the wilderness was Barren Mountain. I found it tough but doable, one step at a time. We crossed the crest of Barren and then stealth-camped near Cloud Pond Lean-to.

The next day brought steep climbs up Fourth Mountain and Columbus Mountain. We just kept pushing through the wilderness—our 243rd day of moving northward. After passing mile 2,100, we camped for the night by a stream.

Gulf Hagas — Last Call

After a long, slow climb up Gulf Hagas Mountain, I had enough signal to call Bonnie. It was good to hear her voice in the lonely wilderness, but we didn't talk long. I checked with Shaw's to tell them where I was and to discuss our food drop. They asked me to update them when I got to the summit of White Cap.

Thunderstorm

At the Sidney Tappan Campsite, I put my phone in a mesh pouch that hung from the wall of the tent at my head. In the middle of the night we were hit with a fierce thunderstorm, which soaked my phone. It was dead.

After breakfast and packing, we climbed West Peak, Hay Mountain, and then White Cap, arriving at the top a little before noon. I tried to activate my phone so I could report to Shaw's and make final arrangements with Bonnie. It briefly displayed a message saying it needed a system reset. I plugged in my backup battery, but after an hour of trying, it still wasn't working. I had my tablet, but I needed an Internet connection along with it to communicate with anyone.

Many days in the wilderness were wet and oh, so beautiful

We began our descent off White Cap. AWOL notes: "View of Katahdin from north side of mountain." This would be a milestone for most NOBOs, but we'd already been there and back. Besides, today was overcast. Cut off from the outside world, we carried on. I'd get to Jo-Mary Road, a day away, and figure things out from there.

We passed the Logan Brook Lean-to around 2:30 and came to our destination for the night at East Branch Lean-to around 5:00. I was almost asleep when a hiker showed up, guided by his headlamp, and quietly got himself settled. We chatted a bit before turning in. I told him about my dead phone, and he said he'd see if he had enough charge and signal in the morning for me to make my calls. He was southbound and had just forded a fast-moving river. We'd face it first thing in the morning.

Jo-Mary Road

On waking, my shelter-mate tried to call without success. I told him about Shaw's and Bonnie and asked if he would try again when he got to the summit of White Cap. He didn't seem to grasp my situation. I'd done my best to no avail. Perhaps he was out of charge.

At 9:11, I took a picture with my tablet of the stream we were about to ford. It was indeed fast-moving and rocky. At our first ford in the wilderness, I had put on my Crocs, keeping my boots and socks dry for the other side. This time my boots were so wet from rain and leaves, I didn't bother to remove them.

I had to take each step very carefully. I gingerly located my boot between or among several submerged rocks and made sure my foot was secure before transferring my weight to it. With the force of the water, and the certainty that the rocks were slippery, I dared not step on them lightly one by one. I held tightly to the handle of Theo's saddlebags so he wouldn't wash away.

We made it to the other side without incident and kept walking. It started to snow. We were cold and wet. The leaves were colorful but fewer now. The season, the cold, and the weight of the snow were stripping the trees. Little puddles of water collected in the countless leaves on the ground, and so I walked, day in and day out, in water with wet boots and wet feet. My hands and toes were becoming numb. My gloves served only to separate my fingers, exposing them to cold air all the way around. Mittens would have allowed them to huddle together, reducing the chances of their freezing. Getting my hands and gloves wet would make matters worse.

The goal for the night was Jo-Mary Road. There was a slight rise after fording and then we were onto a long, level stretch. In time the long, dirt road from civilization came into view. It was 3:30. To the

Theo checking on me in the 100-mile wilderness

right was a bridge over Cooper Brook, which was now high from all the rains.

We crossed the road, and I pitched the tent in a clearing not more than 20 feet from the travel lane. I set up everything inside the tent and crawled in to get warm, or at least to get out of the breeze. I had to conserve my fuel for the few days ahead. All I had left was a small, partially used canister.

I went to the brook and collected water to filter. I was hanging the filter bag from a tree on the side of the tent away from the road when a logging truck came by. I was using my left arm to do the hanging because I could not raise my right arm. Nor could I raise it to signal to the driver that I needed help. He passed right by.

While I was in the tent over the next several hours, I heard a couple of trucks go by, but there was no way I could get out of the tent in time to flag them.

In spite of the cold, I decided to take off my white shirt and hang it from a branch I would position at the bridge. I found a small, dead pine tree to use as a flagpole and hung my shirt. A couple of trucks went by without stopping.

Now that it was getting dark, I moved my shirt to another location that enabled me to angle the small tree more like a flagpole fixed to a house. I set my headlamp to strobe and put it inside the shirt. A truck went by without stopping.

I decided to turn in for the night and, on waking, pace the road all day if necessary.

Truck Stop

The next day was Monday, October 24th. We awoke, ate, and "hit the road." I was determined to keep pacing back and forth until someone came along.

Maybe Shaw's would send someone. I considered how they might reason: 1) He's hurt, unable to make it to Jo-Mary Road, and is without service so he can't call; or 2) He hasn't called because his phone died and he's already at Jo-Mary Road, keeping the pace he had predicted.

If no one from Shaw's showed up, surely there would be another truck in time.

Soon a large 18-wheeler came over the knoll west of me, and I waved him down. He stopped and opened his window. I told him my plight and that I had put out a white shirt to stop someone.

"I saw that last night but didn't know what it was," he said somewhat incredulously.

He was a decent looking, rough-hewn, middle-aged guy. I told him I needed him to call Shaw's Hostel in Monson.

"I don't have any service out here."

"No. But you're going into town, right?"

"Yes. That's 35 miles away."

"That's all right."

I gave him the number for Shaw's and asked him to give the person answering two messages:

> Sojo is at Jo-Mary Road and needs his food drop.
> His cell phone got wet and died.
>
> Would someone from Shaw's please call my wife,
> Bonnie, at [phone numbers] and tell her I will be at
> Abol Bridge on Thursday at 3:00.

I wanted to pick a time that I was all but certain I could make so she would not be waiting around for me in the cold. Of course my timing and hers were dependent on my food arriving soon, so Theo and I could get underway.

The trucker would have to get to town and make the call. Then Shaw's would have to find a driver, and the driver would need to travel the 1½ hours to where we were. We could wait.

Food-Drop

A driver in his 60s arrived in time and delivered our bucket loaded with the food I had stored in it. He also had hot coffee and something for me to eat. I was cold and glad for both. Hippie-Chick reached Bonnie with my message. All was well.

I added the food to my pack and we were on the trail around 1:00, heading north into our final days. Of course, all Theo knew was that we were moving again. Bless that dear dog!

We crossed a few more streams and passed nearby lakes, whose deep, grey waters made the air cold, adding to the bleakness under deep, grey skies.

With just a slight bump at the end of a long, level stretch, we came to the Potaywadjo Spring Lean-to around 5:00. Google tells me this word may mean "wind blows over the mountain."

Their Love

The next day was again a long, level stretch ending with a bigger bump this time: Nesuntabunt Mountain. Again AWOL notes: "16 mile line-of-sight view of Katahdin's summit from here." Still overcast.

Incidentally, a section of trail that AWOL says has a "level" profile, most certainly does not mean smooth. Nor does it mean flat. I had long ago noted that the scale of the AWOL profile does not show a climb if it's between 50 and 100 feet.

I discovered endless subtle, and not-so-subtle, opportunities to fall in this final stretch of the AT. While some hikers were able to make time on these relatively long, level sections, I had to take extreme care over their pervasive roots and rocks.

When we got home, Bonnie said, "You were running on fumes at the end." She was right. I clung to my family during this final push. After a couple of wet days and cold nights, I repeated another mantra slowly and deliberately to a measured pace.

> THEIR. . .LOVE. . .WILL. . .SEE. . .ME. . .THROUGH.
> THEIR. . .LOVE. . .WILL. . .SEE. . .ME. . .THROUGH.

I would say this softly to myself, meaning every word and building my conscious awareness of my surroundings with each utterance. I had been alone for nine days, and wet and cold for four of those. I had two more to go.

In spite of the cold and the dark coming on, we had to make tracks because I had given a time certain for when we would finish. We descended toward Crescent Pond as night fell. The woods were thick, and I had a strong sense that Theo and I were very much alone in this deep, dense wilderness. I could feel the air turning colder as we neared the pond with snow at the water's edge.

I could hardly find a spot to pitch the tent, but it was getting late and I would make do. Because of the awkward terrain and limited ways to extend the guys, I had to improvise with one of the vestibule flaps to make it stay closed.

I got water from Crescent Pond and hung it across from the tent. My hands and feet were wet and cold, but I still slept pretty well that night. We had only one more night to go, but I wasn't really thinking that way. As always, we just took each day as its own challenge. Theo and I had survived much, and we would survive whatever lay ahead.

Last Night

Next morning I took one picture of the snow at the pond before leaving and another of the footprint left by the tent after packing it in its outside pouch. It was 8:30. The woods were wet-lovely.

We had lunch at the Rainbow Stream Lean-to and then moved on.

Hiking this afternoon seemed to go on and on. I was looking for a turn-off for Little Beaver Pond just off the trail. Get us to water and we would bed down.

Finally, through fairly dense pine woods, I saw the trail east and followed it. It wound through trees and climbed around a bend to a knoll overlooking Little Beaver Pond below.

I found a spot for the tent, got water, and began filtering. I cooked supper and turned in.

I felt no elation—no MY LAST NIGHT ON THE TRAIL! WE DID IT! It was just another night. We could have had a hundred more to go, and I would have experienced it the same way. Of course I knew, almost devoid of sentiment, that this was our last night on the trail. My immediate challenges were now to meet my wife and get ourselves home.

Father

Thursday, October 27th. The last day on the trail. The feeling was not quite ho-hum, but I had very little emotion. Sort of like the recovery room after surgery. I wasn't ready to take on the world. I wasn't in a mood to party or be exuberant. I needed to be quiet for a while. I needed to get my bearings.

I fixed myself a warm cup of coffee and the fuel canister gave out. Perfection! I had slept well and had a good breakfast. I was ready to pack for the last time and move forward to greet my wife.

I have no pictures of this final campsite all set up, but I do have one of the footprint, barely noticeable, in the spongy pine needles. I remember well hanging my gravity filter bag on a small pine tree across from where the tent stood.

We moved out, back the winding side trail through the low pines to the AT and turned right, northward, to Abol Bridge. My family knew of our location because of my GPS posts. They tried to communicate to me their sentiments on my finishing, but I wouldn't see or hear them until I got home and got my phone up and running.

My oldest son texted me, "If I read it correctly, you have only 7.4 miles to go." He was right.

My second son left me a message at 4:00 a.m. his time in Australia, where he was lecturing on Saint Pope John Paul II. He was so appreciative of what I had accomplished, saying that he thought it was significant in the whole West bloodline. He thanked me for the gift my accomplishment was to the whole family and our posterity.

My niece Hollie's voicemail message was filled with awe and gratitude for me because of what I had done, saying "I uncle-love you."

In time I would feel the significance of finishing the AT.

In prep school, I had looked out over silhouetted pines standing tall in the cold, winter nights of northern Massachusetts, the sky deep orange-red behind them, and confronted perhaps the deepest mystery of all—someday I would be a father. A FATHER!

Well, I have fathered five, and they are all grown. Now the family I needed so desperately for each step was finishing the trail with me. My oldest had been in tears as I crossed into Maine nearly a month and a half before, and he knew my steps now. They were also celebrating even on the other side of the planet.

I had done the trail because of something that stirred in me when I was just a boy away at camp. It took root in me and never left. Its work in my soul will never be done. I hold it aloft as the father of Kunta Kinte in *Roots* held him aloft, as a newborn, like a sacrificial gift to some divine presence in the night sky. This accomplishment rests upon an unseen altar. It is a humble sacrifice of my spirit to my progeny, to life itself, to the gift of traveling this planet for a time.

This was for me. I did it because I had to.

But it is also for all who follow me. May they take sustenance from the fact that their relative walked through the wilderness at the age of 75 with his dog—because he had to.

Our lives are ordained. Let us live our individual mandates to the full—you, my children, my friends, even you whom I pass on the street and will never see again. All of you, whoever you are, however long from now you walk this earth, I give you all the love God put in my heart beyond measure. I cannot contain it.

I pray that as you face your days, you are able to ride the torrent that rises up within—that you ride it for all its worth and never, never, never give up on its promise swelling within you. Live large, knowing there is no judgment in the smooth waters of a river turning white over rocks.

A torrent of life has compelled me these many months. Soon I will reunite with the woman God gave me to be my partner. The woman he has given me to love and care for—to cherish. It is she and our family who have seen me through.

Final Steps

Theo and I climbed Rainbow Ledges where AWOL says there is a view of Katahdin—again, not for us on another grey day. The Rainbow summit was a mound of rock like the back of a whale, reminiscent of other peaks in the North.

Before long we could see Hurd Brook Lean-to with its "baseball bat floor" (AWOL) off to our left. We ate lunch and moved out.

I remember well coming upon the last boardwalk over marshy land just minutes before the Golden Road came into view.

We walked toward that road at the northern end of the 100-mile wilderness, perhaps a little bit numb, just another series of steps forward. The leaves on the ground were now more tan than colorful. I was aware of their rustling underfoot.

For fun, I filmed and counted my final steps: 4,999,995, 4,999,996, 4,999,997, 4,999,998, 4,999,999, 5,000,000.

I took my last step on the AT on Thursday, October 27, 2016, at 1:45 p.m.

The final step

Just as I counted that last step, a heavily loaded logging truck came whizzing past from the west.

A Short Cold Wait

Theo and I turned right on the road we had hiked before, across Abol Bridge over the Penobscot River to the camp store. I took another picture of Katahdin. She was bedecked in five inches of snow. An ascent, if permitted, would be very difficult going. The hike up and down had taken me 13 hours. It would be impossible for me to make it up and back in one day in the conditions now. Climbing Katahdin early was the right move.

The camp store was closed. The air was cold. Bonnie would not be arriving for a little over an hour.

I took off Theo's saddlebags and my pack and left them at the side of the road for Bonnie to see. We huddled under an eave of the store, hoping for protection against the cold.

The Monarch under 5 inches of snow

Nearby, a garbage can was filled with paper and other fairly soft trash in a large, clear plastic bag. I took it out of the can, tied it tightly at the top, and stuffed it into a corner to sit on until Bonnie appeared.

Theo did what he always did when his pack was off. What he had done at Abington Gap Shelter on April 19, Day 59, when I had to climb down a steep hill for water. What he did again a few days later, north of Damascus, Virginia, on April 22, Day 62, when he

almost went over an embankment. Countless times. In dust, in leaves, in snow, on rock—wherever—Theo rolled on his back, twisting with all sorts of contortions like an injured caterpillar. I'm sure it was ecstasy for him.

A couple of vehicles came by from the east. A pickup truck and a white sedan. I hadn't been sitting more than 10 or 15 minutes when a shiny, black car showed up and slowed. I saw a familiar face inside. Stiff and tired, I made my way to the driver's door for a hug. A lot more pleasant for me than it was for her, I'm sure. More on this later.

It was not an ecstatic reunion with both of us jumping up and down. Instead, we both kind of shrugged: "Well, here we are. It's done."

I put my gear in the trunk and Theo on the back seat. Then I crawled in front next to Bonnie.

She had received my projected arrival time and was prepared to come at 3:00, but then thought, "What if he arrives early?" And, being the extremely thoughtful person she is, she came early—just in case. . . . It's beautiful when two people love and care for each other.

Across the Lake

We turned and headed for Millinocket.

Now the interior of a car is close quarters. Even though I had just spent 10 days in the wilderness in the same clothes, not to mention the eight months of odor our packs accumulated, Bonnie did not put up a fuss about the way Theo and I smelled. And she even hugged me on arrival. But she insisted—never mind the cold air—that we open the windows!

At Shaw's, I had made a reservation for a place in town which Bon learned could be canceled without charge. She had come in the day before and scoped out the place. Because a tasteful décor means a lot to her, she opted to look around.

What she found was to die for. I was almost too dead to appreciate it but, without a doubt, this, too, was Shangri-La! While I showered, Bon searched out a groomer for Theo. It had been the better part of a year, and he surely needed some attention. The fur under his pack and beyond was matted in clumps, and I'm sure it smelled. Not that I could tell.

As a service dog, he could fly home with us. Bon had been very clear when she made the reservations that her husband was coming home with a service dog. "Is there going to be any problem getting the dog on the plane?"

"No, Ma'am."

"Are you sure?"

"Yes, Ma'am."

We hoped she was right, and, in deference to the passengers and the public generally, we needed to spruce up the canine.

Bon found a groomer who could see Theo at 10:00 the next morning. Now it was time to dress in the new clothes Bon had purchased for me. They would fit a scarecrow, but I managed to squeeze myself into them and was more than ready to eat!

After a great meal in Millinocket, we returned to our room and soon crawled into the high, spacious bed. At the foot was a sitting area next to a wall of large windows looking out on the lake, with Katahdin in the distance beyond. What a fitting end to an adventure I could not have completed without the one next to me, an end with far more comfort and charm than I had known for months.

A Banquet

Friday, October 28. Our flight out of Bangor was not until the afternoon, so we had time for a satisfying breakfast at the lodge, then a stop at the groomer, and an unhurried ride to the airport.

We sat at a big table in the large kitchen, and the husband and wife owners served us incredible French toast with eggs, juice, and coffee. As we got to know each other in casual conversation, in view across the lake was the countenance of the Lady whom Theo and I had greeted cheek to cheek. The deep emotion of all that led up to our hike, all that occurred during it, and the endless, even infinite, resource it has proved to be since, are more than can be grasped in a morning view out a window. It was all there like a spiritual banquet to be consumed slowly, bit by bit over time.

Our hosts were warm and kind. They fed us well, and we loved hearing tales of the lodge.

Groomer and Gift

Theo got great attention at Gail's Gentle Grooming in East Millinocket. His collar was so dirty and smelly that Gail put a burnt-orange bandana around him in its place.

I had not driven for months on end, and I didn't miss it at all. Bonnie, who endured my years of shakedown hikes, my intense preparations over months before departure, the endless trail talk (still), and my prolonged absence, drove, even through snow, to fetch me home.

I don't know how to key into Bonnie's goodness any more than I know how to digest the trail. She has laid down her life for me—for us—for our family. She rarely thinks of herself. She will deny this and claim that she is selfish, but countless are the times she sets her own desires aside to tend to the needs of someone else. She cannot think ill of anyone—literally—and she cannot harbor anger or a grudge. She is a treasure, a companion, and a gift in my life far beyond my deserts—no less a mystery than Katahdin rising and the winds howling.

Canceled

When we got to the airport we learned that our flight had been canceled, there were no more flights out that day, and all motels were full because of the cancellations.

Regardless, we tried the airport motel just across from the concourse. It was supposed to be full and expensive, but the kind gentleman behind the desk had one room left and cut us a break on the price. And Theo could stay.

We settled into our third-floor room where, to Bonnie's chagrin, I laid my wet backpack on the radiator to dry out. I insisted, and we went down for supper in the motel's quiet, comfortable restaurant.

As we enjoyed a cocktail, Bon returned to the subject of the backpack. Having lived alone with Theo for more than eight months, civilizing me was going to take a little work. Bon was up to it. I tried to convince her that everything would be fine if the pack stayed where it was.

"Oh, Soren. Please don't do that!"

"Why? What's the matter?"

"Soren! That thing stinks to high heaven. It's going to make the whole room smell terrible."

"Oh, c'mon. It's not that bad."

"Soren! It is! It's horrible! Please!"

I guess she knew something I didn't. I obliged.

I rose, found a waitress, and asked if she had a large garbage bag I might have. She was gone for a bit and returned with two. I thanked her and headed for the room.

After removing my toiletries, I stuck the entire pack inside the garbage bag, tied it tightly at the top, and put in the back of the closet.

Bonnie was relieved.

We had a good meal and a good night, after I took Theo out to water the grass.

CHAPTER 16

Home

Surprise

On Saturday, October 29, we headed for the concourse, Theo in tow with his burnt-orange bandana around his neck. I checked my backpack, now released from its plastic confines, to the likely displeasure of the baggage handlers. Theo just marched onto the plane and down the aisle behind me, unperturbed. I put his saddlebags in an overhead bin. He fit under the seat in front of me and remained there peacefully until we landed in Philadelphia.

I hardly remember the flight or the ride home from the airport. But arriving at our back gate and heading into the house, I will never forget.

It was a bright, sunny day, and, as I came through the back gate with my pack over one shoulder, I said to Bonnie, "I think I'll just set up my tent so it can dry."

"Oh, why don't you come inside first?"

"Okay."

I opened the back door and went in. Bonnie knew what I would see. There in the foyer, sitting across two dining room chairs, was a 30" x 37½" picture of me on Franconia Ridge when the wind and

I were howling at each other, Theo at my feet—the finest of all moments on the AT.

I instantly filled with tears of joy and gratitude. How exhausted and blessed I was. I had received gifts beyond grasping. I was back in the bosom of my loving family. They were happy to have me home and proud of what I had done.

Depleted

A surprise at home brought instant tears

I have so much to say about arriving home and trying to adapt each day to living with my family and friends—in society.

I am a man of routines who does many things on autopilot. I take pleasure in small details of living. I feel blessed to enjoy the efficiency of small movements—emptying the coffee grounds from the drip coffee maker, and loading the dishwasher, followed by a little upward push with the toe of my left foot to close its door. I enjoy the rapid, front-wheels-up 180 with the lawn mower.

But I had forgotten all of these and more. For example, I had to relearn the steps I did automatically to get my breakfast ready. It took some time.

Bonnie observed that all I wanted to do was sit.

We have a second refrigerator in the basement. When I'd get something from there, climbing the stairs back up to the first floor would wear me out. More than once, I said, "I don't get it. I just climbed 510 mountains with 30 pounds on my back, and now I'm exhausted from just climbing these stairs carrying nothing."

My wife's inevitable response was a questioning look, meaning, "That's exactly why you're worn out." She was right.

For months I felt a little off-balance, and my legs hurt—both muscles and bones—when I walked on pavement. I couldn't lift a cup of coffee with my right arm because of the badly torn rotator cuff.

I was skin and bones at the end of 2016. I had lost 30 pounds. The veins under my skin were completely visible, and I knew every step of why that was. Every step had consumed some of my flesh and pushed a bit of what I had known as normal life out of my conscious mind, replacing it with trees, rocks, bogs, climbs, descents, rain, sleet, snow, cold, and heat.

Many were the times on the trail that Theo stood by me, squinting in rain, sleet, or driving snow, waiting as I took pictures or video, abiding his master's wishes without question. He stood silently in fierce elements, wearing his saddlebags and waiting. Was there ever such a sermon as this?

Please Don't Go

The AT, which has silently occupied most of my life, has sung its riches to me in full chorus, and I will mine its treasures for the rest of my days. Surely the AT never ends!

Yet after my first year back home, I began to wonder if I was mistaken. I noticed that I was less offended by TV ads of machines tearing up the earth in a grand show of dominance. I was being absorbed by society again, and I didn't like it.

Where are you, natural world? I miss you, silent one. I miss connecting with you. We've traveled a long way together. You were my partner in the wild. I can't let you go. But, if it happens, let it be only for a time. I trust that the breezes in the trees will return—that you will speak to me again. That the busyness of life in society will not drown you out. That I will still see you in the sunrise and its setting and know that you are always here with me in the beauty under heaven.

Beyond Katahdin

I was back in the realm of what I had known as normal life, but almost nothing was normal. So much was strange and troubling. I experienced a real sadness about my return. I love my family dearly. I could not have done the trail without their generous support. Their love DID see me through.

But I have experienced something that very few know much about. The vast majority of people have no real comprehension of how my psyche has changed. It's lonely. I miss the hikers who know. I miss the AT thru-hikers of 2016.

I know it's hard on those who have lost a major part of me. The sun on our backs is not the same. They haven't experienced the physical calluses, nor the mental and spiritual endurance, nor the constant grace of natural beauty on a thru-hike.

My dear family and friends have lost a part of me to an experience very much out of the ordinary, one causing profound changes, leaving me with a quiet, sad loneliness that lies somewhere in the distance beyond Katahdin. The Appalachian Trail runs through my conscious mind like a river, and only those who have done such a thru-hike know how deep and wide it is.

Many soldiers have hiked the Appalachian Trail to deal with the stress of returning from war. Earl Shaffer did so in 1948 over 124 days, averaging 17 miles per day. He had enlisted in the army in 1941, the year I was born, and served in the South Pacific until 1945. He hiked the Appalachian Trail "to walk the army out of my system, both mentally and physically."

Earl Shaffer's statement speaks to the profound influence of a thru-hike of the Appalachian Trail. If only for a time, it is powerful enough to displace memories of war.

Beauty

My doctor said it could take me six months to regain my weight. Bonnie got me whole milk, which I hadn't had in decades, ice cream, and anything she thought might bring me back to life and restore my energy. I went along with the program. After a few months of being on a heavy fat diet, people started saying, "You look good."

In addition to hearing loss, I have some problems with my feet. Their padding is gone. When I walk barefooted on hardwood floors, it's bone on wood and a little painful, but nothing I can't live with. I'm told that won't change. Also, my second toe on each foot is permanently curled without pain or loss of function.

I'd said often before doing the trail that I wanted my post-AT life to be different than my pre-AT life. It is. It is very clear to me now that I don't want the business of living to be my reason for living. I am blessed with knowing how little I need to survive and how great a home, orchestra, art gallery, and library our pristine planet is. Persisting within me is a natural reverence at odds with our all-consuming, throw-away culture.

In a recent science documentary I heard a commentator say with pride, "Twenty-first century technology allows man to master nature in more ways than ever before." His comment stood in stark contrast to the profound, lifelong connection I have felt with the natural world.

The AT allowed me to detox from society and the enculturation that had eroded the natural man and wild heart of my youth. The AT was hard, demanding endurance and perseverance, but I was free from the influences of a culture built on excessive consumption. We love what demands much of us. The AT demanded enough that it has forever changed me.

In a reflection not long after returning home, I wrote:

> Mother Nature cleans out debris in your soul. She baptizes you in her waters, cleanses you in her rainstorms,

strengthens you in her mountains, shelters you from the sun under her canopy, chastens you in her snows and frosts, and she never abandons you. In her indifference to your thoughts and situation, she is sublimely present, a perpetual provider and a supremely objective participant in your most superficial and most profoundly substantive life. She gave you birth, and she embraces you for eternity.

And this:

> I beg God to lead me on the trail ahead. May my experience, with the help of family and friends, inspire many to keep on going through life's difficulties. We can all trust that the effort builds the sinews of mind and heart, and that the scenery along the way pierces the soul and syncs the heart to a primordial drumbeat known only in surrender. Life is difficult but beautiful beyond reach, known best in the painful joy of reaching. . . .

I pray not to lose the chastening, not to fail to see the sweetness of the natural world, and never to turn my back on the wind that blows over the mountain.

The Ones We Love

I have too often taken Theo for granted. I don't know why. Perhaps it's because he doesn't know about the mortgage, and I have been anxious about such things my whole life. He can't help me with these concerns—directly. There's an out-of-sight, out-of-mind tendency in me regarding Theo. But when he comes into view, my worries fly away like bats at sunrise.

I've mentioned my loneliness on the trail many times, but how much worse it would have been without Theo. He was my constant companion.

Oh! I never told you about the third time I got angry with him. Theo often slept under the back vestibule of the tent. This was the perfect arrangement in a heavy, summer rain. I was out of my wet clothes inside, and wet-furred Theo was protected from the deluge outside.

One night in the North, I was in the tent getting ready to sleep. Theo was outside looking in at me through the front vestibule. Totally forgetting that I was addressing a dog's mind, I patted the ground in the back vestibule and said, "Theo, back here," trying, at the same time, to indicate with my other hand that he should go around to the back.

It was raining hard, and I was intent on getting him to go around the tent *outside*, while I remained inside.

As I patted the ground at the back vestibule and urged Theo to go there, he tried to bolt right through the tent over everything of mine that was dry. Of course he saw me patting the ground behind me, and he saw a direct path there through the tent. He was doing exactly what I wanted.

Sort of.

I pushed him back out. Now he was partially in the rain and partially under the front vestibule flaps.

Why wasn't he understanding that I wanted him to go around to the back?

I directed him again, and again he tried to bolt through the tent. NO, SIR! AROUND TO THE BACK!

After Theo's third effort to bolt through the tent, in complete exasperation, in my dry white socks and dry clothes for bed, I forced my way under the front vestibule flaps, pushing Theo out as I went, grabbed his ample coat, and both lifted and dragged him to the back.

I crawled back in the front, satisfied that he was where I wanted him to be on this wet night. Once calmed down inside the tent, I was full of apologies to my furry friend as he lay obediently in the back vestibule. I removed my wet things and managed to get a good night's sleep.

Of course, I had never taught him a "go around" command and had no right to get upset.

We always hurt the ones we love.

All Is Well

Since Theo has been in my life, I have seen a lot more of his face than I have of mine. I tend to think I am looking at a part of me when I look at him—his black nose, his flews which curve so sweetly from his nose to the back of his muzzle, his greying hair and brown eyes that look so attentively right at me, perhaps into me.

I hover over him in the morning, or any time during the day, when he insists or I can't resist. I get down on the floor and scratch his big, powerful, canine chest, rub his belly, and massage his powerful hind legs. I lean down, mindful of his space, to speak softly to him.

"Him-iiizz. 'Cause I love 'im. Him knows dat I love 'em. I can't help myself. It's your fault you know. God made only one of you, and you're da best! DA BEST! 'Cause him-iiizz."

Who needs grammar? Tone of voice tells him all he needs to know.

Theo was a silent partner on the trail, and he's a silent partner in my life. I don't know how I'll react when he goes to the endless trail in the sky, but there will most definitely be a hole in my heart and in each of my days.

I'm not one, however, to anthropomorphize my close companion. He's a dog. In some ways he's as incomprehensible to me as God is. I'm SOJO. Traveling on this earth somewhere between Theo and God.

While I am sometimes mindless of Theo, I doubt he is ever mindless of me. It never seemed so as we wandered together in the wild kingdom, and it certainly doesn't seem so since we're home. When

I go out for a while, he lies on the rug by the back door, eye on the portal that will bring me home.

We set out together, Theo and I, and we brought each other home again. Back in the familiar space of our lovely home in Lancaster, Pennsylvania, Theo took immediately to his normal routines. He went directly to his water bowl and was soon chewing on one of the large bones he always gets when he is exceedingly happy. He held it between his paws, and then, at home, at peace, he looked toward me to confirm that all was well.